A YEAR OF
SPORT TRAVEL

EXPERIENCE THE GREATEST SPORTING EVENTS IN THE WORLD

01.   02.   03.   04.   05.   06.

MELBOURNE | LONDON | OAKLAND

A YEAR OF ↗ SPORT TRAVEL

CONTENTS

LET THE
GAMES BEGIN!

Sport sits alongside our capacity to imagine, our ability to speak and our nimble thumbs in the things that make us human. And often in under an hour, sport allows us to exercise all those faculties: screaming our support, imagining a win and using those nimble digits to give an emphatic thumbs-up – or perhaps to hold a beer.

As well as being 'the great leveller' – bringing together a bunch of disparate characters for a common cause – sport is also a window into the histories and societies of its players and spectators. It's a unique set of circumstances that gives rise to the sport of kabaddi (see p18), for example, India's national game of chasey in which the 'raider' can only attack on a single out-breath, all the while chanting. Similarly, where else but America could successfully fuse elements of feminism, kitsch and rockabilly to create the high-energy entertainment-on-wheels that is roller derby (see p180).

A Year of Sport Travel profiles more than 200 sports from around 50 countries. It explains the rules, rituals, clothing and equipment integral to each activity. It tells of the struggles and the glory, the hierarchies and the prizes of sports. It tells what it takes to be a professional in any given field: from social and physical conditioning to actual competition. And it provides tips on what it takes to be a fan, with insights ranging from when it's OK to throw your seat-cushion into the sumo ring, to whether to take a tent or sleeping bag to Wimbledon's overnight ticket queue. The book also profiles games (as distinct from sports), because you'd kick yourself if you left town without seeing the Great Fruitcake Toss or Pooh Sticks

Championship, and features essays on historical sports – before big-wave surfing, there was big volcano surfing.

A Year of Sport Travel redefines the calendar year. Every week of every month profiles four events. One of them could be the inspiration for your next trip. Instead of finding Christmas in the fourth week of December, for example, you could find yourself among 200 or so participants running the streets of Kirkwall, Scotland, in a frenzied mass-football match (see p200). It also nails pegs into the ground by which to navigate, so you can coordinate your next trip to coincide with the Olympics (see p134) or the Camel Cup (see p113). You can either plan your next adventure using the world's sporting calendar as a compass, or travel the world without leaving the couch: *A Year of Sport Travel* makes both possible.

However you use this book, you'll find sport travel transforming. It traverses continents, cultures and time. It adds to our knowledge, our self-awareness and tantalises our taste for adventure – all elements that make us human. And the opportunities are there all year, every year.

Matthew Hayden (facing) celebrates with teammate Justin Langer after hitting the winning runs of the Fifth Test in the 2006–07 Ashes series.

THE ASHES

WHERE England or Australia **WHEN** Biennially, in the host country's summer **GETTING INVOLVED** Generally, tickets are readily available, particularly on days two to four. If it's a close match, tickets may be harder to come by.

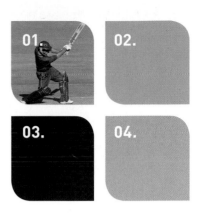

It was outrageous. Beaten by a colony. On English soil. Australia's win over England in 1882 was the genesis of what would become one of the world's greatest sporting rivalries.

England's shock loss prompted a local newspaper to run a satirical obituary that read: 'An affectionate remembrance of English cricket, which died at the Oval on 29th August 1882. Deeply lamented by a large circle of sorrowing friends and acquaintances. RIP NB: The body will be cremated and the ashes taken to Australia.' And so the series became known as the Ashes.

Ever since, England and Australia have been playing every two years, during alternating summers – bar the war years. They're playing for the lofty qualities of honour and respect. And they're playing for a weeny cup – a crystal replica fashioned from a terracotta urn that was gifted to the English captain Ivo Bligh in the 19th century, and said to contain the ashes of a cricket bail. (There have also been reports of it containing the singed remains of a lady's veil.)

Nearly 130 years on, and 65 series later, Australia and England are still wrangling over that little replica trophy (the original of which is displayed at the Marylebone Cricket Museum, at Lord's). And thank goodness. In what other sport can you say you're just going to watch the game, and come home five days later. That's almost a week of sitting under the summer sun, glaring white uniforms, red balls and sightscreens being trundled around the perimeter. That's a working-week's worth of a game of strategy, elegance and grace. A game that mirrors the times.

The 1980s was all moustaches and paunches; cricketers celebrated a win with a ciggy and a drink. That was before the days of media-training, dieticians and zinc cream. These days it seems we're all too time poor and results driven to appreciate the stately (some would say soporific) pace of Test cricket. (That, and the fact that the Aussies just wouldn't lose for 15 years.)

Watching Test cricket is the perfect excuse to slow down. And, for many, a quintessential element of summer: like beach holidays, sunburn, melting ice creams, and those other charred remains – barbequed sausages.

MORE INFO Cricket Australia (www.cricket.com.au), England and Wales Cricket Board (www.ecb.co.uk)

JANUARY
WEEK.01

'Watching Test cricket is the perfect excuse to slow down and, for many, is a quintessential element of summer'

FOR THE RECORD

↗ In 1948, needing just four runs to take his career batting average to 100, Bradman made a duck, going into retirement with an average of 99.94.

↗ To date, Australian batsmen have made 264 centuries in Ashes Tests and English batsmen 212.

'The Count', Ted Hankey of England, goes for blood in the first round match of the 2009 Lakeside World Darts Championships.

NATIONAL THROWBALL CHAMPIONSHIP

WHERE India **WHEN** Early January **GETTING INVOLVED** Check out the website for specific game locations and ticket information.

For a relatively young sport, debuting in its current guise in 1998, throwball has had an enormous influence in India. Played by more than 45,000 schools and colleges, plus clubs, factories and bigger businesses, throwball games are easy to organise and to play, bringing together people from different states, genders, classes and religions. It's played at night and during the day, indoors and out, in the cities and the countryside, and by young and old.

Not unlike volleyball, throwball is a non-contact ball sport, the difference being that players catch and throw the ball rather than 'volley' it. The Young Men's Christian Association (YMCA) is credited with bringing the game to India in the 1940s. And while it was popular almost immediately, especially with women, it wasn't until it had a rule makeover in '98 that it really came into its own.

The new rules prescribed that there be only seven players a side (where there used to be nine). The fewer players allowed individuals room to manoeuvre and fully display their court skills. Players can jump when they're serving, and the ball must leave their hands within three seconds of a catch. The other change to the game, also credited with adding more attraction to the game, is the use of a multicoloured ball during competitions.

The Throwball National Championship is celebrated in typical clamorous, enthusiastic style. With more than 40 teams competing, the participants alone equate to a decent crowd. The host city makes a veritable festival of the tournament, decorating the venue, putting up the players from various states for free, and providing entertainment.

India is so spectacularly, chaotically diverse that it's near impossible to feel like you're just one of the flock, unless you're barracking with the rest at a throwball game.

MORE INFO Throwball Federation of India (www.throwball.co.in)

LAKESIDE WORLD PROFESSIONAL DARTS CHAMPIONSHIP

 WHERE Surrey, England **WHEN** Early January **GETTING INVOLVED** Tickets available through the Lakeside World Professional Darts website.

There's something deeply satisfying about watching what is essentially a pub sport at professional level. You can actually imagine yourself there, hitting triple-20 after triple-20, your hand-eye coordination wildly enhanced by those beer goggles. But the competitors in the World Pro are the cream of the crop, rising to the surface from a field of more than 800 darts events – all of which are officiated by the British Darts Organisation.

A quick refresher on the rules for those who need it: each player starts the game with 501 points. The objective is to get to zero (exactly) in as few turns as possible.

The Pro has a men's and a women's competition, and boasts a rich purse of prizes, as well as a championship trophy for the winner of each competition. And, although the game purportedly attracts the single largest audience for any darts game on earth, don't expect to be seated among hundreds of thousands of darts fans. The majority of viewers are doing so from the comfort of their lounge rooms, as the game is televised across Europe.

The event is hosted by the Lakeside Country Club; has been since 1986. And what better location for a world darts competition than idyllic Surrey, credited with being the most wooded county in Great Britain and for being home to the highest population of millionaires in the UK.

MORE INFO Lakeside World Professional Darts Championship (www.lakesideworlddarts co.uk), British Darts Organisation (www.bdodarts.com)

NATIONAL INDOOR DODGEBALL CHAMPIONSHIP

 WHERE USA **WHEN** Usually around 3 January **GETTING INVOLVED** Tickets are easy to buy online. To participate in the competition, you'll need to have a team of six players and register by early December.

This one's open to spectators, as well as participants. And, if you believe the official spiel, it's a rewarding game to play that requires very little athletic ability or playing experience. Anyone can play.

Traditionally a sport played in PE classes, dodgeball is the antidote to the jocks and cheerleaders who tend to dominate school sports. It's a game of teamwork and strategy, and, to the newcomer, utter mayhem. Picture this: 12 players in a confined space scrambling for one of six balls with the intention of hitting an opponent with it. And it's all over in three minutes. Rules between competitions vary, but for the National Amateur Dodgeball Association (NADA), there are six players per side. The object of the game is to eliminate all opposing players by getting them 'out'. You can get the opposition out in one of three ways: by hitting them below the shoulders with a 'live' ball (ie one that hasn't bounced); by catching a live ball thrown by the opposition before it hits the ground; and by forcing a player to 'dodge' out of bounds.

Deemed violent and inappropriate for schools by its detractors, dodgeball has endured its fair share of criticism (not to mention lawsuits). But the NADA competition adheres to strict rules, is closely overseen and uses regulation rubber-coated balls. So get out of the stands, assemble a posse, and sign up.

MORE INFO National Amateur Dodgeball Association (NADA; www.dodgeballusa.com) and the professional National Dodgeball League (NDL; www.theNDL.com)

JANUARY WEEK.01

'It sure is swell. But, say, when's the game itself going to begin?'

Groucho Marx, after watching a couple of hours of cricket at Lord's

FOR THE RECORD

- - - - - - - - - - - - - - - - - -

↗ In 1992 Hubert Auriol became the first person to win the Dakar in both the motorcycle and automobile classes.

↗ Jutta Kleinschmidt was the first female to win Dakar, in 2001.

DAKAR RALLY

 WHERE South America, but route changes frequently **WHEN** Early to mid-January **GETTING INVOLVED** It takes a year of planning to compete in a Dakar. To watch, just turn up at the start of one of the race stages.

Even if motor sport isn't your thing, it's hard not to be impressed by the spectacular production that is the Dakar Rally. The sheer organisational feat that's required to manage 530 vehicles coming from 50 different countries, fuel stations, campsites, transport between stages for support mechanics, and food for 2000 people is mind-bending.

For spectators on the ground, watching the Dakar is volunteering to be hit with intermittent bursts of grit and dust as a competitor races past. Positioning yourself at the start of one of the 15 sections, which range from 520km to 840km each, allows you to smell the drivers' anxiety, inspect the heavily modified vehicles and hear the deep rumble of the engines. For the drivers, it's another thing entirely. It's two weeks of following a chewed-up track, negotiating sand dunes and patches of quicksand-like *fech fech*, which

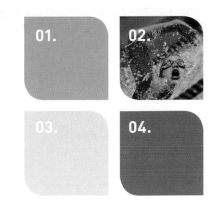

01.   02.

03.   04.

'Positioning yourself at the start of a section allows you to smell the drivers' anxiety and hear the deep rumble of the engines'

JANUARY
WEEK.02

Carlos Sainz invites rival rally drivers to eat Argentine dust as he steers his way to fourth-stage victory during the 2009 Dakar Rally.

means driving blind in a plume of yellow powder at 80km/h over a potholed surface. The drivers are constantly wrestling with trying to achieve a balance between speed and vehicle damage-limitation. As you progress through, the course claims more and more vehicles, the roadside littered with spent motorcycles, trucks and cars. The off-road sections of the course are known as 'the special'. These most challenging sections, 6000-odd kilometres of a 9500km course, are the ones Dakar drivers live for. It is, after all, why they're here: for the adventure.

The Dakar is traditionally run from Paris in France to Dakar in Senegal. Its ever-optimistic founder, Thierry Sabine, dreamt it up while lost in the desert in '78, and the first Dakar ran the following year. The route has changed over the decades, mainly for geopolitical reasons, and was cancelled for the first time in 2008 – a day before it was due to begin – due to terrorist threats. The race re-emerged on a different continent in 2009, running from Buenos Aires, Argentina, through Chile, and back to Buenos Aires. The South American route takes in the plains of Patagonia, the Atacama Desert and the passageway through the Andes mountains. And, true to its ethos, it takes the hard way there.

MORE INFO Dakar (www.dakar.com)

NUDE OLYMPICS

WHERE Maslin Beach, South Australia **WHEN** January **GETTING INVOLVED** Just turn up and strip off.

Since the mid-1980s, a windswept beach just south of Adelaide has hosted the annual Nude Olympics. But long before that, in around 720 BC in Ancient Greece, it's said, one of the Olympic runners lost his loincloth. He went on to win, and so others followed suit, sans suit. As a result, nude Olympics were fashionable for centuries before modesty, again, intervened.

Fast-forward a few thousand years to Maslin beach – Australia's first official nude beach, proclaimed in 1975. On one auspicious day in January, you'll find athletes participating in a range of events – all seemingly chosen for their innuendo potential – including the three-legged race, sack race, and tug of war, to name a few. Other events include the best-behind competition ('perky', 'sticking out a bit' and 'slightly tanned' all being desired attributes) and, the female equivalent, Ms Maslin competition – senior and junior categories. There's also the 'discus' (a Frisbee-throwing competition) and flag race. Sunburn is the most common injury reported, and slightly scorched feet; temperatures have been known to reach 40°C.

These modern Nude Olympics have flaunted the freedom to be nude for more than 20 years. There's no doubt that sport can be the glue that binds a community, and the Nude Olympics has brought the naturist population together, with people travelling from around the world to participate, and has also promoted naturism in the broader, clothes-wearing community. But it seems that the popularity of nudism is shrinking. The Nude Olympics organisers, Southern United Naturists club, has been struggling to survive recently, forced to cancel the event in 2008 and '09 – replaced with a Family Funday: a more informal social gathering. But there are big hopes to relaunch the Olympics under the auspices of the Australian Nudist Federation. So, nudists, clubs need more than just skin, they need financial support too.

MORE INFO Southern United Naturists (www.southernunitednaturists.org.au), Australian Naturist Federation (www.aus-nude.org.au)

BEACH VOLLEYBALL

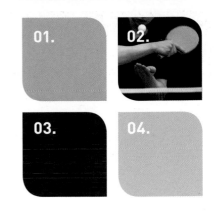

WHERE Ipanema Beach, Brazil, is famous for its beach volleyball matches and balmy conditions **WHEN** Year-round **GETTING INVOLVED** Beach volleyball lessons are available all along Ipanema Beach. Take a class in the morning, then switch to spectator and watch some serious stuff in the afternoon.

Growing slowly in the 1920s and 1930s, it took a while for a beach volleyball tournament to actually offer contestants some sort of incentive for their efforts. When it finally happened, in 1948, tournament organisers didn't exactly go all out. The prize for the winners: a case of soft drink. Hope it was cold.

Less than 50 years later, beach volleyball became an Olympic sport and is currently played all over the world by more than 2000 players for millions of dollars in prize money. Not bad for a sport that began in California and was mainly played by families on holidays.

Played on sand instead of a hard floor, other differences from traditional volleyball include the number of players per team (two instead of six), barefoot instead of sneakers, and bikinis or swimming briefs instead of, well, clothes.

Official matches are played in a best-of-three-sets format. The first team to win two sets wins the match. The first two sets are played to 21 points, and the third set, if needed, is played to 15 points. For all sets a two-point advantage is required, with no maximum.

Seating is designed so that you'll be close to the action as these top-class athletes dive around the court, serving, setting, blocking and spiking. The sand will fly, and so will the hand signals – made with both hands behind the back to indicate to playing partners which type of block to play. There's usually live music and commentary to boot.

MORE INFO Federation Internationale de Volleyball (www.fivb.org/EN/BeachVolleyball), Beach Volleyball Database (www.bvbinfo.com), Volleyball Worldwide (www.volleyball.org)

ASIAN BOWLING FEDERATION TOUR OF CHAMPIONS

WHERE Location changes each championship **WHEN** Mid-January **GETTING INVOLVED** Tickets available through the website.

Ever been tenpin bowling and thrown a strike? Yes? Then followed it up with another? That's called a double. Three strikes in a row? That's known as a turkey. Four in a row?! Never mind what it's called, but that's exactly the sort of form you can expect to see at the Asian Bowling Federation (ABF) Tour of Champions.

The Tour of Champions brings together the top 16 men and top 16 women bowlers throughout the region, which consists of Asia, Australia and the Western Pacific. To get to this level, competitors must first earn ranking points by competing in the six lead-up tournaments, usually staged in Thailand, Saudi Arabia, Kuwait, Hong Kong, the Philippines and Indonesia. This is the highest regional level of competition, with prize money totalling US$75,000. There are two other zones, the European and American. The best players in the regional competitions then go on to compete in world comps – generally held every second year.

The glorious hollow sound of toppling pins is guaranteed with every throw at these championships. If you like what you see, and you're a citizen of the participating countries, maybe think about joining an upcoming tour. The first of the six legs usually starts in April, a good nine months before the Championships – plenty of time to get those colourful shoes fitted and pick out a ball. But then, being an athlete at this level is not all beer and skittles, mostly just skittles.

MORE INFO ABF (www.abftour.com), World Tenpin Bowling Association (www.worldtenpinbowling.com)

AND ANOTHER THING

Great Fruitcake Toss (Colorado, USA)

The Christmas gift that keeps on giving: fruitcake can be hurled (by hand or pneumatic device) for distance or accuracy. Fruitcakes are categorised by weight, and must not contain anything inedible. There's also a fruitcake relay and even a fruitcake art show. (www.manitousprings.org)

FOR THE RECORD

↗ The average men's serve speed is 190km/h.

↗ There are around 360 umpires and more than 300 ballboys and girls at each open.

↗ The AO was played in New Zealand in 1906 and 1912.

↗ Ken Rosewell is both the youngest and oldest man to win the AO: aged 18, in 1953, and 37, in 1972.

AUSTRALIAN OPEN TENNIS

 WHERE Melbourne, Australia **WHEN** Mid-January to early February **GETTING INVOLVED** Tickets are easily booked online; get in early for the finals.

The stars of the Australian Open win more than the public's adoration, earning the highest number of world-ranking points and a share in a bulging purse: winners take home A$1,400,000 of a total A$6,665,000 in prize money. One of four Grand Slam events (the others being Wimbledon, p101; the US Open, www.usopen.org; and the French Open, www.french.open-tennis.com), the Australian Open (AO) is among the world's most important tennis events. But it wasn't always the case.

Attracting the world's top-ranked players to one of the most geographically isolated continents hasn't always been easy. For about half of its 100-odd-year history, the AO was a colloquial affair. Little wonder considering it took 45 days to travel there from

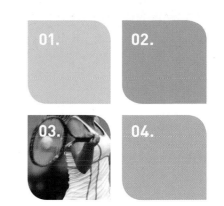

'Each year's attendance breaks the previous year's record, and each year the festival atmosphere just gets thicker'

JANUARY
WEEK.03

A row of tennis spectators wear matching hats as they watch a men's singles match at the 2008 Australian Open in Melbourne.

Europe in the 1920s. Until 1972, the tournament was itinerant, and even travelling from one side of the country to the other kept competitor numbers low. Melbourne has been the Open's home since '72, with its contract up for renewal (or for grabs) in 2016.

Australia's is a particularly hard-won tournament. Held mid-summer in a city famous for its fickle weather, it has a history plagued by rain and, more so, extreme heat. Before the Open moved to Melbourne Park, with its state-of-the-art retractable roof, commentators regularly fried an egg on centre court, just to show that it could be done. The heat can cause the balls to shrink or expand – havoc for a player's game – not to mention the fatigue of running around a court at 40°C for four-plus hours. In 2008, the courts were resurfaced with a cushioned acrylic that holds less heat. Organisers also recently introduced a heat policy to counter the extreme conditions.

Since the open moved to its current venue in 1988, attendances have soared, exploding past the 60,000-mark in one day/night. Each year's attendance breaks the last's record. Add to that mass media coverage, and Australian Open players rival Hollywood mainstays for column space and air time. The festival atmosphere gets thicker each year, and you can expect neighbouring ovals to be transformed by Spiegelworld: a lavish portable salon staging burlesque and live music performance till late. Although maybe not as late as some of the men's finals, which have been known to finish around 4.30am.
MORE INFO Australian Open (www.australianopen.com)

Duelling over a lady: male camels neck-wrestle for love (or lust?) in Turkey.

EURO WORLD ICE-BOATING CHAMPIONSHIPS

WHERE Location changes each championship **WHEN** Around mid-January **GETTING INVOLVED** Check location and dates with the International DN Yacht Racing Association.

Who says the sailing has to cease when the lakes freeze over? Uh-uh. Hard-water sail-racing or ice-sailing is a kind of extreme sport, where speed and generally unfriendly conditions (freezing temperatures and high winds) are deemed favourable.

Popular in North America and Europe, ice-sailing was born out of practical considerations, having its genesis in the Netherlands more than 300 years ago as a means of transporting goods across large bodies of water in the winter months. It gradually developed into a hobby sport, practised by wealthy sailors, before evolving into the competition sport it is today – set to join the Winter Olympics as a demonstration sport in 2010.

The season generally runs from mid-November to early April. There are a variety of classes within ice boat-racing, the most popular being the DN class: for a portable, affordable class of yacht that's often built in the backyard. These fairly basic wood-frame 3.5m-long vessels are composed of a 2.5m crossbar carrying a 5m-long mast. DN class is named for the *Detroit Newspaper*, which ran the first races in the mid-1930s.

The European DN-class Championship has the capacity for 200 sailors, which requires an expanse of around 160 sq km of thick, preferably smooth, ice, without a covering of snow. Known as 'black ice', it makes for a smoother, faster run. Yachts race three times around a course of two markers, upwind and downwind, set about 1.5km apart, keeping the markers port-side (left). Lying flat on their backs, sailors typically skate across the ice at 60km/h. From onboard the sound is not unlike a jumbo taking off. For the spectator, the sight of up to 200 yachts skimming across the surface of a glassy lake isn't one you'll forget in a hurry.

MORE INFO Europe International DN Ice Yacht Racing Association (www.icesailing.org), International DN Ice Yacht Racing Association (www.idniyra.org)

CAMEL WRESTLING FESTIVAL

WHERE Near Pamucak beach, 9km from Selçuk, Turkey **WHEN** Third Sunday in January **GETTING INVOLVED** Arrive on the Saturday before the match, as the camels are paraded through town by their owners who talk up the virtues of their camels, like a boxing promoter spruiking the invincibility of his prize fighter.

Thousands of spectators, musicians and food stalls (camel sausage anyone?), and hundreds of camels all come together for this uniquely Turkish event. And while camel wrestling has a devoted following along the Western Mediterranean and Aegean coasts, no single event is greater than Selçuk's festival.

Essentially, two male camels are pitted against each other in response to a female camel (in heat) being led before them. It's a familiar scenario, as old as the story of King Arthur, Guinevere and Lancelot. The actual camel-wrestling match is an absolute lottery, depending on the temperament of the camels involved. They might be genuinely and equally grumpy, chasing one another and trying to pin the other down with their necks. Or they might just stand there and growl at each other. Or spit.

There are three ways a camel can triumph in camel wrestling. By making the other camel retreat, scream or fall. The owner of a camel may also throw a rope into the field to declare a forfeit if he is concerned for the safety of his animal – like a boxing trainer throwing in the towel. There are generally around a dozen *urganci* (ropers) close by to separate the camels if necessary.

Usually the bout ends when one of the camels decides he's had enough and runs off into the crowd. Avoiding the oncoming camel can be a sport in itself.

There's music everywhere, so if you're struggling to get your head around camels wrestling, enjoy the tunes and festivities.

MORE INFO Selçuk Tourism (www.selcuk.gov.tr)

NFL CONFERENCE CHAMPIONSHIP

WHERE USA **WHEN** Third week of January **GETTING INVOLVED** Tickets available online, but get in early. Should you miss out, find a sports bar and enjoy a day with the locals, scoffing beer and pretzels.

Big men wearing helmets, running fast and scoring touchdowns. Sound good? You're not alone. The most popular sport in the USA is not baseball, basketball or hockey. It's football. Outside of America, it's also referred to as American football or gridiron.

If you've ever watched a Super Bowl (and there's been 43 of them), this is where the two finalists come from. The National Football League (NFL) is split into two conferences, the American Football Conference (AFC) and the National Football Conference (NFC). After 16 regular season games and three weeks of playoffs, two teams are left in each conference. On this championship weekend, the two best teams from each conference go to battle. The prize: a trip to the Super Bowl.

So, on Conference Championships weekend, you have two games to choose from. The venues for the National Conference Championships are not fixed and depend on which city's team is winning. The team with the best record during the regular season earns the right to play their playoff games at home, so the games could be held anywhere.

This home-field advantage naturally attracts wildly parochial, enthusiastic supporters cheering and rooting for the home team, beautifully juxtaposed with a stony silence that meets any good play by the visiting team.

Then when the weekend is over and just two teams remain, enjoy the revelry and excitement of the two crazy weeks leading up to the biggest party, sorry, game of the year: the Super Bowl (p22).

MORE INFO National Football League (www.nfl.com)

JANUARY
WEEK.03

'Sports do not build character. They reveal it.'

Heywood Broun, sportswriter, NYC

FOR THE RECORD

- - - - - - - - - - - - - - - -

↗ India won the first ever kabaddi World Cup 55 to 27 against Iran.

↗ The Silguri women's team created history in 2008, becoming the first team to win all three state titles in a season.

KABADDI WORLD CUP

 WHERE India **WHEN** Every three years (funding permitting) **GETTING INVOLVED** Get your World Cup tickets in advance; seating is limited.

The Iranians might chant *'jhoo-jhoo'* and the Indians *'hu-tu-tu'* or *'ha-do-do'*, but it's all in the name of kabaddi (car-bad-ee) – a combative team sport indigenous to India. Possibly the only hectic sport to integrate yoga, kabaddi requires the so-called 'raider' to run onto the opposition's side of the court, tag them (deeming them 'out') and return to his or her side of the court without being caught by the remaining opposition members, in one single out-breath – all the while chanting *'kabaddi'* (*'jhoo-jhoo'*, *'hu-tu-tu'* etc, depending on where the game is being played). The chant has been likened to the yogic practice of Pranayama in which the breath is held to exercise the internal organs.

Kabaddi's long history is believed to date as far back as prehistoric times, and there are references to the game in the Indian epic Mahabharata. Even Gautama Buddha, according to Buddhist literature, was partial to the odd game. Purportedly, Indian

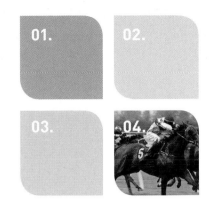

'The Kabaddi chant is likened to the yogic practice of Pranayama in which the breath is held to exercise the internal organs'

JANUARY
WEEK.04

Pakistani 'antis' (in white) surround an Indian 'raider', trying to stop him from returning to his home side.

princes of yore used to prove their mettle in a game, and win a bride – more than the T-shirts and gift bags kabaddi champions of today win.

Kabaddi games are 45 minutes long, with two 20-minute halves and a five-minute break, after which the teams swap from defence (called 'antis') to attack ('raider'). There are seven players per side, but only one raider attacking a defence-side of seven. Antis touched by a raider are 'out'; these players are only allowed back into the game when their side scores points against the opposite side during their raiding turn, or if the remaining players catch the opponent's raider. Remember: the lone raider is facing seven opponents and isn't breathing through any of this.

The first World Cup was played in India in 2004, attracting about 7500 spectators (modest in per-capita terms). Twelve countries and territories participated including Japan, South Korea, Nepal, the West Indies and, home-side champs, India. Kabaddi was recently included in the Asian Games and the Afro-Asian Games, and was played as a demonstration sport in the 1936 Berlin Olympics. If you can't make it to a World Cup, there are loads of national and state-level tournaments. But instead of chanting *'here-we-go, here-we-go, here-we-go'* from the bleachers, listen for the raiders' *'kabaddi'* chant.

MORE INFO International Kabaddi Federation (www.kabad diikf.com)

Pond hockey as far as the eye can see – competitors and spectators brave the ice on Minneapolis' Lake Calhoun.

KORFBALL EUROPA CUP

WHERE Netherlands **WHEN** Finals last week in January **GETTING INVOLVED** If possible, buy tickets in advance for any of the international competitions.

Played in more than 50 countries, korfball is a lot like mixed netball, with four males and four females per side. Men and women play side by side. But, while playing, it's man-to-man or woman-to-woman only. One man may guard one man and one woman may guard one woman, so it's not two against one. A woman may not defend a man, nor may a man defend a woman.

Like netball, korfball players score a point by throwing the ball into the other team's basket. And it is a basket (*korf* in Danish), rather than a plain old ring. It can be played indoors or outdoors, and there is even a beach version.

There are two zones on a korfball court, with a 3.5m-high pole positioned in each – two-thirds of the way between the centre-line and backline. After two goals, teams change zones, with defenders becoming attackers, and vice versa. Teams change ends at half-time. Rules prevent any argy-bargy: there's no blocking, tackling or holding, and the ball cannot be dribbled, kicked or punched.

Of the numerous national and international competitions, the Europa Cup is the premier international event for the clubs, as opposed to the national teams in Europe. Eight of 13 qualifying teams make the finals. The first Europa Cup was played in 1967 as a three-region tournament between Great Britain, Belgium and the Netherlands (at the time, the only three regions with competitions).

A Dutch school teacher is credited with founding korfball in 1902 after he adapted the Swedish game of *ringboll* by simplifying the rules, replacing the ring with a basket and making the game mixed-gender.
MORE INFO International Korfball Federation (www.korfball.org)

US POND HOCKEY CHAMPIONSHIPS

WHERE Minneapolis, USA **WHEN** Penultimate weekend in January
GETTING INVOLVED Just turn up; it's free. Participants are also encouraged, but you'll need a team; register online.

Watching ice hockey played by slick professionals from the comfort of a cosy indoor stadium on an artificial rink is not for everyone. Some prefer to watch hockey as it was originally played: outdoors on a frozen lake. The US Pond Hockey Championship sees 150 amateur teams battling it out for the Golden Shovel trophy: a competition whose program features tips on how to spot signs of hypothermia and frostbite.

In 2005, a businessman (and hockey fanatic) suffering a mid-life crisis dreamt of a national pond hockey championship. A year later the dream was realised with the first US Pond Hockey Championships in Minneapolis drawing nearly 120 teams of pond-hockey players from across the nation, cheered on by thousands of traditional hockey fans.

The event consists of four divisions: the open (men and women aged 18 or older), 40 plus, 50 plus and the rink rats – where you won't see the skills of former NHL or division-one players that you will in the open division, but the passion of these 'rats' more than makes up for that. The pond hockey rink is 50% longer than a standard NHL rink, and has no boards or glass surrounding it – usually a barrier of snow keeps the puck in play. Great old-school stuff.

The US Pond Hockey Championships is free and, in addition to the unique and amazing hockey action, supplies a public skating rink and huge 'warming tent'. The tent is open from 7am and dispenses hot drinks and comfort food.

MORE INFO US Pond Hockey Championships (www.uspondhockey.com)

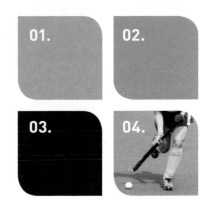

EXTREME UNICYCLING CHAMPIONSHIP

WHERE Munich, Germany **WHEN** Late January **GETTING INVOLVED** If you know what you're doing, register online to compete. Places are at a premium and limited to 150 riders. If you're just interested in having a look, go along and enjoy the ride.

Why use two wheels when you can get by with one? That's the spirit of the unicycle, and extreme unicycling has taken that spirit to a whole new level. A relatively new sport, extreme unicycling is a broad term used to define the emergence of unicycling into the world of physical recreation. No longer the domain of clowns in the circus, extreme unicycling involves riders testing their skills in the city, in the country – anywhere really.

Extreme unicycling consists of two forms: mountain and trial unicycling. Similar to mountain biking, mountain unicycling involves the same rough terrain and dangerous, uneven surfaces as the two-wheel activity. Trial unicycling finds its home in the streets, using railings, curbs and ramps, similar to skateboarding. No surface is too steep or too uneven. These guys are hard-core. And you need to be if you want to be competitive in the Extreme Unicycle Championships (EUC).

The inaugural EUC was held in 2009, with more than three days of competition and workshops. The main events include the backwards long jump, high jump (over a bar) and flatland battle in which competing pairs go head to head performing a line of tricks, which are judged; the winning duo goes through to face their next challengers while the losers are eliminated. Competition is categorised according to age, and with the senior category being for over 15s, you can guess the demographic. These fearless teens test their balance and skills, as well as enjoy some healthy camaraderie in a newly developing sport.

MORE INFO Extreme Unicycle Championship (www.e-u-c.info)

AND ANOTHER THING

Outhouse Races (Conconully, Washington, USA)

Bringing new meaning to the term 'having the runs', wooden privies on skis, with a rider and two pushers, are raced along a snow-covered street. All race vehicles must be equipped with a toilet seat and toilet-paper hanger (www.conconully.com)

FOR THE RECORD

↗ Joe Montana holds the record for Most Valuable Player awards (three), most career passing yards (1142), most touchdown passes (11) and highest passer rating (127.8).

↗ No team has ever won more than two consecutive Super Bowls.

↗ The Pittsburgh Steelers hold the record for the most Super Bowl wins, celebrating their 6th in 2009.

SUPER BOWL

WHERE USA **WHEN** First Sunday in February **GETTING INVOLVED** Find yourself a big telly like everyone else; or prepare to fork out thousands for a ticket.

Professional American football's championship game is big. Reportedly, the most watched TV broadcast of the year (with around 90 million American viewers) and the second-largest day of food consumption in the US after Thanksgiving, Super Bowl Sunday is a kind of surrogate national holiday. Half-time and pre-match entertainment is an event in itself, with stars like Bruce Springsteen, Stevie Wonder, Billy Joel, Justin Timberlake and Janet Jackson's nipple. And for home-viewers there's the added entertainment of creative commercials with high production values (advertisers paying US$2.7 million for a 30-second slot can apparently afford to go all out with Bowl-specific campaigns). Not to mention the 22 heavily padded gents doing combat on the field.

Though not yet named as such, the first Super Bowl was played in 1967 between the top teams of the USA's two leagues: the American Football League (AFL) and National

Linebacker Larry Foote (L) of the Pittsburgh Steelers performs a pre-game dance before a Super Bowl match against the Arizona Cardinals in 2009; the Steelers defeated the Cardinals 27–23.

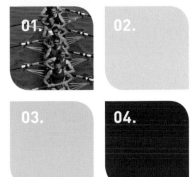

01. 02. 03. 04.

'Reportedly, Super Bowl Sunday is the the second-largest day of food consumption in the US after Thanksgiving'

FEBRUARY
WEEK.01

Football League (NFL). After the leagues merged in 1970, the 'Bowl became the NFL's championship game, played between the champions of the league's two conferences: American Football Conference (AFC) and the National Football Conference (NFC; p17). It was after the merger that the game was dubbed the Super Bowl – another merger, but this time of the name of those bouncy little balls popular with '70s children (Superballs) and 'bowl' being the name for post-season college games (after the bowl-shaped Rose Bowl stadium venue). The actual Superball credited with inspiring the name is on display at the Pro Football Hall of Fame in Canton, Ohio.

Since the football season runs into the new year (from August to February), the Super Bowl uses Roman numerals, rather than years played, to distinguish between games. The first Super Bowl to be numbered was III.

If you're not prepared to part with thousands to attend the actual game, there's a makeshift theme park in the lead up to Sunday's game where you can get into the spirit by padding up and having your photo taken, inspect a huge football-card display and maybe even add to your autograph collection. The majority of Americans go to a party, with a television at its centre, and eat snack food. Gauging by the 20% increase in antacid sales the following day, a decent amount of beer accompanies those snacks.

MORE INFO National Football League (www.nfl.com/Superbowl)

LUGE WORLD CUP

WHERE Various locations throughout the season; aim for St Moritz, Switzerland **WHEN** Finals early to mid-February **GETTING INVOLVED** Tickets earlier in the season are easier to come by than finals tickets.

Animated applause in Oberhof, Germany as compatriot Silke Kraushaar-Pielach celebrates her 2007 World Luge Cup women's single event win.

You only have to look at the origins of luge to discover why it looks like such a hoot. In the 19th-century equivalent of going for a shopping-trolley ride, English tourists at a St Moritz resort used delivery boys' sleds to zoom around the streets and alleys of the village. It became such a popular activity that in the interests of public safety, the owner of the resort, one Caspar Badrutt, was forced to construct a purpose-built track for his guests. Officially opened in 1904, remarkably, the track still exists and is used during the World Cup season. The Olympia Bobrun St Moritz Caterina is one of the few tracks in the world that doesn't rely on artificial refrigeration for its existence.

Technically, those cheeky Brits were riding 'skeleton': head first and face down. Luge is feet first, supine and aerodynamically flat. Lugers steer their sleds, fitted with razor-sharp blades, by shifting their bodyweight, and they brake only with their spike-fitted shoes. Skeleton was replaced by luge in the 1956 Winter Olympics, ensuring its popularity. (As if skidding along the ice on a sled needs any help in the popularity stakes.)

A number of world competition events flourish, including the multi-race World Cup. Like all competitions, World Cup courses are timed, and qualifying runs determine start positions – which are important considering that that smooth track becomes increasingly churned up after each run. The luger or pilot is required to arrive at the finish with the sled and in sliding position; they may no longer push their sleds across the finish line. Two runs determine the winner of the men's, women's and doubles events. The winning country is determined by adding together the individual men's, women's and doubles times – the quickest wins.

MORE INFO International Luge Federation (www.fil-luge.org)

NORWEGIAN REINDEER RACING CHAMPIONSHIP

WHERE Tromsø, Norway **WHEN** Early February as part of Saami Week
GETTING INVOLVED Leave the racing to the pros. Line the course or enjoy the traditional Saami dishes, including reindeer stew, that are part of the festival fare.

As a mode of transport, a reindeer-pulled sleigh is a rather fabled notion. But it's not the exclusive right of Mr Claus on his annual jaunt from the North Pole to a chimney near you. The Norwegian Reindeer Racing Championships that take place in Tromsø's main street are another much-anticipated annual occurrence. Reindeer racing is a featured sport among the indigenous northern European Saami people's celebrations of culture.

The Saami pilots, clad in Lycra and helmets, stand on skis behind their specially trained reindeer at the start of the 201m-long track. The fastest equipages (one reindeer and a skier holding two lines behind) hurtle down the snow-covered street reaching speeds of up to 70km/h, and finish in around 15 seconds. At these speeds falls are fraught with danger, and some of the crashes can be quite spectacular. Each race is between two pilots and their reindeer, and the championship consists of qualifying heats that narrow the field to the eventual final. Traditional dress is favoured by many of the Saami people on the day, so look for reindeer-hide shoes turned up at the toe and heavy dresses fringed in red, yellow and green in the crowds lining the street.

The main town of Troms county – by far the largest in northern Norway – Tromsø is lively with cultural landmarks, an animated street scene, a respected university, the hallowed Mack Brewery and more pubs per capita than any other Norwegian town.
MORE INFO Midnight Sun Marathon (www.msm.no)

EMPIRE STATE BUILDING RUN-UP

WHERE New York City, USA **WHEN** First week in February **GETTING INVOLVED** Ballot application available online.

So, you're in New York and the day's itinerary includes visiting the iconic art-deco Empire State Building. You already know that New York's highest building, with 102 floors, is such a popular attraction that the entry queues are 'as legendary as the building itself'. But there are two ways to beat the queues. One: pay an extra fee and skip to the front. Two: come in February and run up the stairs.

The Empire State Building Run-Up is a foot race that ascends the stairwells to the 86th-floor observation deck. Held annually since 1978, each year more than 100 'lucky' runners (also called climbers) are selected from piles of applications to participate in this calf-burning race up a total of 1576 steps. Part of a growing worldwide circuit of organised runs up the staircases of buildings, competitors in the Empire State Building Run-Up come from the winners of events in Sydney, Moscow, Vienna, Detroit, Toronto and Munich.

There is a mass start in two waves – ladies first. Five minutes later, off the men go. The record time is nine minutes and 33 seconds, achieved by Australian professional cyclist Paul Crake in 2003.

It's a high price to pay for a unique entry to the Empire State. If the souvenir T-shirt, post-run refreshments in a plastic cup and 360-degree views from the finishing line aren't enough, maybe the all-expenses-paid ride down to the bottom in one of the building's elevators will make it all worthwhile.
MORE INFO Empire State Building (www.esbnyc.com)

'[Football] is the last thing left in civilisation where men can literally fling themselves bodily at one another in combat and not be at war.'

- - - - - - - - - - - - - - - - - - - -

Former US president Ronald Reagan, who played football in high school

Competitive DanceSport dancers, such as Adam Blakey and Meagen Alderton of Australia, undergo grueling training sessions to stay at the top of their game.

DANCESPORT WORLD OPEN

WHERE Location changes annually **WHEN** Mid-February
GETTING INVOLVED Check the website for scheduling and ticketing info.

DanceSport embodies the old sport-versus-art rivalry. It broke away from the 'strict confines' of competition ballroom dancing and resolutely defines itself as a sport. The justification for this seems to lie with some scientific research that showed the muscle exertion and breathing rates of a two-minute DanceSport routine to equal that of an elite runner over a distance of 800m.

The range of dance styles recognised in international competition include Latin American, ten dance and rock and roll, primarily falling into two categories: standard and Latin. As you'd expect, there are coat-tails, vests and bowties, colourful gowns and exaggerated facial expressions. Dancing partners are male-female, and remain close throughout the dance – mirroring each other's elegant, sweeping movements. Things heat up for the Latin dances, with lots of hip action, dips, head flings and skimpier, shinier outfits.

A routine is judged according to 'technique, with elements of athleticism, artistry and aesthetics', in direct comparison with other competitors. So, along with technical prowess, there are certain intangibles that judges look for. According to the International DanceSport Federation (IDSF): 'Every competitive couple seeks to develop its own personal style and transmit charisma on the parquet.' For open competitions, there must be a minimum of seven adjudicators from at least six IDSF countries pacing around the dancing couples, of which there are around six on the dance floor at the same time.

The World Open competitions determine couples' world rankings, and their standing going into the biggie, the World Championships, which has competition grades in junior (11 to 16 years), youth (17 to 18) and adult (19 to 34).

In 1997, the Latin and standard events were included in the sports program of the World Games, with acrobatic rock and roll added in 2005. DanceSport also features regularly on the program of the Asian Games. DanceSport has its eye on the Olympics, vying for inclusion in the 2016 Games of the Olympiad, the Paralympic Games and the Youth Olympic Games.

DanceSport is also partly responsible for the scourge of dancing programs on our televisions. The IDSF co-produced the inaugural Eurovision Dance Contest in 2007. Sixteen couples represent 16 countries and perform two dances – one 'freestyle', which exhibits the character of the country being represented. And, like the more famous song contest, audience members vote for their favourite. But that's where the similarities end. Recent changes to the competition excluded one professional DanceSporter from each partnership to allow the inclusion of a celebrity.
MORE INFO International DanceSport Federation (www.idsf.net)

'Scientific research has showed the muscle exertion of a two-minute DanceSport routine equals that of an elite runner over a distance of 800m'

01.
02.
03.
04.

FEBRUARY WEEK.02

FOR THE RECORD

↗ The world number one DanceSport couple is Paolo Bosco and Silvia Pitton. Bosco has been described as 'a whirlwind, with his own strategies as to where to go, what to do and how to play to the music as well as other couples on the floor'.

01. **02.**

03. **04.**

MIDMAR MILE

WHERE Midmar Dam, near Howick, South Africa **WHEN** Second weekend in February **GETTING INVOLVED** Get applications and admission fee in by mid-January.

Things get rather hectic at the otherwise peaceful Midmar Dam come mid-February when around 18,000 people churn up the surface in their attempt to swim 1.6km in the world's biggest open-water swimming event.

It began in 1974 with 153 entrants, and has operated every year since, in all weather conditions, with the exception of a few individual events. These days, it's a slick and sophisticated event. Spectators can make sense of the frothing rabble in the dam thanks to commentary and big-screen TVs focusing on the action. The winner usually runs through the timing pad in under 18 minutes, and is wearing a red cap. Seeded entrants take off at three-minute intervals and are categorised according to cap colour. So, the beginning of the race is a sea of red caps, followed by a wave of blue, yellow, green and white, until they merge to resemble confetti bobbing about in a turgid sea.

If you can swim 1600m in a pool in under 50 minutes, then you're a contender to enter the event. Everyone's a winner, with all swimmers awarded a medal and T-shirt. Only seeded entrants are eligible for the prizes (up to R1500), and no wetsuits are allowed.

Adjoining the southern shores of the 1450-hectare lake is a 1000-hectare wildlife reserve, with wildebeest, zebra and springbok. The Midmar Nature Reserve is a member of Ezemvelo KZN Wildlife, a government organisation responsible for maintaining wilderness areas. Located near the town of Howick, it's also in the thick of the Midmar Meander – an association of rural businesses selling curios, art and craft, food and furniture.

MORE INFO Midmar Mile (www.midmarmile.co.za)

FEBRUARY WEEK.02

CANE-TOAD RACING

WHERE Pubs, particularly in Queensland, Australia **WHEN** Most weekend nights **GETTING INVOLVED** Purchase a raffle ticket to go into the draw to be a toad jockey for a night.

What's a place to do when it finds itself overrun with giant poisonous toads, but race them at the local pub? A bit of backpacker-pub shenanigans, cane-toad racing generally takes place after a few lagers have been sunk and after people have finished dining. Wise decision.

A toad master (commentator) takes charge of proceedings. If yours is the lucky ticket drawn from a hat, then you'll be handed a warty, slimy toad. You will be encouraged to kiss it, but this is optional. Toads already have names, often silly (Potential Prince, Jerry Springer) or with an international flavour (Irish Rover, Italian Stallion, Japanese Jumper or Little Aussie Battler). They are identified by numbers on their backs.

Depending on your location, you may encounter one of a number of variations on racing rules. In one version you may coax your toad with a party blower to promote movement; the winner is the first to hop off the table and be placed in the 'finishing bucket.' Another form of competition has toads released from the starting gates (beneath a bucket), with the victor being the first toad to leap out of the designated area.

The toad master whips the crowd into a cheering frenzy, with people encouraged to barrack for the toad bearing the name of their country. The victorious toad owner wins beer in a variety of quantities. So if you decline to push your lips onto a cane toad you may still be able to wrap them around a beer courtesy of a toad instead.

MORE INFO Queensland Tourism (www.destinationqueensland.com)

AND ANOTHER THING

Westminster Dog Show (Madison Square Garden, NYC, USA)

Among the world's most prestigious dog shows, Westminster has been judging purebreds (more than 2500 of them in recent years), since 1877. There are around 160 breed and variety judgings, which culminate in the Best in Show – the dog-world's equivalent to an Oscar. (www.westminsterkennelclub.org)

SUPER 14 RUGBY GAME

WHERE Southern Hemisphere **WHEN** February through to May (finals late May) **GETTING INVOLVED** Check the website for an up-to-date schedule. Tickets can be bought from the ground on match day.

Pedrie Wannenburg of the Bulls is taken down by a Cheetah during a Super 14 match in 2008.

Rugby. For many, it's the game they play in heaven. Not to mention all over the world.

Played in over 100 countries and on six continents, the sport is hugely popular in Australia, Argentina, England, the Pacific islands, France, Ireland, Italy, Japan, New Zealand, Scotland, South Africa and Wales. But can you name the current Olympic rugby gold medallists? Rather incongruously, it's the United States, which won gold the last time that rugby was played at the Olympics, which was in Paris, 1924. So, until rugby is reinstated as an Olympic event, the USA has bragging rights.

The Super 14 competition is the largest rugby union club championship in the southern hemisphere, consisting of four teams from Australia, five teams from New Zealand and five teams from South Africa. The union has a reputation for robust, attacking rugby. Bonus points are given to every team that scores four tries or more in a game, which ensures passionate and intense play, right into the dying minutes of each game. Don't leave early to beat the traffic.

Those whose interest in rugby only extends to the World Cup (held every four years) have the opportunity to see some of the players from the stronger teams (the All Blacks, Wallabies and Springboks) at a club level, up close. With three countries to choose from, there's really no excuse to not get to a Super 14 match. Unless of course you'd like to take your chances in heaven. Not sure about tickets though.

MORE INFO Super 14 Rugby (www.super14.com)

FOR THE RECORD

↗ Curling has a curse. It was the 1972 Silver Broom championship, and the as-yet undefeated Canadian team needed two points to win. The opposition's skip, American Bob LaBonte, slipped during a celebratory jump (thinking they had won) and accidentally kicked the Canadian stone. A kerfuffle ensued, and though the Canadians went on to win the game, thereafter they experienced an eight-year losing streak – said to be courtesy of LaBonte.

SCOTTISH CURLING FINALS

WHERE Edinburgh, Scotland **WHEN** Third week in February
GETTING INVOLVED Tickets are readily available from the club.

To the casual observer, curling looks like lawn bowls on ice, with the notable addition of compulsive cleaners. But it's commonly referred to as 'chess on ice' – for the strategy the game involves and the complexities of stone placement and shot selection, or 'the roaring game' – for the sound the stones make skidding across the ice.

It's an ancient sport referenced in poetry and paintings, with actual stones inscribed with the date '1511' found when a pond in Dunblane was drained; 'hard' evidence that the sport existed as early as the 16th century. An official sport of the Winter Olympics since 1998, there are plenty of international competitions, but there's something profound about watching a curling match in its home country, at the 'mother club of

01. 02. 03. 04.

'Curling is characterised by its strong sporting ethic. If a sweeper touches the rock, it's expected they will fess up'

FEBRUARY
WEEK.03

The Swedish curling team send their stone towards the 'house' during the World Women's Curling Championship.

curling', the Royal Caledonian Curling Club. Founded in 1838, the club is also the governing body of curling in Scotland, affiliated with a number of international clubs and across the range of competitions.

Curling competitions involve two teams of four players. Teams take turns sliding a polished granite stone weighing up to 20kg along the ice towards the 'house' – painted with concentric circles, the centre of which is the 'button'. Meanwhile, teammates sweep the path of the stone. Aggressive sweeping temporarily melts the ice, which has the effect of straightening the trajectory of the stone and lessening its deceleration. There's generally much yelling during play, with the 'skip' (team strategist) calling out directions to the sweepers. There are essentially two shots in curling: the 'draw' shot, to reach the house, and the 'take out',

to remove stones from play. After both teams have delivered eight rocks, the team with the rock closest to the button is awarded a point for each rock that is closer than the opponent's closest rock.

The iced run that forms the area of play is known as a curling sheet. It must be as close to level as possible, and have the all-important 'pebble' – droplets of water on the surface that allow for friction between the stone and the ice, causing the stone to curl.

Curling is characterised by its strong sporting ethic. If a sweeper accidentally 'burns' (touches) the rock, it's expected they will 'fess up. No one celebrates an opponent's error, and it's common for a team to concede a game before it is played out if there is little or no chance of them winning, and there is no shame in doing so.

MORE INFO Royal Caledonian Curling Club (www.royalcaledonian curlingclub.org), World Curling Federation (www.worldcurling.org)

NORDIC WORLD SKI CHAMPIONSHIPS

WHERE Location changes each championship **WHEN** Late February, in odd-numbered years
GETTING INVOLVED Check the website for scheduling and ticketing details.

All that is missing is the old-fashioned outfits. Championship challengers pedal their penny farthings, at speed, through the streets of Tasmania's Evandale.

The real crowd pleaser of the World Ski Championships is the ski jump – where seemingly fearless athletes launch themselves from a ramp and fly, with grace and aplomb (ideally), great distances. Ski jumpers earn points by landing on or over the K-spot (90m or 120m, and 200m in the ski-flying event) and for style, judged according to whether their skis were steady during the flight, their balance, body position and landing, which is tele-mark style – one foot in front of the other, if you don't mind. It's a breathtaking and teeth-clenching event to watch.

But the ski jump is just one of three disciplines in the Nordic World Ski Championships: along with cross-country skiing and Nordic Combined – a combination of cross-country and ski jumping.

Cross-country skiing has two main styles: the 'classic' diagonal stride and the 'freestyle' skating stride, which is faster. Championship competition is composed of 12 different events, including the popular 'mass start,' with all competitors surging forward simultaneously and racing to the finish line, sprints and relays. There are four events to choose from in the Nordic category, each with varying length cross-country courses and varying numbers of jumps. The combined number of winning points determines the overall winner.

The Championship itself has been wowing winter crowds since 1925 for men, and 1954 for women. It's run by the International Ski Federation, which is the main organiser of international ski sports, with 101 national ski association members.

Norway is widely considered to be the cradle of cross-country skiing, with the famous Huseby and Holmenkollen races run here from the late 19th century, so Oslo hosting the 2011 championships is something of a homecoming. Italy's Val de Fiemme, the host in 2013, is no slouch either, with two previous World Championships under its belt and facilities to accommodate 35,000 people.

MORE INFO International Ski Federation (www.fis-ski.com)

NATIONAL PENNY FARTHING CHAMPIONSHIPS

WHERE Evandale, Tasmania, Australia **WHEN** Second last Saturday in February **GETTING INVOLVED** Accommodation in Evandale is limited, so book early or stay in Launceston and drive down for the day. Races in the streets of Evandale are on the Saturday from 10am to 4pm.

Forget the Tour de France and its fancy bicycles with two wheels of equal size. Get along and see the 1871 invention of British engineer James Starley at the National Penny Farthing Championships, and witness a true test of speed, endurance and balance.

Held annually since 1983, this is the largest penny farthing event in the world. Farthing aficionados from New Zealand, England, USA, Ireland, Sweden, Holland, Czech Republic, Japan, Singapore, Germany and Australia all converge on the small town of Evandale.

The fastest eight riders advance through heats to the final, which is over four laps of the circuit. Total distance: 1 mile in old imperial measurements (seeing as we're measuring old-style bicycles) or 1.6km. While it's definitely the feature race of the day it's by no means the only one. Other races keep the crowd entertained throughout the day including the slow race (last over the line wins), sprint (200m dash), novice race (first-time riders), relay (teams of four pedal one lap each) and a real favourite, miss 'n' out (last rider on each lap eliminated).

Held in conjunction with the Evandale Village Fair, the races take place through the immaculately preserved streets of town, which seem made for penny farthings. Market stalls, food, music and entertainment are all part of the fun.

MORE INFO Evandale Village Fair and Penny Farthing Championships (www.evandale villagefair.com)

SHOWA-SHINZAN INTERNATIONAL YUKIGASSEN

WHERE Hokkaido, Japan **WHEN** End of February **GETTING INVOLVED** Register your team online; applications accepted from December – get in early as quotas are reached very quickly.

Do you have fond memories of childhood snowball fights and remember the glory of a perfectly aimed snowball hitting its target? Then you are perfectly prepared for the snowball fight of your life at the Showa-Shinzan International Yukigassen.

Originating in Japan in 1988, the competition was inspired by the desire to attract more people to Sobetsu Town during the slow, winter season. Most tourists visit the young mountain, which sprang up in a wheat field as recently as 1943, during summer. The competition has been an unqualified success, re-energizing the mountain during this previously quiet time, while also spawning tournaments in Finland, Norway and Australia.

Yukigassen involves two teams of seven players on a 10m-by-40m pitch, which includes a series of snow walls to hide behind. Three sets of three minutes each are played, with each team having 90 snowballs (made before each game by a machine) to throw. Each team has to defend a flag while trying to capture their opponent's and avoid being hit by a ball. If a player is hit they are out for the whole set. A set is won by either capturing the flag or by having more players left on the pitch at the end of the three minutes. If there is a tie, then the team that used the fewest snowballs wins.

Organisers expect more than 2500 teams to compete in the annual heats of the Showa-Shinzan International Yukigassen, with the number of participants increasing every year.

MORE INFO Showa-Shinzan International Yukigassen (www.yukigassen.jp/english)

Firm on his cramp-bits stands the steady youth

Who leads the game: low o'er the weighty stone

He bends incumbent, and with nicest eye

Surveys the further goal, and in his mind

Measures the distance; careful to bestow

Just force enough; then, balanc'd in his hand

he flings it on direct...

Early poetic description of curling, James Graeme, 1773

FOR THE RECORD

↗ Only two countries south of the equator have ever won medals at Winter Olympics: Australia and New Zealand.

↗ In 2002, Georg Hackl won his fifth consecutive medal in the same event (luge singles), a feat never before achieved by any Olympian.

WINTER OLYMPICS

WHERE Location changes each games **WHEN** Every four years **GETTING INVOLVED** Each country has its own official ticketing agent handling ticket sales. Obviously, the earlier you book, the better your chances of securing the events you want.

The Olympics' humble raison d'être is to promote a peaceful and better world through sport, practised without discrimination. But until 1924, the year of the first Winter Olympics (28 years after the first modern Olympics), countries with colder climates were mostly discriminated against via their exclusion.

The first separate 'International Winter Sports Week' (which would later become known as the Winter Olympics) was held in 1924, in France. It was a roaring success, with 200 athletes from 16 nations competing in 16 separate events. The Winter Olympics have run quadrennially since – except for the few years interrupted by world wars.

Fewer countries participate in the Winter Olympics than the Summer Olympics, due to the fact that there are simply fewer countries with the kind of winter

01.

02.

03.

04.

'These days the Winter Olympics have more than 5500 athletes competing, from around 80 countries'

FEBRUARY
WEEK.04

Team Canada's Mathieu Turcotte leads during the men's speed skating 5000m relay final at the 2006 Winter Olympics in Turin.

conditions required for athletes to develop in winter sports. That's not to say that competitors from tropical countries are excluded from Winter Olympic Games; more, they provide the human-interest element. The Philippines sent two alpine skiers to Japan in 1972 (neither finishing the slalom event), and although finishing 14th in the 2006 Olympics, the Jamaican bobsled team were indisputably the crowd favourites.

The Winter Olympics has all the elements of the summer version: a showy opening and closing ceremony, cutesy mascots, the torch relay (which travels from Olympia and passes through the host country's participating towns), associated cultural festival (showcasing premier artistic performances from the region), and sporting events that attract the world's best athletes, including those with differing disabilities.

Each year, the Winter Olympics program is extended to include more sports. There are 20 sports in the 2010 Olympics (each with up to 10 events). Among them is speed skating, which has been an Olympic sport since the first Winter Games and is the fastest non-mechanical sport in the world, with skaters reaching speeds up to 60km/h. Other events include figure skating, wheelchair curling, snowboarding, ski jumping, ice-sledge hockey and the biathlon (which combines cross-country skiing and rifle shooting).

The Olympics would have to be the world's premier events for bringing together the greatest number of athletes from the largest variety of countries. These days the Winter Olympics have more than 5500 athletes competing, from around 80 countries. And if you're from the southern hemisphere, attending a Winter Olympics is a grand opportunity to watch the world's best compete at some rather unfamiliar sports.

MORE INFO The Olympic Games (www.olympic.org)

Concentration as the fleece flies – competing for the Golden Shears in wool handling requires strength, style and a great deal of skill.

GOLDEN SHEARS – SHEARING & WOOL HANDLING CHAMPIONSHIPS

WHERE Masterton, New Zealand **WHEN** Late February or early March **GETTING INVOLVED** Tickets are available at the door.

How long does it take to shear a sheep? Less than two minutes, if you're a 'gun shearer', the likes of which will be vying for the Open Shearing Title at the Golden Shears Championships. More than 90 shearers compete in the open, heralding from Australia, New Zealand, South Africa, Norway, Scotland and Wales. And watching them has been described as 'physical poetry'.

The 'tally-hi' technique is preferred (generally thought to be fastest and causing the least stress to the sheep). Instituted in 1963, the tally-hi starts with the animal's tummy, then moves to its sides and back until the fleece is removed in a fluid routine. A gun shearer will tally between 400 and 500 sheep in a day's work, and will hardly nick the animal.

Other events of the Golden Shears include the wool handling: flinging a fleece onto a slatted table, 'skirting' it (picking out undesirables such as poo, leaves and twigs) and throwing it into the correct wool bin – according to its class; and the wool-pressing competition, which organisers describe as 'muscles in motion'. This is the final part of the shearing process, where wool is pressed into bales for storing and/or transport.

The Golden Shears is closely linked to the nation's identity, New Zealand being the world's largest producer and exporter of crossbred wool, and second only to Australia in the export of all wool. It's little surprise then that the competition attracts a crowd, albeit a mostly rural-oriented one. In its early years, the army had to be called in to control the unexpected surge of spectators. Running since 1961, the Golden Shears is one of the world's premier shearing and wool handling competitions. Things kick off before 8am, so get there early.

MORE INFO Golden Shears (www.goldenshears.co.nz)

BATTAGLIA DELLE ARANGE (BATTLE OF THE ORANGES)

WHERE Ivrea, Italy **WHEN** Concludes Shrove Tuesday **GETTING INVOLVED** Anyone can take part. Just get in early to enlist in one of the sides. If you're a spectator, in theory you're safe from an orange attack. In reality, keep your eyes open for flying oranges and watch your footing on the sea of fallen fruit.

Three days, 3500 people, two sides, 400,000kg of oranges, and a whole lot of pulp. The beautiful old town of Ivrea, 35km from Turin, celebrates the town's history with an annual carnival, the incontestable highlight being the Battle of the Oranges.

Taking place in the town square, this gigantic food fight is inspired by the story of a miller's daughter who, during the Middle Ages, rebelled against the evil ruling tyrant after he had proclaimed the right to sleep with any woman about to be married. The refusal by the miller's daughter sparked a revolt by the entire town, which is now re-enacted annually.

Today, carriages represent the duke's guard (who rode through town in horse-drawn carts) and the orange throwers represent the rebellious townsfolk (who pelted them). Anybody can take part by enlisting in one of the nine orange pelting teams or, if tyranny is your thing, becoming a member of a carriage crew.

Why oranges? Well, originally people threw beans. Then, in the 19th century, girls started throwing oranges at boys they liked, who would throw them back if they in turn liked the girl. Many a romance may have been lost due to a boy's true feelings not being revealed through his simple distaste for oranges.

Spectators are not permitted to throw oranges. Red hat wearers are considered part of the revolutionaries and are not to be targeted. So, enlist in a team and warm up your throwing arm, or stand back, marvel at the spectacle and look out for errant flying oranges.
MORE INFO Il Carnevale de Ivrea (www.carnevalediivrea.it)

WORLD TUG OF WAR INDOOR CHAMPIONSHIPS

WHERE Location changes each championship **WHEN** February
GETTING INVOLVED Check the website for scheduling and ticketing info.

Pick up the rope. Take the strain. Steady. Pull. It may sound easy, but reserve judgment until you've seen the machine-like efficiency of teams competing at the World Tug of War Indoor Championships. This pure contest of strength predates any written history and permeates modern parlance in the form of metaphor.

While it mightn't be at the forefront of your hometown sporting news coverage, it's quite possible that your country is a member of the Tug of War International Federation (TWIF). There are more than 50 countries represented including England, Ireland, Australia, Canada, Israel, China, France, Latvia, Russia and the USA.

The World Tug of War Indoor Championships involves teams of eight competing in a qualifying round, semi-finals and finals in different weight categories. Categories include ultra flyweight (where the total weight of the team cannot exceed 480kg), heavyweight (maximum team weight of 720kg) and catch weight (no maximum weight limit).

Like any sport, tug of war is governed by strict rules: staying on your feet being the most important. No sitting, leaning (touching the ground with any part of the body other than the feet), locking (any hold preventing the free movement of the rope), propping, climbing or rowing is permitted.

The tug of war was once an official Olympic event – from 1900 to 1920. While it hasn't been represented since, it is recognised by the International Olympic Committee (IOC) and there was talk of it being included in the 2012 London Games.
MORE INFO Tug of War International Federation (www.tugofwar-twif.org)

01. 02. 03. 04.

FEBRUARY
WEEK.04

AND ANOTHER THING

Pari Roller (Place Raoul Dautry, 14e, Paris)
Up to 20,000 skaters have been known to roll through the streets on these highly organised events, which run every rain-free Friday night. Pari Roller is non-competitive and exists for the sheer joy of rollerskating, en masse, along the boulevards and byways of Paris. (www.pari-roller.com)

FOR THE RECORD

↗ Portsmouth beat Reading 7-4 in 2008; the game was the highest scoring in Premier League history.

↗ Former Blackburn Rovers and Newcastle United striker Alan Shearer holds the record for most Premier League goals with 260.

↗ The highest paid players earn £150,000 a week.

ENGLISH PREMIER LEAGUE

 WHERE England **WHEN** Season runs from August through to May
GETTING INVOLVED Obtaining tickets ranges from easy to near impossible, depending on who's playing; each club has its own process and allocation.

It's the world's most watched football league and the world's most popular sport. It's also the most lucrative league – luring the best players from around the world. So it's hard to believe it has such a short history, with the first Premier League ball kicked as recently as 1992.

Of course, it didn't just materialise overnight. The league pre-existed, under the auspices of the English Football Association, established in 1888. Through the 1970s and '80s, football in England ebbed to an all-time low. Hooliganism was rife: 39 mostly Italian fans were killed after English supporters breached a fence to charge and attack them in 1985 in Brussels. English teams were subsequently banned from Europe.

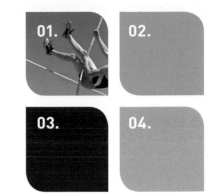

'To watch an English Premier League game is to hear thousands of supporters singing their hearts out'

MARCH
WEEK.01

West Ham's goalkeeper Rob Green (in yellow) punches the ball out under a challenge from Arsenal's Emmanuel Adebayor during a Premier League match in 2009.

Stadiums were in poor condition: 56 people died when a fire destroyed one side of Bradford stadium. Spectator numbers were in decline.

A radical restructure ensued. English first-division clubs withdrew from the Football League en masse, and joined the newly created Premier League – which promised lucrative television-rights deals.

The home-and-away season consists of 38 matches. Manchester United has won the EPL 10 times, making it the most successful club in the last 20 years. The top four teams in the English Premier League qualify for the UEFA Champions League, along with the top teams in Europe. Liverpool was the last English club to win the coveted trophy for a fifth time, back in 2005. The bottom three teams heartbreakingly drop to the Championship (2nd division), and three teams from the Championship rise ecstatically to the Premier League.

Local-derby matches are also vehemently contested (and vehemently followed). The big derby rivalries have their roots in the clubs' histories and communities, such as Manchester City and Manchester United, Arsenal and Tottenham, and Liverpool and Everton.

To watch an English Premier League game is to hear thousands of supporters singing their hearts out. All teams have one defining team song and dozens of chants – some about the club, others about the manager (coach) or even about particular players. Apart from venting some of that pent-up energy, the ruckus is intended to influence the teams, by urging on their beloveds or putting off their opposition. Part of the football-watching culture is finding a nearby pub afterwards in which to celebrate with like-minded folk.

MORE INFO Premier League (www.premierleague.com)

Vasaloppet – it could very well be Swedish for ski scrum. Competitors in the 2007 event put their endurance and woollen hats to the test.

THE IDITAROD

WHERE From Anchorage to Nome, Alaska **WHEN** First Saturday in March **GETTING INVOLVED** Parts of the trail are open for public recreation; otherwise you can cheer for the dog-sled teams trail-side and at checkpoints.

More than 1000 wolf-like Siberian huskies lunge out of Anchorage every March, marking the start of the epic Iditarod dog-sled race. Teams of 12 to 16 dogs and their mushers traverse 1850km of Alaskan winter wilderness in a tough 10 to 17 days.

The first race ran in 1973, as a kind of ode to the importance of dog-sled racing in Alaskan history. Up until the mid-1920s, sled dogs were the only means to transport goods across the frozen Alaskan countryside. The Iditarod trail was first mapped and marked in 1908, and originally used as a mail-run and supply route, connecting coastal towns with gold-mining towns in the state's interior. A crack team of 20 of Alaska's best mushers and their dogs also famously transported much-needed serum to the city of Nome, cut off by winter ice in 1925 and facing a diptheria epidemic.

The route is now honoured as a National Historic Trail commemorating the importance of the run in American history. Parts of the trail are open to the public, especially in Chugach National Park. The race, named after the once thriving gold-mining town of the same name in the state's interior, honours sled dogs for their part in humans surviving and thriving in Alaska.

It's a punishing race covering wild terrain with equally wild weather, frequently below zero. Mushers sometimes put shoes on their dogs to protect their pads from the cutting packed ice. The race follows a southern route in odd-numbered years (with 27 checkpoints, and passing through the ghost town of Iditarod) and a northern route (with 26 checkpoints) in even-numbered years. Traditionally, the last musher over the line is awarded a red lantern – the Iditarod equivalent of the wooden spoon. The longest time for a red lantern was 32 days, 15 hours, nine minutes and one second by John Schultz in 1973.

MORE INFO The Iditarod Trail Sled Dog Race (www.iditarod.com), The Iditarod National Historic Trail (www.iditarodnationalhistorictrail.org)

VASALOPPET

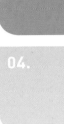

> **WHERE** From Salen to Mora, Sweden **WHEN** Early March **GETTING INVOLVED** Register online. If competing is not for you, find a vantage point at the start or finish of the race, and visit the Vasaloppet museum beside the famous Portal that marks the finishing line.

Imagine a mass of humanity on skis stretching out for more than 1km. The start of the Vasaloppet, a 90km cross-country ski race – the oldest, longest and biggest cross-country ski race in the world – provides such a spectacle. A total of 14,000 anxious, shivering skiers stand there in the village of Salen, in subzero temperatures, seeded into 10 groups with 350 elite skiers at the front of the field. Novices stand with those that have competed 30 times. Not long after getting underway at 8am, skiers find themselves climbing 'the Hill'. They strive for rhythm, speed and to simply catch their breath over the rolling course, in a race that is a true test of endurance.

The Vasaloppet, so named after King Gustav Eriksson Vasa and *loppet* (Swiss for 'race') was first held in 1922. In all its history, Nils 'Mora-Nisse' Karlsson's nine victories are the most by any one skier. His sister placed the winner's wreath over his head after his 1943 triumph, she was the Kransukulla (Garland Girl), which has been a prestigious role in the race's history. Peter Goransson holds the current record of three hours 38 minutes and 57 seconds, which he skied in 1998.

Drinks stations en route dispense warming cups of soup or salty bouillon to sustain skiers. After they see the church spire in Mora the cheers of hundreds of onlookers carries them to the finish line, completing their marathon under a sign that bears the race's now-famous motto: 'In the footsteps of our forefathers for the victories of tomorrow'.
MORE INFO Vasaloppet (www.vasaloppet.se)

EUROPEAN ATHLETICS INDOOR CHAMPIONSHIPS

> **WHERE** Birmingham, England **WHEN** Biennially, in the first week of March **GETTING INVOLVED** The championships routinely sell out, so get in early.

The simple solution to the problem of performing certain athletic disciplines in unfavourable conditions has resulted in a separate and very popular athletics competition of its own. The indoor championships have attracted Europe's top athletes since 1970. Initially an annual event held in different cities all over Europe, since 1990 it has been run biennially.

Around 500 athletes from around 45 countries compete in an intense and exciting three-day event. Indoor running events generally take place on a six-lane, 200m track – smaller than an outdoor track, athletes must alter their technique to accommodate the tighter turns. Many of the distances (400m, 800m and 1500m) will be familiar to outdoor athletics fans, although the 60m sprint, which takes slightly less than seven seconds to run, is peculiar to the indoor arena. Other well-known events include the high jump, pole vault, long jump and shotput. All heats and qualifications are contested on the Friday, with the finals spread between the Saturday and Sunday afternoons.

These championships have provided many junior athletes with their first opportunity to compete internationally in the senior ranks. Many world indoor and national records are broken here. Athletes strive for gold, while countries battle to top the medal tally.

The fans are further entertained by musical performances and are kept well informed about the event schedule, specific disciplines and results via the stadium announcer. The enclosed space allows the considerable noise that the fans generate to help exhort the athletes on to their personal best.
MORE INFO European Athletics (www.european-athletics.org)

MARCH
WEEK.01

'We'll still be happy if we lose. The game's on at the same time as the Beer Festival.'

Cork City Football Club manager Noel O'Mahoney before a game in Munich, 1986

- - - - - - - - - - - - - - - - - -

↗ Athletes have been known to compete in the pentathlon in as many as four Olympic Games: while age has an adverse affect on times for the swim and run, experience tends to sharpen technical skills in the riding, fencing and shooting.

↗ Pavel Lednev is the oldest Olympic gold medallist, aged 37 when he won the modern pentathlon at the 1980 Moscow Games.

MODERN PENTATHLON WORLD CUP

 WHERE Various locations throughout the series **WHEN** Four to six competitions and one final throughout the year **GETTING INVOLVED** Tickets are readily available online.

Whatever the sport, athletes strive to be the best. But, it is argued, there is only one event that yields the 'complete' athlete, revealing their moral qualities as well as their physical abilities and skills. Introducing the modern pentathlon, where athletes fence, swim, ride a horse, run and shoot – the latter two almost simultaneously.

Touted as 'the true Olympic sport', the pentathlon was included in the 18th Olympiad of 708 BC, with athletes running the length of the stadium, jumping, throwing a spear and a discus, and then wrestling. The modern pentathlon has been an Olympic sport since the Stockholm Games in 1912. And since 2009 the shooting and running events have been combined, so, not only would the athletes make

'Introducing the modern pentathlon, where athletes fence, swim, ride a horse, run and shoot'

MARCH
WEEK.02

Andrea Valentini of Italy completes the run, which is one of the five disciplines of the modern pentathlon.

better criminals, but the overall time of the event is reduced (previously extending to around 12 hours) making it a more friendly sport for athletes and spectators.

There's mass movement in pentathlon events, as spectators move around, following the 36 competing athletes from one playing field to the next. It begins with the fencing. Every athlete fences with the other, once, in a sudden-death bout lasting just one minute. The action is swashbucklingly fast, with 18 athletes fencing on nine pistes at any one time. To the pool next for the 200m freestyle; athletes are seeded according to their personal bests. But it's the third leg where things start to get really interesting. Athletes randomly draw an unfamiliar horse to ride over a 350m to 450m course that includes a dozen show jumps. Anything can happen, and usually does. It's not unheard of for athletes who were

previously in the lead to choose a horse that decides it simply doesn't want to jump that day. And, finally, the run-shoot event. By now it's pretty clear which athletes are likely contenders for a win, but again, a fast runner may lose the lead with a few bad shots. Athletes run (at handicap intervals) a short distance to the shooting range where they fire off five shots. They then run 1km to the next firing range and fire another five shots, repeating the run and shoot three times in total, so firing 15 shots and running just over 3km. Complete athlete or what?!

MORE INFO Union Internationale de Pentathlon Modern (UIPM; www.pentathlon.org)

01.

02.

03.

04.

OXFORD & CAMBRIDGE BOAT RACE

WHERE River Thames, London, England **WHEN** Mid- to late March, depending on the tides **GETTING INVOLVED** There's usually no problem getting a possie by the river along with the other 249,999 spectators.

For those boys who find the rigours of studying at one of London's top universities not tough enough, there's some serious rowing training available, and a serious rivalry in which to partake: the annual rowing race between Oxford and Cambridge Universities.

The rivalry goes back to 1829, when the race began, in Henley. Today the eight-class, 6.8km race is rowed on what's known as the Championship Course, from Putney to Mortlake, an S-shaped section on the tidal reaches of the Thames. Before the race, the clubs' presidents call a coin toss (using an 1829 sovereign); the winner decides on which side of the river (station) they will row. During the race, the boats compete for the fastest current (found at the deepest part of the river), which frequently leads to clashing oars and warnings from the umpire.

It's all done in just over a quarter of an hour, with the record finishing time being 16 minutes and 19 seconds, set in 1998 by Cambridge which, incidentally, also holds the record for the slowest winning time (36 minutes, in 1836) and has the most wins.

The race attracts around a quarter of a million spectators, with millions more tuning in via television or radio broadcasts. And, as is tradition since the race was first run in 1829, the losers will challenge the opposition to a re-match, and you can guarantee it'll go on again the following year.

The Head of the River Race runs the same stretch of the Thames, usually the week prior – sometimes the day prior. It's considered to be the peak of the head-race season (time-trial rowing) and attracts 420 crews including the top UK crews as well as foreign clubs.

MORE INFO The Oxford and Cambridge Boat Race (www.theboatrace.org), Head of the River Race (www.horr.co.uk)

MARCH
WEEK.02

AND ANOTHER THING

- - - - - - - - - - - - - -

Calligraphy Competition (Lamu, Kenya; part of the Maulid Festival)

Among the festivities to celebrate the birth of the Prophet Mohammed is the artful practice of writing Swahili in Arabic script – as it was originally written before the Latin alphabet was adopted. There are also poetry readings, donkey races and quivering-sword dances.

NATIONAL SHEEP DOG TRIAL CHAMPIONSHIPS

WHERE Canberra, ACT, Australia **WHEN** Mid-March **GETTING INVOLVED** Apart from the trials, there's a sausage sizzle, plenty of other food and drink, and visiting dogs are welcome – as long as they're on a lead and well behaved.

If horse racing is the sport of kings, then sheepdog trials must be the sport of the queen – if the attendance of Her Majesty Queen Elizabeth II and His Royal Highness the Duke of Edinburgh at 1970's National Sheepdog Championships is anything to go by. Not only were they there, but Her Majesty presented the winning trophies. She must have enjoyed herself, because in 1975 the right to use her name on a trophy received the royal nod, and the 'Queen's Trophy' became *the* prize.

The Australian National Sheepdog Trials involve dogs moving a flock of sheep around a field, fences, gates or enclosures, under the direction of their handler. Apart from being a necessary element on sheep farms in Australia and New Zealand, such trials are also popular in the UK, Ireland and South Africa.

An average of 50 competitors enter approximately 250 dogs, usually kelpies, border collies or a mix thereof. They compete for trophies, prize money and a shot at winning the Queen's Trophy, the Duke of Gloucester Sash and the Governor General's Sash. There are three different grades in which the dogs compete: maiden dogs (dogs that have never won a trial), improver dogs (dogs that have won a maiden trial) and open dogs (dogs that have won both maiden and improver trials).

The competition runs for six days, with the maiden-class dogs trialling early in the week. Why not stay for the entire championship? If it's good enough for the Queen...

MORE INFO National Sheepdog Trials Association (www.nationalsheepdogs.webone.com.au)

Cambridge wins the battle...this time. Kieran West roars to the sky after winning the race's 153rd bout.

CYCLE-BALL WORLD CUP FINAL

WHERE Various countries host qualifying and finals matches **WHEN** Qualifying matches run year-round, with the finals in mid-March **GETTING INVOLVED** Check the website for scheduling and ticketing info.

In 1893, New Zealand granted women the right to vote, the US Supreme Court legally declared the tomato to be a vegetable and the sport of cycle-ball was born. The result of a magical fusion of artistic cycling and football (soccer), cycle-ball is a unique sport that blends the characteristic skill and raw power of its parent sports.

A quick reminder: artistic cycling involves athletes performing tricks atop their bikes before a panel of judges. Cycle-ball players apply the same bike-handling skills and combine it with ball-handling skills to create quite a spectacle.

Played indoors and contested by two teams of two, on a 'field' that measures 14m by 11m with a goal at each end, the game consists of two fast-and-furious seven-minute halves. Riding bicycles, the players trap, pass and shoot the ball at goal by manipulating the front wheel. Players interchange between offence and defence depending on the ebb and flow of the game. Each player may in turn act as a goalkeeper. Cycle-ball players ride specifically designed bikes that are modified in shape and strength to accommodate the movements the sport requires. The bicycles are set in a fixed gear, which enhances acceleration and control.

Ten teams, representing their country, contest the World Cup, which is played in a round-robin format, with each side playing four games. The two best sides contest the final. The proximity of the crowd to the field is close enough to hear the clash of metal, and the frenetic pace of the play makes cycle-ball a wonderful spectator sport. **MORE INFO** Union Cycliste Internationale (www.uci.ch)

Ekaterina Rubleva and Ivan Shefer of Russia perform their 'free' routine during the 2008 ISU World Figure Skating Championships in Gothenburg, Sweden.

WORLD FIGURE SKATING CHAMPIONSHIPS

WHERE Location changes each championships **WHEN** Late March **GETTING INVOLVED** Tickets are readily available; check online.

To read about it is a confusing, clumsy-sounding jumble that goes something like this: triple toe loop, loop, salchow, twizzle, camel spin, death drop, choctaw, outside-edge spiral in catch-foot, lutz, walley jump, axel. To watch it, though, is something else entirely. It's to see bodies defying reason, and jumping gazelle-like through the chilled air, spinning tightly like highly tuned pistons and stepping like ballerinas into another awesome jump or spin.

With that kind of agility, all performed on ice, it's not surprising that figure skating is one of the world's most popular winter sports. And the World Championships is considered to be the most prestigious competition outside of the Olympics. The 'worlds' (as they're known) were established in 1896, and included male-only events. But with no rules actually preventing women from competing, Madge Syers-Cave competed in 1902, and won silver. The governing body was quick to create separate female events (1906), and followed soon after with pair-skating events (1908).

With a history dating back to the mid-19th century, figure skating began as a stiff and formal sport. Even up until the 1960s, figure skating was a very different beast to the one practiced today. It was originally true to its name, with skaters judged on their precision in executing various figures, such as the figure 8. Apparently watching 8 after 8 after 8 was less than riveting. When television came along, the figure-skating component of the competition was gradually reduced until it was finally dropped altogether in the '90s.

Another telly-friendly change to the sport was a restructure of the competition format to include a short and long program. The short program involves the skater performing a list of elements (jumps, steps and spins) of which there are many sorts of each: there are six types of axel alone. The long program allows the skater more freedom to choose which elements to include in their routine.

Ice dancing is a relative newcomer in the history of the competition, included in 1952. As the title suggests, the focus is on the footwork of the male-female couple who are locked closely and are moving to music.

Like the names of the manoeuvres, the scoring process is long-winded, and quite technical. It's best left to the judges. It doesn't take an expert to appreciate the skill and old-school beauty of a figure-skating routine.

MORE INFO International Skating Union (www.isu.org)

'To watch figure skating is to see bodies defying reason, jumping gazelle-like, spinning tightly and then stepping into another awesome jump or spin'

MARCH
WEEK.03

FOR THE RECORD

- ↗ Male skaters may not wear tights; they must wear pants.

- ↗ Only once in the history of international competition has a woman been credited with a quadruple jump.

- ↗ Sonja Henie is popularly credited with setting the fashion for ladies to wear white boot skates back in the 1920s.

TRUGO

WHERE Melbourne, Australia **WHEN** From August through to April **GETTING INVOLVED** The VTA needs new players; look them up if you're in Melbourne.

There's only one small pocket of the world where you can see, and even play, the unique game of trugo. And if the current trend of low club membership continues, you should hurry lest the game becomes extinct.

Something like a hybrid of lawn bowls and croquet, trugo was invented by Melbourne rail workers in 1924. Not surprisingly, every aspect of the game relates to trains. Solid rubber rings used as buffers between carriages were knocked about with a sledgehammer, since replaced by a lighter wooden mallet. The pitch's length is that of a train carriage and the goals are the same width apart as an open doorway to a carriage.

What began as a way for rail workers to kill a bit of time during their breaks at work grew into an organised sport, popular in the city's working-class areas. It's a highly sociable game played by both men and women – mostly in their 80s.

Until the '90s, trugo club membership was reserved for over 65s, but it soon became clear that the game could use some young blood, and it was opened to all. But the younger generations aren't replacing the original players, at the same rate. The game's future is uncertain.

So, if you live in Melbourne, think about picking up the mallet and having a go – maybe even a 'true go'. The game involves two teams of eight players. Each team has six turns at hitting four rings through the goals: a 'true go' according to legend. Men prefer to take a swing backwards through the legs, while the ladies often prefer the putt-style swing. Even if you're in town briefly, watching a game and chatting to the players goes straight to the heart of Melbourne's local heritage.

MORE INFO Victorian Trugo Association (http://home.vicnet.net.au/~vtrugo)

WORLD GOLF CHAMPIONSHIPS

WHERE Florida, USA **WHEN** Mid-March **GETTING INVOLVED** Be a part of the huge galleries that walk the course, following around the greatest golfers in the world. You can purchase daily tickets and weekly tickets at the gate on the day or from the website.

Golf is many things to many people. It's 'a good walk spoiled' if you're Mark Twain and it is 'a game played on a five-inch course – the distance between your ears', according to Bobby Jones. Find out what golf is to you by getting along and seeing the best male golfers in the world walking and battling their minds (and swings) at the prestigious World Golf Championships.

This event is one of the three annual tournaments that make up the official World Golf Championships. The other two are the World Golf Accenture Match Play Championships in February and the World Golf Championships Invitational in August. These championships are fully supported by the International Federation of PGA Tours.

The best players from around the world come together for 72 holes of stroke play with no cut. That means you're guaranteed a full four rounds from all the players competing. Originally created to bring the golfing elite together more regularly than just for the major championships, it was seen as a chance for the formation of a World Tour – although this concept seems to have lost some momentum recently. But what hasn't been lost is the interest and quality of players competing, as can be seen by a roll call of past winners: Tiger Woods, Ernie Els and Geoff Ogilvy. See the world's finest golfers battling for ranking points and substantial prize money. We're tipping this is one walk even Mr Twain may have enjoyed.

MORE INFO World Golf Championships (www.worldgolfchampionships.com)

WORLD FLY-FISHING CHAMPIONSHIPS

WHERE Location changes each championships **WHEN** Usually around mid- to late March **GETTING INVOLVED** Apply online.

'A trout is a moment of beauty known only to those who seek it', Arnold Gingrich once said. Mr Gingrich, editor of *Esquire* magazine, would be very proud of participants in the World Fly-Fishing Championships, who have been seeking that moment of beauty, using ancient technique, for 30 years. The event, and fishing in general, continues to grow in popularity to the point where there are now more than 20 fly-fishing teams from around the world that gather annually to compete for the world title. The week begins with a couple of practice days before the competition opens and spreads over three days and over several chosen fisheries in the area.

During the three days of competition each individual fishes for five sessions of three hours each. Their catches are scored and the total score of their 25 individual session scores is added to the total team score. Judges supervise the sessions and volunteers are in charge of measuring the fish.

Massive numbers of large trout are caught both in practice and during the competition. It is not uncommon for the winning team to snag almost 400 fish over the three days. Even the bottom teams capture almost 100. Teams can be off the pace after day one, then storm up the standings by the end of day two, due to some individual brilliance. It's exciting stuff.

It's often been said that a bad day's fishing is better than a good day at work. Ask the losing teams at the World Championships if they agree.

MORE INFO FIPS-Mouche World Fly-Fishing Championships (www.worldflyfishing championships2009.com)

'Golf is deceptively simple and endlessly complicated; it satisfies the soul and frustrates the intellect. It is at the same time rewarding and maddening – and it is without a doubt the greatest game mankind has ever invented.'

Arnold Palmer, American golfer and instructor

Under a blazing sun, and carrying all their equipment on their backs, competitors trek over Saharan sand dunes during the 2008 Marathon des Sables.

MARATHON DES SABLES

WHERE Morocco **WHEN** End of March to beginning of April
GETTING INVOLVED Allow six months of training prior to the event, plus
be prepared for the hefty entry fee.

For those who consider running the sorts of distances most people would only
drive a 'walk in the park', this one's for you. The Marathon des Sables (Marathon
of Sands) may not be the longest, at a not-so-modest 243km, but make those
kms across the Sahara, and you've got what's widely considered to be the
world's toughest footrace.

Run over six days, the trail crosses uneven rocky terrain, between dunes and
over seas of soft sand (think of your calf muscles after a short jog on the beach).
Desert temperatures are extreme. Competitors are advised to wear shoes two
sizes bigger than normal and wider at the toe to allow for swelling from the heat.
Temperatures can go from 48°C during the day to 4°C at night. Any anti-chafing
creams quickly collect sand, which equates to having sandpaper between your
legs, and thorny trail-side plants will stab anyone who passes too close.

Added to this is the fact that competitors must carry everything on their
person: that's enough freeze-dried food and energy bars for the journey, a
sleeping bag, enough water for quenching thirst between checkpoints and a
credit card. Yes, a credit card, for those satellite phonecalls home, and emails
(over the six days of the event, the organisers receive around 40,000 messages
to pass on to competitors). At the end of each race stage, which includes a non-
stop 82km section that has most competitors running after nightfall, there's a
Berber-tent camp (provided by the organisers). Competitors sleep eight to a tent
on a carpeted floor.

Sound insane? What's more insane is that it's been operating for more than
25 years, and more than 800 people from 30 different countries sign up for it. As
with all endurance races, runners are battling themselves as much as the other
800-odd entrants. Along with the obvious stress on the body, the mental stress
is intense. Competitors must overcome pain and the internal chatter that says,
'You're not cut out for this, c'mon, let's pull over here'.

Still keen? Some final words from the organisers: 'If you have never run, or
if you are not used to training at least three times a week for several months, it
would not be reasonable to consider entering the Marathon des Sables.'
MORE INFO Marathon de Sables (www.darbaroud.com)

MARCH
WEEK.04

*'Competitors are advised to wear shoes two
sizes bigger than normal to allow for swelling
from the heat'*

FOR THE RECORD

- ↗ The MdS is equal to almost
  six regular marathons.

- ↗ Moroccan Lahcen Ahansal has
  won the marathon 10 times;
  his brother has won twice.

RIP CURL PRO

WHERE Bells Beach, Victoria, Australia **WHEN** March or April **GETTING INVOLVED** Tickets are available each day at the entry gate.

'The Bell is arguably the best trophy you can win in surfing.' So says eight-time world champion Kelly Slater. Formerly the Bells Beach Surf Classic, the Rip Curl Pro is held in and around Torquay, with the event itself staged on the famous Bells Beach, although it has moved further down the coast in the recent past due to a lack of surf. It is Australia's longest-running and most-famous professional surfing event, and a big favourite of the international surfing community. Quite simply, everyone loves coming to Bells.

Bells has been surfed since the 1930s but access was a considerable problem until 1960 when local surfer and Olympic wrestler Joe Sweeney hired a bulldozer and cleared a road along the Bells cliff down to the beach. He charged £1 per surfer to recover his expenses.

If the world's best surfers cutting up enormous waves is not enough action, there is a music festival on the Easter Saturday and Sunday, with local and interstate bands performing on the Bells cliff top.

If you're a fan of the 1991 movie *Point Break*, you're probably aware of the final scene, in which a friendly fugitive is free to surf to his death on the giant waves at Bells Beach. You're also probably aware that it wasn't actually filmed at Bells. You'll need to make your way to Cannon Beach, Oregon for that particular filmic location. If you want the real thing just get to Bells Beach in March.

MORE INFO Rip Curl (www.ripcurl.com.au)

MARCH
WEEK.04

AND ANOTHER THING
- - - - - - - - - - - - - - - -
World Pooh Sticks Championship (Day's Lock, River Thames, Oxfordshire, England)

Not nearly as bad as its name suggests, Pooh Sticks is the game made famous by Winnie the Pooh. It involves standing on a bridge, dropping sticks into the river and seeing whose emerges on the other side of the bridge first. This simple game, popularised by a fictional bear, attracts hundreds of Pooh-mad spectators each year. (www.pooh-sticks.com)

HONG KONG SEVENS FINAL

WHERE Hong Kong **WHEN** Late March **GETTING INVOLVED** Tickets are available online. Should you miss out, the Rugby Village is just outside the stadium where, for a small cost, you can watch the action on a big screen within earshot and punting distance of the stadium.

Can you name the sport in which the Cantabrians defeated the Wallaroos in the inaugural final? If you said the IRB's Sevens World Series, played annually on the last weekend in March, you were right and have just described the Hong Kong Sevens. The 40,000-seat Hong Kong Stadium plays host to arguably the biggest event on the Hong Kong sporting calendar. The competition consists of 24 national sides in a round-robin format in six pools of four teams with the best-performing teams progressing.

Sevens rugby is the red cordial–fuelled little brother of the 15-a-side game. Everything is fast and action packed: games are 15 minutes long, coaches have two minutes at half-time to reorganise their team, and players can be sent off – for two minutes. With fewer rules, the rugby purist will enjoy the sight of the ball carrier running at his opponent, while for the rugby novice the frenetic pace and high scoring will appeal.

A festival atmosphere pervades throughout the weekend, both around the stadium and inside the ground. Try for a seat in the South Stand (over 18s only) where fans dress in wacky costumes, dance, sing and lead the Mexican wave. While traditional rugby powers New Zealand and Australia have performed well in this tournament, Fiji, with their unpredictable style, have been crowned champs 11 times. So pick a country to support, clear your throat and add to the pageant and noise that is the Hong Kong Sevens.

MORE INFO Hong Kong Sevens (www.hksevens.com)

DUBAI WORLD CUP

WHERE Dubai, United Arab Emirates **WHEN** Last week in March **GETTING INVOLVED** Admission to the
public enclosure is free; reserved seating in various ticketed areas is available online.

It's the world's richest horse race in an opulent city-state at the convergence of three major continents, so it
easily attracts 50,000 highfalutin racegoers from around the world. With a total purse of more than US$20 million,
the winner of the invitational Dubai World Cup receives a tidy $6 million. Yet, despite all the cash, gambling is
illegal in Dubai, so the exchange of money is limited to the prize giving.

It's a Group 1 thoroughbred race on dirt over 2000m, and something of a homecoming for racing. All
thoroughbred horses can trace their pedigree back to three Arabian stallions from the 17th century, exported
to England to breed with 74 English mares. The Dubai Cup thus proudly brings thoroughbred racing back to the
Arabian Peninsula.

Dubai's ruler, Sheikh Mohammed, created the race in 1996. He is also the founder of Godolphin Racing – one of
the world's leading thoroughbred breeding and racing operations, and currently the holder of the most Dubai Cup
wins. Godolphin, incidentally, is the name of one of those three original Arabian stallions.

Like the attendees, the Nad al Sheba Racecourse gets dolled up for the event, with marquees and terraces of
varying levels of opulence. The race brings together two world–renowned ostentatious elements: the city-state
of Dubai itself and thoroughbred racing, so it's not surprising there's a conspicuous display of clothing, hats,
sunglasses, shoes, cufflinks, hair-dos and bags. Dubai is, after all, also home to the Shopping Festival (mid-January
to mid-February), which attracts three million people annually to shop – all part of living in a tax-free business haven
and world capital of excess.

MORE INFO Dubai World Cup (www.dubaiworldcup.com)

DEAD SPORTS
BULL LEAPING

If your mate suggests that you grab the bull by the horns it is more than likely they are trying to motivate you to rise to a particular challenge. But if you had been living in ancient Greece 4000 years ago they might have meant something a bit more literal, like: 'See that bull charging at you with its head down snorting madly through its hairy nostrils. Well, wait until it's just about to gouge your guts out then grab it by the horns and, as it jerks its head back, use the momentum to launch yourself into the air to perform a series of outrageous somersaults before landing on your feet to rapturous applause from your audience, members of which you will notice are assembled safely high up in the amphitheatre.'

Exactly what possessed the first of our mythical Greek ancestors to risk life and limb by launching into such a dangerous dalliance with a bull is a mystery. But the result was clearly fascinating enough to lead to the development of one of the great extreme sports of Mediterranean Antiquity. We know this from the depictions of bull leaping contained in artefacts and artworks recovered from archaeological sites all over Crete – the island that spawned bull culture and spread it across the then known world.

Back in the day, Crete was serious bull country. It was the home of the fabled half-man, half-bull beast, the Minotaur, and of King Minos, son of Zeus and Europa, whose lunar symbol was the cow. In a nutshell, the islanders, or Minoans as they were known, thought bulls were the dog's nuts. And they developed the rituals and sporting events to prove it.

Minoan culture flourished from around 2700 to 1450 BC and marks the romantic pinnacle of the Bronze Age. The main palace was at Knossos and it is here that archaeologists believe bull leaping formed part of the ceremonies to honour and entertain Minoan royalty and their gods. There is fierce debate about the mechanics of bull leaping. Some experts say the style of acrobatics found in frescos found along the palace walls would have been physically impossible and far too dangerous to have been accomplished in real life. Others reckon the bull leapers were elite athletes capable of vaulting the horns of charging bulls and landing on the beast's backs.

While the true form of bull leaping remains a secret of the Bronze Age what we do know is that by the time the volcanic island of Thera (present-day Santorini) erupted and, along with its subsequent tsunami, triggered the Minoans demise, bull leaping had already been exported throughout the Mediterranean. Long after the Minoans disappeared, their love of the great bull-leaping spectacle was being replicated at royal courts and outdoor arenas in other

Greek city states as well as in India and Egypt.

Pansy versions of the sport have survived in parts of France and Spain with the modern version using cows or juvenile bulls, as opposed to the much more aggressive adult males. It's still dangerous though, as demonstrated by the untimely death of champion French leaper, Jean-Pierre Rachou, who died of blood loss after his femoral artery was gashed by a bull's horns in 2001.

FOR THE RECORD

↗ The fastest finishing time is eight minutes 47.8 seconds, run by Mr Frisk in 1990.

↗ The year 1928 saw the fewest horses finish ever, with Tipperary Tim, a 100-1 outsider, the first of two past the post.

GRAND NATIONAL

WHERE Liverpool, England **WHEN** Early April **GETTING INVOLVED** There is a range of attendance options, with varying degrees of access; check online.

On a wintry Saturday afternoon every April for the past 170-odd years, spectators have gathered, horses lined up, and bookies crossed their fingers for what has become the UK's single largest betting event – responsible for more than £100 million changing hands.

The Grand National is a Grade 3 handicap chase, run over 4 miles, reserved for six-year-old horses. It's a notoriously tough course, with 30 jumps. The difficulty factor is the reason the race attracts so much attention: both good and bad. The course allows for horses with an outside chance to win, and more than 500 million viewers tune in to broadcasts of the race, the outcome of which is famously unpredictable. The course's many jumps, some with steep drops, are also responsible for the relatively high number of injuries to competing horses, often resulting in death.

The hunt race, as it's also known, can be traced back at least 300 years. Traditionally, races were run between two towns with the start and finishing lines being the towns'

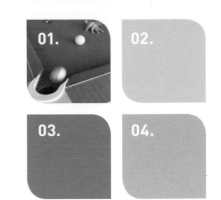

The Grand National is widely regarded as the world's greatest jump race, and is viewed by over 500 million television viewers worldwide.

'The difficulty factor is the reason the race attracts so much attention: both good and bad'

APRIL
WEEK.01

church steeples – hence the name steeple chase. The Grand National goes back to 1839, first instituted by the local publican.

Despite a shaky period in the 1980s when the Aintree Racecourse – the Grand National's home – was slated for redevelopment, the race has a long and solid history. It was deemed void in 1993 after two false starts and cancelled in '97 due to bomb threats. Its most famous horse is Red Rum, the only horse in the event's history to win three times: 1973, '74 and '77. He also came second in the intervening years: '75 and '76. A spectacular accomplishment in itself, Red Rum's run of glory was made all the more honourable due to the fact that he had a debilitating bone disease, which should have seen him put out to pasture. Red Rum lived to the ripe old age of 30 in 1995 and is buried by the finishing post at Aintree.

You can see Red Rum's commemorative stone at the finishing line as part of the many hospitality packages put together each year for visitors to the Aintree races. While the Grand National runs on the Saturday, the racing events begin on the Thursday prior, with Ladies Day on the Friday.

MORE INFO Aintree Racecourse (www.aintree.co.uk)

Rising from the deep
– Jessica Wilson of
the USA is met by
safety divers after
completing a 90m
freedive in 2008.

AMPUTEE AFRICAN CUP OF NATIONS

WHERE Africa **WHEN** First week in April **GETTING INVOLVED** Check the website for details.

They train hard and their commitment to soccer is the same high level as any professional paid big bucks, but these players also qualify to play by the fact that they have all lost limbs during their countries' civil wars. Four or five teams of six one-legged men and a one-armed goalie play their hearts out in front of around 10,000 to earn the winner's trophy, yes, but also to earn respect for the thousands of others mutilated by rebels.

Though winning the All Africa Cup doesn't bring a lot of, if any, financial benefit to the players, the personal benefits are priceless. Amputee football players enjoy being recognised in the street as elite sportsmen, rather than victims. The football field is also friendly common ground for relations between neighbouring African countries to regenerate, after years of uncertainty. The inaugural host, Sierra Leone, played neighbouring Liberia – untangling years of rebel political alliances, illegal trafficking and population displacement.

The first All Africa competition was held in 2007, in Sierra Leone whose Single Limb Soccer Club (SLSC) championed the event from its base at the Aberdeen Amputee Camp. The camp houses machete victims and their children who are desperately short of money and means. Sierra Leone was set to play Nigeria in the first game of the series, but the Nigerian team was still on the road – travelling overland for three days and three nights to attend. Along with Nigeria, Sierra Leone and Liberia, Ghana also participates – each taking turns to host the event. These days, all the All-Africa countries are open to international travellers. If you happen to find yourself over that way in April, you won't be disappointed by being one of the crowd – cheering for the game and the fact that it exists, more than any one team.

MORE INFO World Amputee Football (www.worldamputeefootball.com)

VERTICAL BLUE

WHERE Bahamas **WHEN** Early April **GETTING INVOLVED** A three-day introductory course is available, as well as other classes for more advanced freedivers.

If you've ever held your breath under water at the beach or in the bath, then you've taken the first breath to becoming a competitive freediver. That's what they do. They just do it for longer. Much longer.

Freediving is essentially the sport of breath-holding. Also known as competitive apnea, competitors attempt to conquer great depths, times or distances on a single breath without assistance (so, no oxygen, weights or fins). Static, free immersion, dynamic, variable weight, and no limits are just some of the types of freediving and all relate to the time and depth of the dive.

Vertical Blue is two things. It's a freediving school that operates at Dean's Blue Hole in the Bahamas – overseen by freediving world-record holder William Trubridge. It's also the title of the official freediving competition that takes place there annually in April. In 2008 alone, five world records and more than 20 national freediving records were shattered at Vertical Blue. Who knows how many records will fall in the ensuing years.

Freediving is not a simple case of taking a big breath, holding your nose and jumping in. This is a sweet science with training required and breathing exercises practised both in the water and on land. Competitors are risking drowning, shallow-water blackout, injuries to ears and sinuses, and shark attacks.

So while a freediver may find peace and tranquillity down in the ocean depths, spectators can experience the nerves and tension of competitive freediving and find out plenty about their own fears.

MORE INFO Vertical Blue (www.verticalblue.net)

WORLD SPORT STACKING CHAMPIONSHIPS

WHERE Denver, USA **WHEN** Early April **GETTING INVOLVED** Tickets readily available at the door.

You've probably caught a glimpse of it on TV. It will most likely have been the cute novelty story that ends the nightly news or on a late-night talk show with a perplexed host gawping at a child stacking and unstacking plastic cups with superhuman speed.

Sport stacking, also known as cup stacking, involves the up-stacking (setting the cups into pyramids) and down-stacking (unstacking the pyramids and returning them to their nested position) of specially designed plastic cups. Competition cups are made with holes in the bottom, which allow air to pass through and prevent them from sticking.

Competition sport stackers manipulate cups in pre-determined sequences, competing against the clock or another player. Sequences are usually pyramids of three, six or 10 cups. The elements of speed, pre-determined stacking patterns and an opponent all add up to one crazy, yet strangely fixating sport. It began in the early 1980s in the USA and is spreading all over the world. There is even a governing body – the World Sport Stacking Association (WSSA).

The undeniable Mt Everest of sport stacking is the World Sport Stacking Championships held in Denver, which draws combatants from far and wide to compete for world records, glory and fame. And, while you may not choose to travel halfway around the world to attend, you may be inspired to have a go yourself – it might even catch on with your fellow attendees at the next boring official function.

MORE INFO World Sport Stacking Association (www.worldsportstackingassociation.org)

APRIL
WEEK.01

'Water tastes disgusting without the benefits of whisky'.

- - - - - - - - - - - - - - - -

Captain Becher, Grand National legend, on his experience of being tossed into the brook that was later named after him.

↗ With six wins, Jack Nicklaus has won more Masters tournaments than any other golfer.

↗ Tiger Woods is the youngest man to win a Masters; he was 21 when he first won in 1997. (He has gone on to win another three times.)

THE MASTERS

WHERE Augusta, Georgia, USA **WHEN** First full week of April
GETTING INVOLVED You might luck on a ticket to a practice round: apply for the random ballot a year in advance. Forget about tickets to the actual tournament, unless you can get yourself on the members' patrons list.

Renowned for its manicured grounds, for its exclusion of female members, for its team of staff caddies all dressed in trademark white jumpsuits (all African American until 1982), and for a swathe of traditions, the US Masters is as much about the Augusta National Golf Club course as it is about championship golf.

The first of four in the championship series, (including the US Open in June, the Open Championship in July and the PGA Championship p149), the Masters is the only tournament to be played at the same course each year. And, although the series ranks third in terms of financial reward (after the PGA and European tour), it's up there with the best in terms of kudos, with winners allocated the highest allowable number of world-ranking points (100), automatic invitations to play in the other majors, and attracting lucrative sponsorship deals.

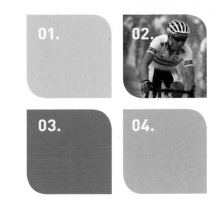

01.   02.

03.   04.

'Although the series ranks third in terms of financial reward, it's up there with the best in terms of kudos'

APRIL
WEEK.02

Australian Robert Allenby gets himself out of trouble on the 8th hole during the first round of the 2008 Masters Tournament in Augusta, Georgia.

In keeping with the course's exclusive reputation, this 72-hole, four-day invitational tournament welcomes the smallest number of competitors (around 90), famously including the winners of amateur tournaments thanks to one of the founder's amateur status. Because of its small field, competitors play in groups of three (instead of the usual four). After 36 holes the field is reduced. To make the 'cut', players must either be within 44 places of the lead, or no more than 10 strokes behind the leader's score.

Probably the most famous of the Masters' many traditions is the ceremonial awarding of the green jacket. Every year, since 1949, the previous year's winner helps the new winner into the club's green jacket, which must be returned to the clubhouse the following year, and passed onto that year's winner. Gary Player broke with tradition in 1961 when he

refused to return his jacket, and Jack Nicklaus helped himself into the jacket after successive wins in 1966.

The Masters has been running since 1934, the year after the Augusta Golf Club opened. And although many of the traditions and features remain, the course itself has seen a few changes, mostly thanks to Tiger Woods' appearance here in 1997. Bunkers were added and the number of green contours reduced after Woods broke the tournament record low, with 18 under (270) to win by the largest ever margin (12 strokes). He incidentally also became the first non-white man to win a Masters.

MORE INFO The Masters (www.masters.com)

Troy Dumais, of the United States, is caught in a moment of pure musculature during the 3m springboard final of the 2008 FINA USA Diving Grand Prix.

DIVING GRAND PRIX

WHERE Location changes for each of the seven stages of the series **WHEN** A series of seven meetings, usually between January and June **GETTING INVOLVED** Tickets are generally readily available and well priced. Check the website for an up-to-date schedule.

It's stunning to watch, and deservedly popular with spectators; however, the dives that most impress the casual observer are not necessarily those that wow the judges.

More akin to gymnastics than swimming, professional diving is broadly judged on three elements: the take-off, flight and entry. Then, there's the degree of difficulty (DD, or 'tariff'). And this is where spectators and judges can diverge in opinion. Some pretty spectacular manoeuvres that stun audiences are actually easier to perform than less extroverted moves. For example, everyone loves an aerial somersault but, in terms of difficulty, it's easier for a diver to control his or her speed while performing somersaults than, say, a straight dive, which all depends on the take-off.

Among other factors, the DD is determined by the number of twists and somersaults within a dive, the height of the platform or springboard (3m to 10m) and the dive group. Dive groups are categorised by forward, backward, reverse, inward, twist, and the platform-only armstand. Divers are required to submit a list of dives before the day of the events, which is composed of some compulsory dives and some 'free' dives – those that are choreographed by the diver.

The Diving Grand Prix was established in 1995 to give the world's best divers the opportunity to dive at a high level of competition and promote the sport. The other competitions are the World Cup and Olympics – where diving has been included since 1904. The prize money for Grand Prix winners isn't much to write home about, but to dive against the world's best is a rare and coveted opportunity for divers. It's also a great opportunity for spectators to be involved, without the fuss of attending higher-level competitions, such as the Olympics.

MORE INFO Federation Internationale de Natation (www.fina.org)

COW-CHIP THROWING CHAMPIONSHIP

WHERE Beaver County, Oklahoma, USA **WHEN** Third weekend in April
GETTING INVOLVED The competition is open to all. Simply register on arrival.

Who knows what the early settlers might have thought of the annual Cow-Chip Throwing Championship being held in their honour, but considering the role the humble chip played in American history it seems a fitting tribute. Arriving in the west, settlers found a drastic shortage of wood or fuel on the vast grassy plains. They soon discovered the benefits of the cow chip – a dried out chunk of cow dung – and began burning them for cooking and heating. Leading up to each winter, townsfolk would harvest the chips and compete (now, this is where things start to get interesting) by throwing them into the back of carts from a great distance.

Beaver County's welcoming slogan of 'No Man's Land, Everyone's Town' sums up the community's positive spin on one of the world's more curious sporting events. Started in the 1970s to boost the town's profile, it soon took on a life of its own. Beaver County is now home to the worldwide chip-throwing community. Local attractions include the town mascot, a cow chip with a crown and sceptre, and a giant beaver holding a cow chip. The tournament is open to everyone and occurs on the third weekend of April as part of the Cimarron Territory Celebration. Activities over the weekend range from carnivals and a chilli cook-off, to team 'roping' and old-fashioned church revivals.

So don't be shy, the Cow-Chip Throwing Championship is a chance for people from all around the world to get together and 'chuck a chunk of moo poo!'
MORE INFO Beaver Oklahoma – World Championship Cow-Chip Throwing Contest (www.beaveroklahoma.net/CowChip.html)

BROOMBALL SENIORS FINAL

WHERE Canada **WHEN** Early to mid-April **GETTING INVOLVED** Tickets are available through the website.

'Ice hockey in slow motion with brooms and no skates' is how some would describe broomball, and to the uninitiated it looks a lot like that. Sharing rules with ice hockey, roller hockey and floor-ball, broomball can be confusing to a newcomer. Rules aside, the most baffling part is how the players manage to manoeuvre themselves around at all without slipping over.

The game is played indoors or outdoors, on ice that's specially prepared to be smooth and dry, with competitors wearing rubber-soled shoes to slide around easily and quickly. Six players make up a team and each member carries a 'broom' (a stick with a moulded triangular head) to hit a ball (not a puck) around the ice. Whichever team hits the most balls through their opposition's goal wins. As in ice hockey, the goals are set in from the boundary, allowing players to move around behind them.

Though played recreationally from the early 20th century, it wasn't until the 1970s that the game began to attract serious attention. Teams now come from all over the country each year to battle it out for the championship. In 2009 the championships were held in Saskatoon where the Canadian Broomball Federation (CBF) celebrated the centenary of the first recorded game of broomball, which occurred in Saskatchewan in 1909. With a national membership of 19,000 registered members and 15,000 participants, Canada's CBF pulls out all the stops for the annual championships. After watching a final, you'll never sweep the floor in quite the same way again.
MORE INFO Canadian Broomball Federation (www.broomball.ca)

01. 02. 03. 04.

APRIL
WEEK.02

AND ANOTHER THING

Bug Bowl (Purdue University, USA)

The headline event at Bug Bowl, sponsored by Purdue Uni's department of agriculture, is the cricket-spitting. It involves placing a dead cricket on the tongue and spitting it as far as you can. The record is almost 5m. Other events include cockroach racing and robotic beetle battles, and there's an insect petting zoo where you can line up for the privilege of having a worm writhe in your palm. (http://news.uns.purdue.edu)

FOR THE RECORD

↗ With a time of 36.190 seconds Maris Strombergs from Latvia became the first male to win an Olympic gold for BMX; Anne-Caroline Chausson from France won the women's race with a time of 35.976.

↗ American Kevin Robinson jumped his BMX a record 8.1m in 2008.

BMX SUPERCROSS

WHERE Location changes **WHEN** A series of four world cup events spread throughout the year **GETTING INVOLVED** It's easy to get tickets; not so easy afterwards to ever ride your bike again without jumping it over a curb.

This one's for everyone who's ever jumped their bike over the curb or popped a wheelie. (And that's all of us, hopefully.) BMX has to be one of the most joyous sports to watch – takes you back to riding around the streets with school friends looking for a plank and a mound of dirt, which would serve as the perfect props for an afternoon's entertainment. And this is precisely how the hugely popular sport of BMX began.

It was the late 1960s in California. A group of kids riding their Schwinn Stingrays in disused lots of land, trying to emulate their motocross heroes – BMX being a contraction of Bicycle MotoCross. The film *On Any Sunday* is generally credited with popularising BMX in America; its opening scene shows kids riding off-road. Kids gradually sought higher jumps and longer tracks. Within a decade, the sport had exploded, providing an accessible, adventuresome and affordable activity for all children. By 1977, the American Bicycle Association was established to sanction the sport. In 1981 the International BMX

01. 02.

03. 04.

'BMX is a younguns' sport, with the majority of competitors well under 30 years'

Riders negotiate a jump at the 2008 BMX Supercross World Cup in Madrid.

APRIL
WEEK.03

Federation was formed, and the first world championships were held the following year. The UCI adopted BMX into its authority in 1991, and in 2008 BMX became an official sport of the Olympic Games. A meteoric rise for something that was essentially a backyard sport.

BMX riders look like they've grown, but have never grown up, hunched as they are over the specially made bikes with 50cm wheels. It is a younguns' sport, with the majority of competitors well under 30 years. There are separate events in competitions for males and females. To watch a Supercross is to watch eight riders explode out of the gate and fly over bumps, burn around banked corners and jump obstacles to get to the finish line first. The course is generally around 350m of dirt track, and it's all over in less than a minute, with cyclists reaching speeds of around 40km/h.

Supercross is distinct from 'freestyle' BMX, where riders perform tricks: cycling backwards while sitting on the handlebars, bunny hopping and jumping. It's also a competition sport, with a number of disciplines, including street, vert, park, trails and flatland.
MORE INFO Union Cycliste Internationale (www.uci.ch)

TOONIK TYME

WHERE Iqaluit, Canada **WHEN** Third week in April **GETTING INVOLVED** Events are not ticketed; just turn up.

This is the place of dog-sledding across white expanses, of icebergs, and of long, dark, freezing winters. So, it's fitting that the people of Iqaluit should celebrate the coming of spring with traditional Inuit competitions – and you're invited.

The weeklong Toonik Tyme sees the community emerge from its winter hibernation to participate in time-honoured Inuit activities. There are seal-hunting events, and subsequent skinning competitions. And for those uncomfortable with the sight of blood on ice, the igloo building is probably more for you. There are also dog-sled and snow-mobile races, pond hockey tournaments, and kite-skiing and ice-sculpting competitions. It's a bit of fun, with games (arm-wrestling and children's relays) and musical entertainment, especially at the opening and closing ceremonies. Even the music comes in the form of a competition of sorts. Inuit throat singing is traditionally performed by women in a kind of duet or duel to see who can outlast the other. Overall, it provides a rare insight into Inuit customs and community, influenced by rare and beautiful surrounds.

The largest and newest territory of Canada, Nunavut was officially separated from the Northwest Territories in 1999. Iqaluit (formerly Frobisher Bay) is the capital, located on Baffin Island in the east. While you're here, consider going whale watching; in these parts it's narwhals that you're looking for, the unicorn-like whale with a long twisted horn, which it uses for jousting, but little else. Alternatively, experience the region by dog sled and be pulled by a team of dogs across the Arctic tundra – the feeding grounds for Peary caribou. Toonik Tyme's location is truly amazing and, as it occurs in the far far north, it's fair to say that you have to travel to the ends of the earth to experience it.

MORE INFO Toonik Tyme (www.tooniktyme.com), Nunavut Tourism (www.nunavuttourism.com)

CLIMBING-BOULDERING WORLD CUP

WHERE A different country hosts each round **WHEN** Nine rounds annually, from mid-April through to November **GETTING INVOLVED** To qualify you must be a member of your country's International Federation of Sport Climbing affiliated association, and be in the top four in your division.

With terms like: 'crash pad', 'dyno', 'crimp', 'smear' and 'sloper' you could be forgiven for thinking that bouldering is some kind of skate-punk-krumping hybrid, but, in fact, it's exactly what the name suggests – climbing big rocks.

Unlike conventional rock climbing, a bouldering route is over a very short distance, undertaken without a rope, and is often called a 'problem' instead of a route. Each problem involves a short sequence of difficult moves that rely on strength, power and dynamics, rather than the stamina required for conventional rock climbing. Boulderers work through a series of problems on a time limit, with points awarded for the fewest number of attempts required to complete the problem. It's important that competitors do not see the boulder before their attempted climb, so as not to give them a chance to work out the problem before physically attempting it.

The origins of bouldering can be traced back to the end of the 19th century when it was used to train rock climbers. In France, during the 1930s and '40s in the area surrounding Fontainebleau (now the home of European bouldering), a group of climbers began to take it more seriously. Over the last 20 years it has become a sport in its own right.

In 1998 bouldering came under the control of the IFSC (International Federation of Sport Climbing) and has since expanded rapidly to be included in many established competitions. The Bouldering World Championship is one of a number of popular bouldering events that take place around the globe culminating in the World Cup Finals.

MORE INFO International Federation of Sport Climbing (www.ifsc-climbing.org)

APRIL
WEEK.03

'Whoever said, "It's not whether you win or lose that counts," probably lost.'

– – – – – – – – – – – – – –

Martina Navratilova, tennis player

MEZZALAMA

WHERE Aosta Valley, Italy **WHEN** Odd-numbered years, for one day in the third week of April
GETTING INVOLVED All athletes must be at least 21 years old and provide a resumé of their skiing/
mountaineering experience and a medical certificate stating they are physically prepared for the event. To enter
you must have a team of three athletes who are regular members of a skiing organisation in your own country.

If clambering over high-altitude snow-covered peaks on thin skis with limited equipment while roped to two
companions is your idea of a good time then look no further. You have found the most dangerous and difficult ski
mountaineering race in the world. However, if the thin air, blizzards, chance of avalanche, and the 45km of rough
terrain all seem a little too taxing, then join the thousands of more sensible folk who are just there to watch.

Held every two years, and named in honour of the famed ski mountaineer, Ottorino Mezzalama (1888–1931),
the Mezzalama is the London Marathon of tour skiing with all the drama and heartache that comes with
endurance races. Participants must do battle with themselves and each other as well as the ever-changing
weather and terrain, which ranges from tough going to very very tough going.

The race is governed by FISI (Italian Winter Sports Federation) and ISMF (International Ski Mountaineering
Federation), and attracts around 800 athletes competing from more than a dozen different countries around
the globe. The race begins at sunrise from Breuil Cervinia and ends at Gressoney La Trinité with the spectacular
scenery en route taking in the Matterhorn, Mont Blanc and the Aosta Valley. There are four checkpoints along the
way, and the record time for completing the course is four hours and 18 minutes.

If you're looking for something else to pass the time, check out the Ice Cave in Cervinia, or if you need an
adrenalin rush after watching the race there's every level of skiing available all year round.
MORE INFO Trofeo Mezzalama (www.trofeomezzalama.org)

FOR THE RECORD

- - - - - - - - - - - - - - - - - -

↗ Sachin Tendulkar has scored 1796 runs in his World Cup career, the most runs in CWC history.

↗ Glenn McGrath dominates the bowling record books, with the most wickets (71), lowest average (19.2), best bowling figures (versus Namibia, seven for 15) and most wickets in a tournament (26).

ICC CRICKET WORLD CUP

WHERE Location changes each tournament **WHEN** Every four years
GETTING INVOLVED Get in early for a seat; check online for up-to-date ticket and schedule info.

Talking World Cup cricket ought to prove a pretty safe topic for small talk, should you find yourself wanting in 2011. Watching it, you'll be among two billion-plus other viewers spread across 200 countries to have seen part or all of the tournament on their televisions. And actually going to the ground to catch the action live puts you in the company of more than 670,000 for the tournament.

Regarded as the showcase event of the cricket calendar, the Cricket World Cup has been played every four years since 1975. The format has changed considerably over its nine-tournament history, mostly to accommodate more teams and more spectators.

The inaugural tournament was played in England with the traditional red ball that was hit, fielded and bowled by men wearing white uniforms for 60 overs each innings. The competition included the eight Test-playing nations, excluding South Africa, which was banned from participating due to its government's apartheid policies. By the next

Australia's Adam Gilchrist scored 149 runs off just 104 balls in the 2007 ICC Cricket World Cup Final between Australia and Sri Lanka in Bridgetown, Barbados.

01. 02. 03. 04.

'The Cricket World Cup is the first tournament of its kind and calibre to be hosted on all six populated continents'

APRIL
WEEK.04

World Cup in '79, non-Test playing nations were included taking the number of teams up to 10. In '87, the number of overs was reduced to 50 per innings, and by the fourth World Cup in '92 there was a veritable revolution. Coloured clothing was introduced, white balls and day/night games came into play, and there were changes to the fielding restrictions; it was also the first year that South Africa was included in the competition.

The 1996 tournament was played in India. The home team's poor semi-final performance (losing eight wickets for 120 runs) led to Indians rioting in the stands in disgust. Sri Lanka won by default, then went on to defeat Australia in the final.

Generally, each tournament is hosted on a different continent, with a number of countries being host to preliminary games. The West Indies hosted the 2007 tournament, consisting of 16 teams and, in doing so, made the Cricket World Cup (CWC) the first tournament of its kind and calibre to be hosted on all six populated continents. Australia won the 2007 CWC, becoming the first team to win three consecutive cups, and is the most successful team with a total of four wins.

MORE INFO International Cricket Council (www.icc-cricket.yahoo.com)

01. 02. 03. 04.

LAND DIVING

WHERE Pentecost Island, Vanuatu **WHEN** April, May and June **GETTING INVOLVED** Book in advance, as transport and accommodation on the island are limited, especially during *naghol* time.

When the first yam crop emerges in early April on the Vanuatu island of Pentecost, the southern islanders begin to build high wooden towers. Once completed, and through until the end of May, village men and boys dive from these rickety structures with only two vines attached to their ankles to break their fall. It's an age-old practice that was 'discovered' in the 1950s when David Attenborough documented it on film. To do it right (because to do it wrong is hard to think about), the vines should pull the divers up just as their hair touches the soil. This is said to fertilise the ground, guaranteeing a bountiful harvest. Also a kind of right of passage, boys jump their way into manhood; their mothers toss away a cherished childhood item after a successful jump to symbolise that the boy is no longer a child.

Fast-tempo drums help to raise the excitement levels of the 300-strong crowd, which is uproarious each time a diver walks away from the tower having successfully had a face-off, at speed, with the ground.

Today, tourism as much as tradition drives the *naghol* (land-diving) ceremonies, with dives taking place mainly for show, though the local people still have to adhere to traditional taboos in order to participate: no wearing of lucky charms and no sex the night before. Failure to do so will have cultural implications (or worse) for *naghol* divers. Most visitors travel to Pentecost simply for the *naghol* ceremonies, but around the villages of Molcici and Vanu there are good walks to gorges and waterfalls. Pentecost is one of 83 islands that make up the South Pacific nation of Vanuatu. Neighbouring Pentecost, the volcanic landscape of Ambrym island is extraordinary.
MORE INFO Vanuatu Tourism (www.vanuatutourism.com)

APRIL WEEK.04

PILLOW FIGHTING

WHERE Toronto, Canada **WHEN** Schedule changes constantly; check website **GETTING INVOLVED** If you feel the need to release some pent-up rage and you've got some time to kill in Toronto, why not give it a go? The Pillow Fighting League has tryouts every Wednesday and Sunday.

Tell the folks back home that you're off to the pillow fights and they might worry that you've copped a hard pillow to the head. But with a stable of female fighters and a rising profile it won't be long before more people hear the catch cries of Boozy Suzy, Olivia Neutron Bomb, Carmen Monoxide and Eiffel Power.

The league has quickly expanded from burlesque show to further afield. There are now 22 registered fighters and these everyday ladies come from all walks of life to don costumes, masks and new personas before tearing each other apart with pillows in the ring. Current two-time world champion, the formidable Champain is, in real life, Stacy, a marketing coordinator who rates Henry Miller and Faulkner among her favourite authors.

Pillow fighters are judged on style, stamina, and the more abstract scale of 'Eye of the Tiger'. It's strictly a female-only affair but this doesn't mean it's headed for the gutter. Rules against biting, scratching and lewd behaviour ensure it's more fun than fear. At these matches you're more likely to see a room full of Toronto hipsters and art students than the placards, giant foam hands and trumpets favoured by the followers of Hulk Hogan.

Home to the Pillow Fight League, Toronto walks the line between American cultural osmosis and staunch northern independence. Torontonians embrace both worlds with verve and open-mindedness: enlightened, multicultural and uniquely Canadian.
MORE INFO Pillow Fight League (www.gopfl.com)

BOSTON MARATHON

WHERE Boston, USA **WHEN** Third Monday in April **GETTING INVOLVED** Entrants must be 18 years of age or older and run a qualifying time at a certified marathon – the qualifying times are determined by your age on the date of the Boston Marathon.

Harvard, the Red Sox, the Pixies and the Boston Marathon… As famous as the city itself, the Boston Marathon began in 1897, just one year after the first modern Olympic Marathon in Athens. The first annual event of its kind in the world, it is now part of the 'Big 5' on the marathon circuit – London, Berlin, New York and Chicago – and attracts upwards of 20,000 professional and amateur runners from all across the globe.

The whole city of Boston stops on the third Monday of April. And they kind of *have* to – approximately half a million eager spectators line the streets on the Patriots' Day holiday to pass drinks and snacks to the high profile athletes and earnest amateurs as they sweat it out over the 26-mile course. Originally an amateur event, with only a wreath awarded to the winner, the prize money now totals around US$800,000.

The Boston Marathon holds the world record for the largest marathon in history, with 38,708 entrants in 1996 – its centenary year. As far as onsite media coverage goes, it is second only to the Super Bowl as the largest single-day sporting event in the world, with more than 1000 media members scrambling for the best photos and stories of the day.

There is also a vast array of cultural activities available in this university city. Whether it's the drama of a Red Sox game, a trip to the Boston Museum of Fine Art or a grungy gig in nearby Cambridge, you won't be disappointed.

MORE INFO Boston Athletic Association (www.bostonmarathon.org)

A colourful sea of competitors surges up the hill in the first wave of the 2008 Boston Marathon.

Buzkashi, which translated literally means 'goat grabbing', is the national sport of Afghanistan.

BUZKASHI

WHERE Afghanistan **WHEN** Usually on Fridays **GETTING INVOLVED**
Spectating is for men only; ask around in major cities.

Involving money, violence, barely contained chaos and relentless power
struggles, buzkashi – the Afghan sport of 'goat grabbing' – has been likened
to the country's political history. Banned by the Taliban during its five-year rule,
buzkashi is again being played with gusto in Afghanistan and neighbouring Central
Asian countries.

A game can involve up to 800 riders, last all day, and invariably involve broken
bones, whippings, and horses slamming into each other in the relentless and
resolute pursuit of a calf or goat carcass. Two teams of riders compete for
possession of the carcass – weighing between 30kg and 60kg. Only the best
riders are allowed to actually lunge for the carcass. The other riders are there to
foil the opposition, either by whipping, hitting, slamming, whatever – there are
few rules in buzkashi.

There are two versions of the game. The first is *tudabarai*, which involves
riding clear of the pack with the carcass. Sounds easy, but you try riding clear of
a scrum of hundreds of horses while carrying a calf carcass. The other version is
called *qarajai*, where the rider is required to ride around a marker and dump the
carcass into the 'goal' hole.

The history of the game is believed to date back to somewhere between 1200
and 1500, during the days of Genghis Khan. The Mongols were said to have
played it, presumably between sweeping up dead bodies – so renowned were
they for their ruthlessness. The Afghans claim to be the first to tame horses, and
their superior horsemanship apparently enabled them to stave off Alexander the
Great for two years.

Watching a game of buzkashi involves being crammed on an embankment or
into stalls with thousands of men (women aren't welcome, although they are
allowed to watch from a distant rooftop if they so desire). The game is something
of a messy scrum, so the play can be difficult to follow for the novice, especially
if there are hundreds of horses. It can just look like a melee of horses and riders.
Occasionally the riders' woollen hats come into focus or a leathery face with a
whip between gritted teeth. The winning rider receives money donations from
members of the crowd, and from the owner of the horse he is riding – which
becomes something of a legend and increases the value of the other horses in
the breeder's stock.

MORE INFO Traveller's info on Afghanistan, Lonely Planet
(www.lonelyplanet.com/afghanistan)

01.

02.

03.

04.

MAY
WEEK.01

FOR THE RECORD

- - - - - - - - - - - - - -

↗ The goat or calf being used
as the ball is prepared for play
by cutting off its head and,
usually, the legs below the
knee, disembowelling it, and
then soaking it in water for a
few days.

↗ The horses ridden in the game
are highly trained; they will
automatically stop if their rider
is thrown.

*'A game can involve up to 800 riders, last all day,
and invariably involve broken bones'*

CLIPPER ROUND-THE-WORLD YACHT RACE

WHERE Round the world **WHEN** For around 10 months, usually September to July **GETTING INVOLVED** Must be over 18 years and prepared to shell out some cash; see the website for training and sign-up details.

Choose your own adventure. Will it be to sail for six weeks on one or more legs of the course, or can you go around the whole world? While this 10-month adventure is a race, for many of the crew, it's more about the journey. And there are surely more clichés to live if you get onboard a Clipper Round-the-World race. You steer your own course (see, there's another one).

Being one of 18 crew aboard one of a fleet of 10 or so yachts forges pretty strong friendships. It's the rollercoaster theory, of having been through something extraordinary together. And, the 'extraordinary' is the ups (dolphins in phosphorescent seas, whales within reach, flying fish and clear night skies revealing gazillions of stars) and the 'downs' (the hard work: of being confined to 68ft of fibreglass for weeks at a time, precariously bobbing on vast seas, working four hours on, four hours off). Depending on your skills, you could be the boat's official videographer, victualier (responsible for food stocks, with no fridge onboard), sail mender, cook, cleaner or engineer. The majority of crew are not sailers, rather: nurses, teachers, government officials or office workers. Everyone has to participate in 19 days of training, and, needless to say, everyone must be committed to the race.

Joining the race in May puts you on about Leg 6, taking in Santa Cruz, Panama City and Port Antonio, Jamaica. Although the course can change from year to year, it generally follows the old trade routes used by spice and tea clippers. It departs from Liverpool, England, where up to 40,000 well-wishers wave off the fleet, and ends where it began 10 months later. Stops include Salvador da Bahia in Brazil; Durban, South Africa; Fremantle, Australia; Qingdao, China; and Nova Scotia, Canada.

MORE INFO Clipper Round the World Yacht Race (www.clipperroundtheworld.com)

WORLD SNOOKER CHAMPIONSHIP

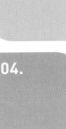

WHERE Sheffield, England **WHEN** First week in May **GETTING INVOLVED** Book ahead as tickets sell out well before the event.

Better known for its rock stars – the Arctic Monkeys, Pulp and the Human League – and as the grim setting for the breakthrough film *The Full Monty*, Sheffield has also been the home of the World Snooker Championships since 1977.

The competition has been running since 1927, when the legendary Joe Davis helped organise the event in and around Birmingham. He went on to win the fledgling tournament a record 15 times. His prize money in the inaugural year was a whopping £6.10. Given its history, the trophy is the one that all snooker players dream of, and now with a £1.3 million purse – the richest in the game – there's plenty more motivation for the world's best to compete.

Held at the famous Crucible Theatre, the World Snooker Championship is the last competition on the annual snooker calendar. The event, one of the longest in world sport, runs for 17 days. But with a large TV audience and tickets often selling out well before the event, there is high demand for seats in the less than 1000 capacity venue. But if you plan far enough ahead you will be rewarded with seats only metres from the action. Only the top 16 players are invited to fight it out after a rigorous qualifying process involving many pre-competition matches.

While in Sheffield, you might also pay a visit to the Yorkshire Sculpture Park for exhibitions of modern and contemporary sculpture set in the lush 18th-century parkland of the Bretton Estate. The collection includes works by Henry Moore and award-winning sculptor Andy Goldsworthy.

MORE INFO World Snooker (www.worldsnooker.com)

HAMILTON TROPHY

WHERE Scotland **WHEN** Early May through June **GETTING INVOLVED** Check with the association for an up-to-date schedule and attendance details.

What it lacks in pace, fervent crowds of supporters and awesome displays of physical ability, it makes up for in majesty. For the spectator, lawn bowls holds a visual appeal quite apart from the skill of its competitors. Watching one white-uniformed competitor after another virtually genuflect, to send a wonky ball down a hyper-green patch of lawn has a ritualistic fascination. It's as though each 'bowl' is a prayer to the god of symmetry, represented by a little white ball.

Though popular throughout the Commonwealth countries, with the Southampton Old Bowling Green established as early as 1299, Scotland has a particular hold over lawn bowls. The game's rules, the flat green and even its dress code is attributed to the Scots. And, while banned in France and England in the 14th century (its popularity threatening archery, which was essential for defence), the game continued uninterrupted in Scotland.

The Hamilton Trophy is the annual competition between Scottish county clubs and city clubs. Established in 1939, it's named in honour of Andrew Hamilton, secretary of the Scottish Bowling Association from 1895 to 1936. He's described as one of the 'greats', both in terms of his bowling ability and service to the game – particularly for popularising it internationally.

Bowls is generally played as much for its sociability as for the physical and mental exercise that it affords. Attending one of the inter-county/city matches in Scotland is bound to have you milling with the locals after the match.

MORE INFO Scottish Bowling Association (www.scottish-bowling.co.uk)

'I like playing in Sheffield, it's full of melancholy happy-go-lucky people.'

– – – – – – – – – – – – – – –

Alex 'Hurricane' Higgins, twice world-champion snooker player

- - - - - - - - - - - - - - -

↗ Two men's world records were broken in 2008, Denis Nizhegorodov (Russia) for the 50km in three hours, 34 minutes and 14 seconds, and Sergey Morozov (Russia) the 20km in one hour, 16 minutes and 43 seconds.

↗ Olimpiada Ivanova (Russia) has held the women's world record since 2001 with her time of one hour, 24 minutes and 50 seconds.

WORLD RACE WALKING CUP

WHERE Location changes each world cup **WHEN** Biennially, around mid-May **GETTING INVOLVED** Easy; check the website for event details.

It seems a contradiction in terms: 'race' and 'walking' – walking generally being something you deliberately do slowly. But, as you would know, race walking looks very different from your average amble. Paul Connolly, author of *World's Weirdest Sports*, describes it as 'cartoonishly camp…the hips sway, the shoulders sashay, the arms pump and the legs make countless little steps'. That's apparently what happens when you defy every urge in your body to break into a run, while moving forwards as quickly as possible, all the while keeping one foot in contact with the ground.

Competition events are over distances of 20km for women, and 20km and 50km for men. Usually street races, the course treads a route through the host city. Planted among the curbside spectators are judges who look to see that athletes retain some

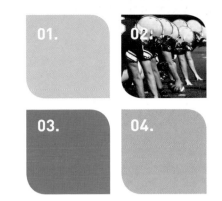

01.

02.

03.

04.

'Inspired by English footmen, walking competitions began around 1780 as endurance races'

Athletes must have a straight lead leg and always retain some contact with the ground during the IAAF Race Walking World Cup.

contact with the tar at all times. If both a competitor's feet should leave the ground at the very moment they happen to pass a judge, then a warning is issued. It's a case of three strikes and you're out, though the athlete isn't aware of the number of warnings issued against them until the race's end.

Inspired by English footmen, who alternated between running and walking alongside their masters' coaches, walking competitions began around 1780 as endurance races, over six days. In 1908, walking was included in the Olympics, with two events: 3500m and 10 miles. Event distances differed between competitions, seesawing between one and two events of varying distance, until walking was altogether scrapped from the 1928 Games due to the inconsistent manner in which judges 'caught' walkers with both feet off the ground. There are two rules of race walking. The first stipulates

that '…no visible (to the human eye) loss of contact occur' with the ground. The second rule requires that the lead leg is straight (no bent knees). Both are judged by sight, without the aid of video-stop footage. And judges were not watching every athlete every minute of every race. It's possible then that indiscretions by athletes wouldn't be detected by the judges, or that the judging method could at least be criticised for being less than thorough.

Olympic walking was reintroduced in 1932, and World Cup event distances mirror those of the Olympics: 20km and 50km. The first World Cup was held in 1961, with women first entering the competition in 1979.

MORE INFO International Association of Athletics Federations (www.iaaf.org)

01. 02. 03. 04.

CORSA DEI CERI (CANDLES RACE)

WHERE Gubbio, Italy **WHEN** 15 May **GETTING INVOLVED** Limber up, and run alongside the *ceri*.

Contested since the 12th century, the Corsa dei Ceri is a strongman contest of mammoth proportions. The entire town comes out to watch and to run with three teams who race through the city's streets forming a human river. The race is about 4.3km long and the course runs up the steep slopes of Monte Ingino, wending its way past gothic buildings to the Basilica of St Ubaldo. Each team carries a so-called 'candle' *(ceri)*, which is actually a 4m-long wooden pillar bearing a statue of one of three 'rival' saints (Sts Ubaldo, George and Anthony) and weighing around 400kg. The challenge for the *ceraiole* (candle holders) is to keep the candle upright, without toppling over. It's a test of strength and skill, acquired through years of practice.

The race begins at 6pm with a blessing by the bishop, and after a sprint around the city, begins the climb to the basilica. Located about 300m above the city, the basilica houses the body of St Ubaldo. The race is a colourful affair, with each of the *ceraiole* wearing the colours of the saint they carry: yellow for St Ubaldo, blue for St George and black for St Anthony. The whole shebang is accompanied by traditional folk music that is played in procession or in small groups while drinking, celebrating and running.

This centuries-old race is run to commemorate the city's patron saint, St Ubaldo, so if you're expecting a fair race, you may wonder how it is the yellow team – running for St Ubaldo – reaches the basilica first, year after year after year.

If you're not running with the *ceri*, and are visiting Gubbio on any other day of the year, don't despair, the open-air funicular ride to the top is almost as exhilarating.
MORE INFO The Festival of the Ceri (www.ceri.it)

MAY
WEEK.02

AND ANOTHER THING

- - - - - - - - - - - - - - - -

Sand-sculpting Tournament of Champions (Harrison Hot Springs, Canada)

A competition for King of the Castle, this sand-sculpting event takes place annually. It's a doubles match, with previous competitions' multiple medal winners paired up and invited to submit a design. The sand flies over 36 furious hours of construction, after which visitors vote for their favourite. Only sand, water and some wooden support panels (which are later removed) are used to construct incredible 3D images. (www.harrisand.org)

ISSF SHOOTING WORLD CUP

WHERE Each round is hosted by a different country **WHEN** Rounds and categories held throughout the year **GETTING INVOLVED** Tickets available through the host country's shooting federation.

The French film director, Jean-Luc Godard famously once said, 'All you need for a film is a girl and a gun', and for many the humble pistol maintains a certain allure. So if you like guns and shooting, but you can live without the James Bond women and sports cars, this is the tournament for you. With slow moving contestants in slacks and sensible hats it may not be the world's most spectacular spectator activity, but the sport has garnered the passionate support of hundreds of thousands of enthusiasts from every walk of life.

The International Shooting Sports Federation (ISSF) World Cup Final celebrated its 20th anniversary in 2008. Since its inaugural year in 1988 it has become the highlight of the competitive shooting calendar. Rivalled only by the Olympics in media attention and spectator numbers, the World Cup Finals attract shooters from all over the world to compete. The powerhouse nations of China, India, Australia and Russia consistently produce competitors of the highest calibre and recently Indian shooting sensation Ronjan Sodhi won the gold medal in double trap and equalled the world record in doing so.

Four lead-up events held throughout the year determine who qualifies to compete in the prestigious World Cup, and these contestants, along with the defending world and Olympic champions fight it out for medals in a range of events in the rifle, pistol and shotgun divisions. All events are decided on accuracy, with shooters aiming for the bullseye on a 10-ring target.
MORE INFO International Shooting Sport Federation (www.issf-shooting.org)

WORLD INDOOR LACROSSE CHAMPIONSHIPS

A rush of colour heralds the arrival of St Anthony's ceraiole into Gubbio's Piazza Grande.

WHERE Location changes each championship **WHEN** Every four years **GETTING INVOLVED** Tickets are available through the host country's federation; check the website for details.

Clashing sticks, battered shins and broken teeth. That's how many remember lacrosse from childhood days, but the origins of this ancient sport stretch back a lot further than you might think.

One of the oldest team sports in the world, the origins of lacrosse can be found among the native tribes of North America. Played as early as AD 1100, the game was very important to the local culture. Games were contested to resolve disputes between tribes, for religious events or as training for soldiers. Early versions of the game included matches with up to 1000 men on each side competing on a field sometimes 2 miles wide. Matches would be played from dawn to dusk and last for three days. The game remained a mystery to westerners until 1636, when the Jesuit missionary Jean de Brébeuf witnessed a game being played and dubbed it lacrosse.

Box Indoor Lacrosse is one of a number of streams of the game. It's played on ice-hockey rinks after the ice has been removed. Encouraged in its infancy by ice-hockey rinks looking to generate revenue during the off-season the game is now Canada's official summer sport.

In May 2003, the first International Lacrosse Federation–sanctioned Indoor Lacrosse Championship was held in Ontario, Canada. With teams from the Czech Republic, USA, Australia and Scotland, as well as the indigenous team of the Iroqouis Nation competing, the game has certainly arrived with a bang on the international scene.

MORE INFO International Lacrosse Federation (www.intlaxfed.org)

FOR THE RECORD

↗ Ayrton Senna has the most Monaco wins, with a total of six – five of them earned consecutively between 1989 and '93.

↗ Michael Schumacher holds the record for the fastest lap time, with 1:14:439.

FORMULA 1 MONACO GRAND PRIX

WHERE Monaco **WHEN** Third Sunday in May **GETTING INVOLVED** Tickets are available through the Automobile Club of Monaco website. You'll also need accommodation, which is often booked out a year in advance; consider staying in Menton or Nice.

The narrow, winding streets of Monte Carlo and La Condamine are transformed annually for the prestigious Monaco Grand Prix. By today's standards, the course would never pass as a Grand Prix circuit and it's only by virtue of its age, run in varying forms here since 1929, that it is included as a World Championship course – albeit the world's shortest at 3.34km.

The narrow course entails many changes in elevation, and tight corners, which has given it the reputation as one of the most demanding tracks, as well as one of the most unpredictable – able to take out four leading drivers in a single turn. But it's

01. 02. 04.

'The circuit includes the slowest corner in Formula One, taken at 50km/h, and one of the quickest, at 260km/h'

MAY
WEEK.03

Heikki Kovalainen of Finland negotiates the Monte Carlo circuit in a McLaren Mercedes during the 2008 Formula 1 Monaco Grand Prix.

not just the difficulty of the course and its longevity where Monaco earns its prestige. The tiny principality of Monaco is a glitzy, warm-weather tax haven, home to some of the world's wealthiest. But being part of a Grand Prix, as a spectator at least, is for everyone. When those five red lights blink off and up to 20 formula one cars thunder out of the grid to complete their 78 laps it's exhilarating. The circuit includes the slowest corner in Formula One – the Grand Hotel Hairpin – taken at 50km/h, and three turns later one of the quickest, taken at 260km/h.

To actually drive in a Grand Prix requires a 'super licence,' awarded based on past performances in junior formulae, and a contract with a formula one team that is entered in the world championship race. That means having a track record that's impressive enough to convince a team to let you drive one of their million-dollar machines.

Formula one cars utilise the latest advancements in technology, though omit driving aids (such as ABS brakes and four-wheel steering) so that the competition remains purely about a driver's ability to handle the car. F1s use commercially viable fuel, a regulation introduced by the Fédération Internationale de l'Automobile (FIA) to steer oil research in a direction that would benefit the consumer in the long run. Petrol samples are submitted before the race to ensure it complies.

After the chequered flag comes down on another year's race and organisers begin the three-week task of dismantling the race course, there's the rest of Monaco to explore, including attractive streets presided over by palaces, lush manicured parks and its glamorous casino.

MORE INFO Automobile Club of Monaco (www.acm.mc)

The King lives – and runs – in San Francisco's annual Bay to Breakers event.

WORLD SERIES OF BIRDING

WHERE New Jersey, USA **WHEN** Mid-May **GETTING INVOLVED** Either sponsor a species or start studying your bird book; the website also outlines winning strategies.

Generally perceived as a peaceful pastime, the birdwatching world can get furiously competitive, especially during the 24 hours of the World Series of Birding competition. The rules are simple, teams of at least three twitchers (as birdwatchers are also known) have just 24 hours to identify the greatest number of birds. At least three team members must see or hear the bird for the species to count towards their tally, however, for every 20 species clocked, just two team members are required to hear or see the bird being added to the list. The competition runs purely on the honour system and organisers say they have never encountered cheating.

The competition coincides with spring and the peak of the bird migration season. It starts at midnight, when serious birdwatchers start looking or listening for nocturnal birds, such as owls. The majority of the day's species tally is picked up between the hours of 5am and 10am. Most teams, of which there are up to 60, have spent the weeks leading up to the event scouting New Jersey for nests that they can return to on the day of the competition, and carefully planning their route to maximise the variety of habitats (eg woodlands, coastal and swamp) and to minimise the amount of time spent in the car. Come twilight, the birders are back looking for night birds before they return to the starting post by the following midnight. The most number of species tallied is 231 in 2003.

While there is no prize money for the winners, teams garner sponsorship by soliciting pledges for each bird species they identify. Since its inception in 1984, the event has raised more than US$8 million for bird conservation.

MORE INFO World Series of Birding, Cape May Observatory (www.birdcapemay.org/wsob.shtml)

BAY TO BREAKERS

WHERE San Francisco, CA, USA **WHEN** Third Sunday in May **GETTING INVOLVED** The race is open to all; register online.

From the flowers and patchouli of the Summer of Love to Alcatraz and the red towers of the Golden Gate Bridge, San Francisco deserves its place among the most famous cities in the world. This is a place that knows how to throw a party, and the enormous Bay to Breakers race is no exception – half sporting event, half all-out costume-filled street extravaganza.

Since its inaugural year way back in 1912 (when the race was still called the Cross City Race), the Bay to Breakers has grown to become one of the biggest races of its kind in the world. The competition even holds the Guinness World record for the largest running race, with more than 110,000 participants, set in 1986.

The course is 12km long and runs from the Embarcadero all the way down to the Golden Gate Park. Participants include professional athletes, enthusiastic amateurs, those running for charity and some who simply want to be a part of the spectacle. People dress up as animals, rock stars, storm troopers and robots, while many – in the spirit of San Francisco – choose to wear nothing at all.

The city stops for the day as more than 100,000 people line the streets to cheer on the runners, marvel at the extravagant floats and chuckle at the elaborately costumed competitors as they stumble by. The diverse colours, traditions and cultures of this great city come together in a family-friendly carnival atmosphere that is quintessentially San Fran.

MORE INFO Bay to Breakers (www.ingbaytobreakers.com)

EUROPEADA

WHERE Location changes each year **WHEN** End of May to early June **GETTING INVOLVED** Check website for match fixtures and ticketing details.

In the 45 states that make up Europe, one in seven people belong to a national minority. These citizens total a staggering 100 million people, and between them they represent 337 different ethnic groups. Out of the 90 languages spoken throughout the continent, 53 are considered 'stateless' and the Europeada, a soccer tournament open to members of these minorities, celebrates this vast array of cultures.

With teams representing the Occitans, the Karachays of Russia, the Lemkos of Poland and the Danes in Germany, most of the nations represented in Europeada are not otherwise recognised as independent football (soccer) associations. Looking at the 20 teams that compete, it's hard not to be reminded of Europe's extraordinary history over the last thousand years. Though some critics of the tournament fear it may reignite ethnic pride, which has had bloody consequences in places like Croatia and Bosnia, the competition aims to use sport as a way of increasing awareness of linguistic diversity and national minorities.

The tournament was held for the first time in 2008. The event took place in the Romansh region of Sulselva, Switzerland, by way of a joint effort between the Austrians and the Swiss. Games were played in relatively small stadiums, and the spectating 'crowd' could perhaps better be described as a 'group'. Subsequent competitions, slated to be held annually, are organised by the Federal Union of European Nationalities (FUEN) – an independent union of national minorities, established in 1949.

MORE INFO Europeada '08 (www.europeada2008.net), FUEN (www.fuen.org)

'For me, it's not only the circuit, it is also the whole weekend that is crazy, because it is completely packed with a lot of people with a lot of money. I think it's great to watch it, just to see things that you normally don't see in life. And as a spectator you also get closer to the cars than anywhere else. If a spectator could come to only one race, I would suggest Monaco.'

Nick Heidfeld, a driver for the 2008 BMW Sauber team

FOR THE RECORD

↗ In 2005, Kettering Town broke the record for most goals in FA Cup history having scored 820 goals between 1888 and 2007.

↗ In 1983 18-year-old Norman Whiteside became the youngest player to score in an FA Cup final.

THE FA CUP

WHERE Wembley Stadium, London, England **WHEN** Season runs from August through to the final, held the Saturday after the Premier League season concludes **GETTING INVOLVED** Tickets to season games are readily available. Get in early for finals seats, and polish up the credit card, with prices in the vicinity of £830 to £1500.

It's the oldest association football competition in the world, dating back to 1871. So, in the same year that the first cup goal was scored by Clapham Rovers, Queen Victoria was opening Albert Hall and, over on the other side of the world, Susan B Anthony was arrested for trying to vote. Apart from its venerable age, the FA Cup has an edge over other competitions for the simmering possibility that anything can happen.

The knockout competition includes clubs from all levels. As well as Premier and Football League clubs, clubs from as many as six levels down compete. This opens the field up for minnows to become giant-killers (which translates to aspiring clubs from lower divisions causing an upset by unexpectedly beating clubs from a higher

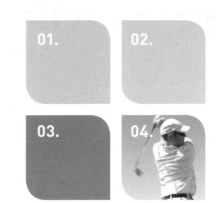

'The knockout competition includes clubs from all levels, opening the field up for minnows to become giant-killers'

**MAY
WEEK.04**

Steven Gerrard (R) of Premier League team Liverpool scores his third goal against minnows Luton Town in the third round of the FA Cup in 2008.

level). Also raising the excitement stakes is the draw, which determines who plays who. It's done by drawing numbered balls from a bag and has developed into a spectacle in itself, becoming a public event where famous footballers draw the numbers. The randomness of the draw means that two top Premier League teams can play each other early on, eliminating the otherwise likely eventuality of them playing each other in the final.

There are 14 rounds in the competition: six qualifying, six further rounds, a semi-final and the final. Until the early '90s, all games that were drawn were replayed until one of the teams came out on top. As many as six matches were sometimes played before a winner finally came through. These days, in the event of a draw, there's one replay, which, if at the end of the game is still drawn, goes to a penalty shoot-out.

There are no replays in finals games. In the 2008-09 tournament, 762 teams competed, and around 90,000 attended the final.

As well as qualifying for the UEFA Cup, the winning team receives *the* Cup. The original FA Cup trophy, used since 1871 was stolen from a shoe shop window in Birmingham in 1895 never to be seen again. The second cup, used between 1896 and 1910 was sold in 2005 for £480, ironically, to the chairman of Birmingham City. A third trophy was used between 1911 and 1992 when it was retired due to fragility. The current trophy, used since '92 is the fourth. (And there is a fifth in reserve, just in case…)

MORE INFO The FA Cup (www.thefa.com)

And they're off and racing... Competitors in the 2008 cheese rolling event at Cooper's Hill brave damage to limb and life in pursuit of a delicious Double Gloucester.

CHEESE ROLLING

WHERE Cooper's Hill, Brockworth, England **WHEN** Last Monday in May **GETTING INVOLVED** Competitors must be over 18 years of age. See the website for more details.

You may have thought the most dangerous thing about cheese was the mould, but then you've probably never stood atop Cooper's Hill on this mad Monday. The premise is simple: a handmade, 7lb circle of Double Gloucestershire is rolled down the hill and a gaggle of people give chase: rolling, sliding and stumbling their way down behind the cheese. The first to the bottom of the hill (or to grab the cheese) wins, and gets to keep the cheese. Which does nothing to explain the mud, the slippery grass, the slope and the injury toll.

A 200-year-old tradition (though a wooden cheese was used during rationing after WWII), it is unashamedly a cheesy event, but it draws around 5000 spectators and an international cast of competitors, with Australians and Kiwis seeming to do particularly well.

The course for the event is a swathe of grass cut through the forest on Cooper's Hill. The slope is at times vertical and at some lesser moments has a 50% grade. The idea may be to run after the cheese, but for most, it means falling, rolling and tumbling down the hill. And even if you catch the thing, it's a whole other matter to grab it while simultaneously trying to defy gravity. Each year competitors are injured – sprains, strains, broken bones – with the toll even reaching 33 wounded in 1997 (police cancelled the event in 1998 in response). And yet, runners return, competing year after year.

The first cheese is rolled at noon and there are five downhill races, 20 minutes apart. At a count of 'three', the cheese is rolled and competitors lurch over the edge on 'four'. Between each of the downhill races there's also an uphill race in which competitors claw, grope and strain to the top of Cooper's Hill.

MORE INFO Cheese Rolling in Gloucestershire (www.cheese-rolling.co.uk)

INDY 500

WHERE Indianapolis, USA **WHEN** Memorial Day weekend **GETTING INVOLVED** Tickets are available online. The city is overrun with tourists and racing teams so book early to ensure a place to crash at the end of the festivities.

Blisteringly fast cars, gasoline alley, women in bikinis, burning rubber and the screams of hundreds of thousands of American rev-heads make up what is for many the 'Greatest Spectacle in Racing'. Motor racing fans of all shapes and sizes – from tattoo-covered bikers to caravan families with petrol in their veins – descend on Indianapolis to be a part of one of America's oldest and most beloved motor races.

After relatively humble beginnings nearly 100 years ago – the first race took place in 1911 – the Indy 500 now attracts up to 400,000 people to Indianapolis each year. Travel agencies offer all kinds of packages for flights and accommodation, from private jet and limo packages to cheaper accommodation for the budget-conscious motor-head.

Race day is preceded by the 500 Festival Parade through the streets of Indianapolis where 300,000 people come out to watch the floats, bands and all 33 drivers parading by in race formation. On race day multicoloured balloons are released to the closing chords of 'Back Home Again in Indiana' before the flag drops and the deafening roar of the engines engulf the stadium. Cars hurtle across the 'yard of bricks' – the final remaining piece of the original brick-paved track – and drivers begin their 500-mile chase for the famed orchid wreath and racing immortality. Everything about the Indy 500 is larger than life – even the enormous Borg-Warner Trophy, awarded to the winner, which features bas-relief sculptures of every previous winner.

MORE INFO Indianapolis 500 (www.indy500.com)

WORLD TABLE TENNIS CHAMPIONSHIPS

WHERE Location changes each championships **WHEN** Biennially, with the singles and team events held on alternate years **GETTING INVOLVED** Check the ITTF website for scheduling and ticketing details.

There aren't many sports that have changed the course of history, and if forced to name one, table tennis would seem an unlikely choice. But in the early 1970s, when the Cold War was creeping across world politics, a simple game of ping-pong helped improve relations between communist China and Nixon's USA. Referred to as 'Ping Pong Diplomacy', the invitation for US players to visit China paved the way for a visit to Beijing by Nixon in 1972, thus bringing to an end the stand-off between the two powers.

In the table-tennis world, 2010 is the year for Moscow. Once the very heart of the Soviet Empire, Red Square is to be the next stage for the ITT (International Table Tennis Federation) World Team Championships. The competition began in London in 1926 and has been held every two years since 1957. The last team world championship was held in 2008 in Guangzhou and welcomed more than 700 athletes from 130 countries for a week of intense competition. More than 13,000 eager spectators attended the final.

An after-dinner activity among the Victorian English aristocracy, table tennis was played with an assortment of household objects and quickly grew in popularity. An informal world championship was staged in 1902, which led to the current global competition and the establishment of high level national leagues in China, Hong Kong, Germany, France and Japan, just to name a few.

MORE INFO International Table Tennis Federation (www.ittf.com)

MAY
WEEK.04

AND ANOTHER THING

- - - - - - - - - - - - - - - - - -

World Beard & Moustache Championships (various countries)

If you're a hirsute man and proud of your facial hair then this one's for you. Over 250 competitors from clubs such as London's Handlebar Club, Germany's First Berliner Beard Club and Beard Team USA compete. Categories include the delicate Dali moustache, the full-beard Freestyle and the partial-beard Fu Manchu. (www.worldbeardchampionships.com)

- - - - - - - - - - - - - - - - - -

↗ Away from the pounding oars, homes fill with invocations of physical and spiritual wellbeing. The herbs calamus and moxa are hung from front doors and pictures of Chung Kuei, the demon slayer, are pinned up.

↗ Another tradition associated with dragon boating that's making a popular comeback, particularly in Taiwan, is the making of aromatic silk sachets, filled with flowers or herbs, which are given to children.

DUANWU JIE (DRAGON-BOAT RACING)

WHERE Hunan Province, China **WHEN** Fifth day of the fifth lunar month **GETTING INVOLVED** To participate in a race, contact the IDBF, which facilitates races internationally. To watch, particularly in Hunan, organise transport and accommodation well in advance.

It's a mass paddle. In each elaborately designed dragon boat are 22 rowers, a drummer and a helm (steerer), packed like sardines. The drummer sets the pace, so that each of the boat's individual members can work together as one, to the same rhythm. With a dozen different drum beats, 264 oars smacking the water, calls from the steerer, and up to 100,000 cheering spectators, dragon boat racing is a spirited spectacle in more ways than one.

Although the customs associated with races vary from place to place, the festival's origins date back to 278 BC when, it's said, Qu Yuan committed suicide by throwing

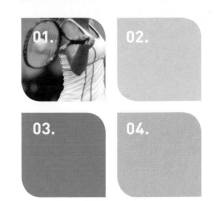

01.

02.

03.

04.

'With 264 oars smacking the water and up to 100,000 cheering spectators, dragon boat racing is a spirited spectacle'

JUNE
WEEK.01

The dragon-boat drummer's rhythmic beating leads the crew throughout the race, indicating the timing and frequency of the paddlers' strokes.

himself into the river. The revered poet and statesman was protesting against the Qin state's invasion of his patch, Chu. Dismayed local people took to their fishing boats, splashed the water with their oars and threw in rice to keep the fish and evil spirits from Qu.

Early June is the time for dragon-boat racing, which takes place in more than 60 countries, from China (where there are 50 million participants) through Hong Kong and the Czech Republic to Australia. The race is run over a distance from 200m to 2000m, and won when a rower straddles his craft's dragon head and grabs the flag, often only fractions of a second ahead of his rivals. Spectators are unabashed in their support, cheering and clapping wildly. The traditional snack on the day are *zongzi,* triangular dumplings made of glutinous rice wrapped in bamboo or reed leaves, in memory of the rice that

was scattered to distract the fish from nibbling on the noble poet's body.

A poignant place to catch the race is along the Miluo River in Hunan Province, where Qu apparently met his end. The river is formed by the confluence of the Mi and Luo Rivers, after joining in Daqiuwan, Miluo city. Races also take place on the WWF–protected Dongting Lake, the country's second-largest freshwater lake. It's home to rare silver fish and 200 bird species, including the Siberian crane and great bustard.

Get to the waterside early to see the blessing of the dragon-head prows, with incense and gongs. The party continues after dark with firecrackers, traditional dragon dances and *hsiung huang* wine (a potent rice-wine concoction).

MORE INFO International Dragon Boat Federation (www.idbf.org), China National Tourist Office (www.cnto.org)

01.

02.

03.

04.

STANLEY CUP

↘ **WHERE** Location changes each championship **WHEN** First week of June
GETTING INVOLVED Finals tickets sell fast, so get in early.

They have to be the world's most macho ice skaters, and watching an intense hour of full-contact ice hockey can be vicariously terrifying. And when the stakes are as high as this, playing for the honour to hold aloft the oldest and most prestigious professional hockey trophy, the play could hardly get more furious.

The Stanley Cup is the National Hockey League's championship cup. The league's 30 teams (24 based in the US and six based in Canada) begin the season in October, with the Stanley Cup playoffs beginning in April until early June. It's an elimination tournament, where two teams play against each other to win a best-of-seven series in order to progress through to the next round. But the Cup's veritable celebrity status predates the NHL championship tournament by 32 years, when a Frederick Walter Stanley had a cup made in 1893 to give the amateur hockey teams in Canada something to fight for.

And fight they do…a tactic governed by a complex system of unwritten rules referred to as 'the code'. More recently, the NHL has imposed more penalties for illegal hits and fights, which has ultimately increased the speed of the game by allowing for more goals to be scored. Which is not to say that it's no longer a physical game. Clashes of sticks and bodies are common. Called bodychecking, and allowed only in men's hockey, players can ram each other with their hips and shoulders in pursuit of the speeding puck.

Though least popular of the four major leagues in the US, the Stanley Cup has a huge following in Canada (as does ice hockey generally). But nowhere is it more popular than with members of the victorious team who each take a turn of having the cup in their homes for 24 hours.

MORE INFO The National Hockey League (www.nhl.com)

JUNE
WEEK.01

ASIA PACIFIC TCHOUKBALL CHAMPIONSHIPS

↘ **WHERE** Location changes each championship **WHEN** Biennially, early to mid-June
GETTING INVOLVED Check the website for match fixtures and ticketing information.

At first glance tchoukball looks like a crowd of high-jumping anarchists who've invented a game where they can hurl balls at trampolines every which way without concerning themselves with rules at all. On closer inspection, however, upon realising teams can score at either end, the object of the game begins to show itself.

The creator of tchoukball, Dr Hermann Brandt once said, 'The objective of human physical activities is not to make champions, but to make a contribution to building a harmonious society', and this is the spirit that underpins the entire sport. After studying the effects of high-contact sports on athletes Dr Brandt aimed to create the 'perfect team game' and though he didn't survive to see the game reach its current heights he lived long enough to see some of his dreams realised.

A zero-contact sport, tchoukball is a curious mix of volleyball, netball, soccer and handball. Nine players make up each team and compete on a court similar to a handball court. On either end is a trampoline tilted at a 45-degree angle, and teams must hit the trampoline with the ball to score.

The sport came to prominence in Taiwan and other parts of Asia during the 1980s, and is fast becoming very popular throughout Hong Kong, Macau, India and Japan. Members of the international body that governs the sport, the Féderation Internationale de Tchoukball (FITB) include Taiwan, Great Britain, USA, Hong Kong and Japan.

MORE INFO International Tchoukball Federation (www.tchoukball.org)

'Goaltending is a normal job, sure. How would you like it in your job if every time you made a small mistake, a red light went on over your desk and 15,000 people stood up and yelled at you.'

– – – – – – – – – – – – – – –

Jacques Plante, Canadian professional ice-hockey legend

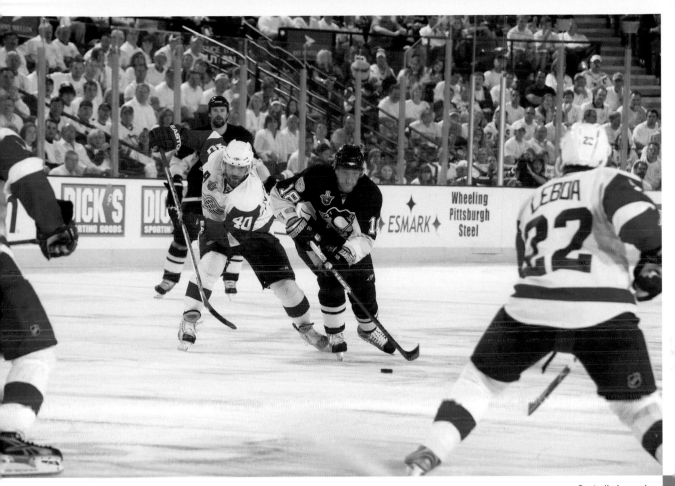

Controlled anarchy on ice – the Pittsburgh Penguins battle the Detroit Red Wings in 2008.

INDIAN PREMIER LEAGUE FINAL

 WHERE India, but subject to change **WHEN** Early June **GETTING INVOLVED** See the website for match fixtures and venue details.

'The most exciting parts of cricket, without the long boring bits' is how some would describe the new twenty20 format and, after witnessing a match in all its high-octane glory, all but the most traditional followers of the game would tend to agree.

Watch in amazement as the world's best batsmen let fly with fours and sixes all over the ground, bowlers charge down the pitch to the screams of jubilant crowds, and fielders leap this way and that to snag spectacular catches and run-outs.

With big business paying the bills, the Indian Premier League has managed to lure the world's first-class veterans and most promising youngsters to create a new competition that aims to please the cricket-mad country of India. Teams are made up of players from all the powerhouse nations of the game (Australia, India, South Africa, England, the West Indies, Pakistan and Sri Lanka) and each team is led by a champion or 'icon' player. Shane Warne captains the Rajasthan Royals, VVS Laxman leads the Deccan Chargers and the great Sachin Tendulkar heads up the Mumbai Indians.

For the first time, cricketers have the chance to make the kind of money offered to those in other sports and they have seized the moment. The fans and the sport, however, are the real winners. Players, formally enemies on the field, are now performing side by side in front of ecstatic crowds. With Warne's Royals grabbing victory on the final ball of 2008's nail-biting inaugural final against Dhoni's Super Kings, you best start planning your trip early to avoid missing out.

MORE INFO Indian Premier League (www.iplt20.com)

FOR THE RECORD

- - - - - - - - - - - - - - - - - -

↗ Michael Jordan holds the record for highest career regular season scoring average with 30.12 points per game.

↗ In 2008 the Boston Celtics convincingly beat high-profile rivals the LA Lakers 131-92 to win a record 17 NBA championships. The final score was the second-largest margin of victory.

NBA FINALS

 WHERE USA **WHEN** Mid-June **GETTING INVOLVED** Buy tickets online well in advance.

From its humble peach-basket beginnings to its 1980's heyday, basketball has given North Americans of all ages something to look up to. And the pinnacle of the National Basketball Association's season, the NBA finals, is no exception.

The men's professional basketball association, NBA, was founded in 1946. Then known as the Basketball Association of America, it consisted of 11 teams. Three years later saw a merger with the National Basketball League, and the birth of the NBA as we know it. Today's league has 30 teams: 29 from America and one from Canada. The NBA playoffs begin in late April, with eight teams in the Eastern Conference and eight teams in the Western Conference vying for a place in the championship, played between the winner of each conference.

Basketball was invented in 1891 by a PE professor as a means of keeping his charges fit during the long Canadian winters, within the confines of a school gymnasium. Much

Derek Fisher of the LA Lakers goes up for a shot against Kendrick Perkins of the Boston Celtics in game four of the 2008 NBA Finals in Los Angeles.

01. 02. 03. 04.

'Basketball was invented in 1891 by a phys-ed professor, James Naismith, who nailed a peach basket to a 3m pole'

JUNE
WEEK.02

to the amusement of the students, James Naismith nailed a peach basket up a 3m pole and jotted down the fundamental rules, which, apparently, make reference to another game, Duck on a Rock – where one person must protect their 'duck' (stone), which is perched on a rock, from other children trying to knock it by pelting stones, and tag them, eliminating them from the game. It wasn't until 1906 that a hoop replaced an actual basket. Getting a goal in those days was equally met with joy and annoyance, as someone had to shimmy up the pole and retrieve the ball from its basket.

The 1950s saw the rise of basketball as a college sport, and it was then that an actual orange basketball came into being. Previous games used a soccer ball. By the 1980s, big names were attracting more and more spectators to the sport. Names like Magic Johnson who led the LA Lakers in five

wins, and Michael Jordan who is not only one of the decade's most outstanding athletes, but one of its most successfully marketed. Jordan inspired a shoe (the Air Jordan), a movie *(Space Jam)* and thousands of spectators to the NBA with his prolific scoring.

Today's NBA playoffs consists of 16 teams, with games attracting around 18,000 fans. Make it 18,001 and see the big men fly.
MORE INFO National Basketball Association (www.nba.com)

Race cars take to the streets during the 2008 24-hour Le Mans endurance race. In the red, Emanuele Pirro attempts to wend through the traffic.

LE MANS

WHERE Le Mans, France **WHEN** Second Saturday in June **GETTING INVOLVED** Tickets are available online; book accommodation early.

With just a few weeks between this and the Formula 1 Grand Prix (p80), there's the perfect amount of time to slowly make your way from Monaco through the Cote d'Azur, Pyrenees and Paris arriving in Le Mans for all the hoo-ha of the world's other famous European race, the 24 hours of Le Mans.

First held in 1923, Le Mans predates Monaco's Grand Prix by six years, and is generally known as the Grand Prix of Endurance. Le Mans is arguably the more friendly of the two competitions, with motorcar innovations having practical applications in the consumer marketplace. For nigh on 90 years, the race has led competing car manufacturers to innovate in the areas of aerodynamics and fuel consumption; both fields in which innovations trickle down into mass-produced cars.

Run on actual streets, rather than a dedicated track, the 13km Circuit de la Sarthe is the ultimate test of a car's reliability and efficient fuel consumption. And, run over a continuous 24-hour period, it's also fairly testing for drivers. Once upon a time drivers attempted to complete the entire race either solo or by swapping with only one other driver. For safety reasons, these days a driver can only drive for a maximum of four hours at a time, and no more than 14 hours total.

But there's much more on offer than 24 hours of race, flag waving, and jet flyovers spraying red, white and blue. Qualifying and practice days begin on the Wednesday before the race, which also includes the Le Mans Legend race for cars that have raced in Le Mans in a particular, earlier, era. Friday is the driver parade and allocated rest day before Saturday's 4pm start when 50 cars start their engines.

Porsche is the race's pin-up car, with 16 overall victories. Ferrari is next, with nine, and Jaguar third with seven. **MORE INFO** Automobile Club de L'ouest (www.lemans.org)

ORIENTEERING WORLD CUP

WHERE Location changes each world cup **WHEN** Events run from mid-May through to September **GETTING INVOLVED** For competition details and ticket enquiries check the website.

Always getting lost? Never know which way is north? Maybe competition orienteering isn't the sport for you. But if you're in Europe from May to September perhaps a visit to one of the orienteering World Cup events will help point you in the right direction. Competitions generally take place in Norway, Finland, Hungary and Switzerland.

Competitors are given a compass and a map and must navigate their way over unfamiliar terrain to various 'control points'. There are four different versions of the sport. These occur on foot, skis, mountain bikes and, finally, trail orienteering, which is not judged on speed and therefore open to disabled competitors.

The history of orienteering goes back 100 years to late 19th-century Sweden when the term was first coined. Initially a military training exercise for the Swedish army before becoming competitive among civilians, the first orienteering competition open to the public was held in Norway in 1897. With the advent of cheap compasses in the 1930s, the popularity of the sport skyrocketed in Sweden and surrounding countries such as Russia, Finland and Switzerland. The sport now has 67 national orienteering federations across the world and a full calendar of events that are staggered throughout the year.

The orienteering World Cup is organised by the International Orienteering Federation and was held for the first time in 1986. The competition was held every two years until 2004, when it became an annual event.

MORE INFO International Orienteering Federation (www.orienteering.org)

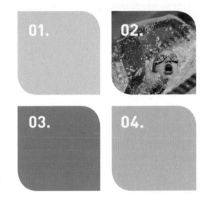

01. 02. 03. 04.

GIOSTRA DELLA QUINTANA

WHERE Foligno, Italy **WHEN** Sometime in June, as well as the second or third Saturday in September **GETTING INVOLVED** Thousands travel to attend the festival each year; book early to ensure your place.

Complete with knights and lances, corsets and lace, horses, high collars and velvet robes, the Giostra della Quintana has everything one would hope to find at a jousting tournament in 15th-century Italy. Foligno, an ancient town in the heart of Umbria, comes alive twice a year for one of the world's greatest equestrian spectacles.

The meet in its present form has been running since 1946, but it has a history that dates back to 1448. The first tournament of the year (the challenge) takes place in June on a Saturday night, with a follow up event (the counter-challenge) held on the second or third Sunday in September. Ten knights gather for the meet and represent each of the 10 wards of Foligno.

Rings of varying sizes are attached to a statue (the Quintana) in the middle of the arena and, while on a galloping horse, the contestants must catch the rings with their lance. As each round of the tournament progresses, the size of the rings gets smaller. The knight who finishes the course in the quickest time is the champion and thus awarded the *palio* (banner).

The entire town takes part and the festivities begin with the opening of the *Fiera dei Soprastanti* – a reproduction of the old market, complete with old currency. Leading up to the event, each ward has a tavern serving traditional dishes from the era, and a colourful Baroque street parade precedes the main event with renaissance costumes, music and dancing.

MORE INFO Quintana (www.quintana.it)

JUNE
WEEK.02

AND ANOTHER THING
- - - - - - - - - - - - - - - -

Goanna-pulling Championship (Wooli, Australia)

No reptiles allowed! Goanna-pulling involves two men connected by a thick leather neck strap, each trying to pull the other over a line – tug-of-war style. The belly-down, backwards scuttle of the competitors resembles the gait of a goanna, albeit one running backwards. The host town, Wooli (population 500), also puts on a parade and kid's activities on the day of the event. (www.visitnsw.com)

FOR THE RECORD

ROYAL ASCOT

WHERE Ascot, Berkshire, England **WHEN** Third week in June
GETTING INVOLVED Tickets are available online, from £65 to £18,630 per person; under-16s free.

Even if you're not an avid race-goer, but you enjoy tradition and pageantry, then Royal Ascot is your target. Royal Ascot Racecourse celebrates its tercentenary in 2011, and the queen and her royal party – who trot to the course from the castle 10km away – attend Royal Ascot race-week each year. It's high fashion and hubbub that could keep you amused for a full five days.

The pinnacle of the thoroughbred racing calendar and the summer social scene, Royal Ascot starts on Royal Tuesday and runs through to Royal Saturday. Over the five days, around £4 million of prize money is awarded – a mere fraction of the amount spent by attendees on champagne and outfits alone, never mind the betting. The Ascot Gold Cup on Royal Thursday (Ladies Day) is the feature. The 2.5-mile race for four year olds was first run in 1807 and, together with the 2.25-mile Doncaster Cup

'More than 300,000 attend Royal Ascot annually – making it the best-attended race meeting in Europe'

JUNE
WEEK.03

Spectators massed in a sea of top hats, feathers and fascinators cheer on Frankie Dettori as he rides Kheleyf to victory in the first race of the second day of Royal Ascot in 2004.

(September) and 2-mile Goodwood (late July/early August), is part of the coveted Stayers' Triple Crown for longer distance races. Only six horses in history have ever won all three, with Le Moss the only horse to do it twice.

More than 300,000 attend Royal Ascot annually – making it the best-attended race meeting in Europe – and her majesty's representative wishes to point out that only formal day dress is appropriate. That doesn't stop you from wearing a giant Stilton cheeseboard on your head (hello madam), or other irreverent headwear. However, if you have hopes of watching from the royal enclosure, 'gentlemen are required to wear either black or grey morning dress, including a waistcoat, with a top hat' and ladies, 'a hat or substantial fascinator', and no off-the-shoulders, halter necks, midriffs, spaghetti straps or minis. 'Overseas visitors are welcome to wear the formal

national dress of their country or Service dress.'

For overseas visitors, there are five opportunities to glimpse a royal. The family attends via horse and carriage, and forms a procession down the track before racing begins each day. And after the flashing silks, the look-at-me hats and fashions, and the majestic thoroughbreds have all departed for another year there is plenty to see elsewhere in the region. Watch the changing of the guard at nearby Windsor Castle or check out the Vikings across the way at Legoland.

MORE INFO Ascot Racecourse (www.ascot.co.uk)

Jose Molina of the New York Yankees watches his hit become a home run, the last in the old Yankee Stadium, during a game against the Baltimore Orioles in 2008.

NEW YORK YANKEES MAJOR LEAGUE BASEBALL GAME

WHERE New York City, USA **WHEN** Season runs from April to October **GETTING INVOLVED** Tickets are available online. Brush up on the words to 'New York, New York' before the game.

It's New York. To not see a Yankees game is to not see a fundamental piece of the city, tantamount to walking around with one eye closed. And most Yankees fans are one-eyed in their support of their beloved team. The Yankees return the love, leading Major League Baseball's 30 teams, winning 26 World Series championships and 39 American League pennants. Yankees games draw more than three million fans each season; even in an away game, stadiums groan under the weight of baseball fans keen to see the famous Yankees in action.

Based in the Bronx since 1903, the club was originally founded in Baltimore a few years earlier (and named the Baltimore Orioles). The Yankees are a member of the American League's Eastern Division, and have a persisting rivalry with the Boston Red Sox that dates back to the 1920s. (If you luck upon a Red Sox vs Yankees game, consider yourself one lucky traveller.) The Red Sox were one of the most successful teams, clocking up five World Series wins between the inaugural match in 1903, and 1919–20, when it traded pitcher-turned-outfielder Babe Ruth. For the next 86 years, the Red Sox would not win a series, often eliminated at the hands of the Yankees. It became known as the 'Curse of the Bambino', as the run of luck (good and bad) had supernatural proportions.

In 2008, the famous Yankee Stadium closed. Since opening in 1923, it had hosted more than 6500 Yankees home games, as well as evangelist conventions, concerts (U2, Billy Joel) and Mass, delivered by Pope John Paul II, among others. Be among the first few hundred thousand to enjoy a hot dog, while watching a Yankees game at the new stadium: located across the road from the original and one of the most expensive ever built at US$1.6 billion.
MORE INFO New York Yankees (www.yankees.mlb.com), Major League Baseball (www.mlb.com)

EUROPEAN TREE CLIMBING CHAMPIONSHIPS

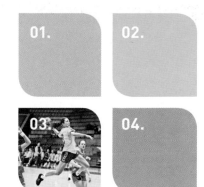

WHERE Location changes each championship **WHEN** Third week in June
GETTING INVOLVED Competitors must represent certified associations.

Tree-climbing championships you say? Yes. You heard right. All those afternoons spent hanging off the branches in the backyard may finally pay off – probably not, but if you love trees and climbing this is the holiday event for you. Held in a different location each year the European Tree Climbing Championships is just one of the many highlights on a full annual calendar of events organised by the international tree-climbing community.

Feeling more like a jamboree than a competition at times, the four-day event includes a trade fair, workshops and demonstrations, as well as competitions. Casual observers mix with seasoned professionals, avid amateurs and arborists to talk trees, climbing and methods of care. Ideas are exchanged and new techniques and products are trialled, alongside recreational climbing and children's activities.

Clubs from around Europe and the UK, associated with the International Society of Arboriculture (ISA), compete against one another in a number of events, which include speed climbing, the throw line, the foot lock, the work climb, and the aerial rescue. Points are scored for climbing technique as well as for speed.

'Improving the understanding of trees and the practice of arboriculture' is the mission statement of the ISA, the governing body of a sport that has found enthusiastic followers across many continents. More than 50 tree-climbing events occur around the globe each year and, as people become more aware of the benefits of environmental protection, this number is bound to rise.

MORE INFO European Tree Climbing Championships (www.eurotcc.org), International Society of Arboriculture (ISA, www.isa-arbor.com)

WORLD LEAGUE WATER POLO FINAL

WHERE Changes **WHEN** Around the third week in June **GETTING INVOLVED** Check the website for event details.

Swimming caps with earmuffs, competitors with giant shoulders, and little soccer goals in a swimming pool – to the uninitiated, water polo can look like an impromptu game at a football players' pool party.

Known in its early years as 'water rugby' or 'aquatic football', the game was first played in Great Britain in rivers and lakes with a ball made from Indian rubber. One of the early versions of water polo involved competitors paddling around on barrels fitted with fake horse heads, hitting the ball with their oars. The game has evolved a great deal since Victorian times and, along with football, cricket and tug of war, was one of the first team sports to be added to the Olympic roster in 1900.

Not many sports are as exhausting or as physically draining. Players must throw, leap and sprint all around the pool, and in between chasing the ball they must constantly tread water. The modern game consists of four eight-minute quarters and includes nine players on each team, with the aim being to score more goals than the opposition.

The FINA Water Polo World Leagues take place between February and June each year and were staged for the first time in 2002. Preliminary competitions take place to determine which teams will participate in the Super Final. Media coverage is increasing with each year and representatives from the strongest water polo nations join with emerging powers to compete for the championship and a share in the lucrative prize money, which now totals more than US$500,000.

MORE INFO Federation Internationale de Natation (www.fina.org)

'I wasn't even supposed to bloody be there. I was on my way to Worcester but there was a monster traffic jam. I phoned my clerk and told him to turn around and head for Ascot instead.'

Bookie Gary Wiltshire on losing close to a million pounds thanks to Frankie Dettorie's Magnificent Seven in 1996

Rafael Nadal (pictured) dethroned five-time Wimbledon champion Roger Federer in 2008 by winning the longest-ever Wimbledon men's final.

WIMBLEDON

WHERE Wimbledon, London, England **WHEN** Late June to early July
GETTING INVOLVED Tickets are available by ballot (application forms
available online from August). Around 500 seats are made available for
those willing to queue overnight; see the British Tennis website for details.

Quite apart from the thrill of being part of an elite sporting event, attending
Wimbledon puts you front and centre for a swathe of only-at-Wimbledon
traditions. Strawberries anyone?

As much a part of Wimbledon as tennis balls, strawberries are the traditional
snack, with fans nibbling through 28 tonnes of fruit and 7000L of cream over the
two weeks of competition. It's a tradition that stretches back to the very first
championship, held in 1877, here at the All England Lawn Tennis club. Back then,
tennis was called sphairistike, and had only been invented a year or so earlier by
Walter Clopton Wingfield.

The tournament's venerable age contributes to the generally held belief that
Wimbledon is the most prestigious of the four grand slams, and the world's
most prestigious tennis event. It attracts top players, and pays singles champions
£750,000. But it's about much more than money. Wimbledon is unique in many
ways. It's the world's oldest tournament and the only grand slam still played
on a grass surface. It requires that competitors wear primarily white-coloured
clothing and that they bow to the queen if she is in attendance – the royal box is
situated at centre court. And female players are represented on the scoreboard
with a Miss or Mrs honorific; men's events are known as the gentlemen's singles
or doubles. And while Wimbledon is as British as the British flag, a British man
hasn't won the singles event since Fred Perry in 1936.

Given its long history, until recently little about Wimbledon had changed.
Traditionally, the ball boys and girls wore green in an endeavour to make them
as invisible as possible against the lawn. In 2006 they all got new blue uniforms,
designed by Ralph Lauren. Interruption of play due to poor weather was as much
of a tradition as the strawberries, though less welcome, until 2009's completion
of the retractable roof.

The prestigious All England private club has 19 courts. Centre court and court
number one are used only for the two weeks of Wimbledon each year (with the
exception of Olympic events in 2011) and host the hotly contested events, such
as the gentlemen's singles events and the finals. And if you delight in others'
misfortune, get yourself courtside at court No 2. Known as the 'graveyard of
champions,' it earned its reputation as the court most likely to eliminate seeded
players early. Just ask Venus Williams, Pete Sampras or Andre Agassi.
MORE INFO Wimbledon (www.wimbledon.org), British Tennis (www.britishtennis
.com/tickets/wqueue.shtml)

FOR THE RECORD

↗ Martina Navratilova holds
the record for winning the
most ladies singles events,
with nine. For gentlemen, it's
a seven-each tie between
Renshaw and Sampras.

↗ Boris Becker is Wimbledon's
youngest champ, being just 17
when he won in 1985.

*'As much a part of Wimbledon as tennis balls,
strawberries are the traditional snack, with fans
nibbling through some 28 tonnes'*

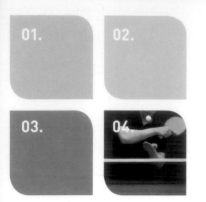

01. 02.

03. 04.

LIFESAVING WORLD CHAMPIONSHIPS

WHERE Location changes each championship **WHEN** Biennially
GETTING INVOLVED Tickets are available online.

For everyone who loved *It's a Knockout* – the popular TV show that pitted local towns against each other via a series of zany games – you're going to love lifesaving games. They're great for two reasons: for their generally entertaining nature, but also for their ability to sharpen the skills of the actual lifesavers competing.

Lifesaving originated in Australia in 1906, after the rule prohibiting bathing during the day (for reasons of modesty) was lifted, spurring an influx of swimmers. Volunteers were trained in rescue and resuscitation, and patrolled beaches. The drills that kept lifesavers fit (and occupied between actual rescues) developed into a competition sport – and the world championships sees the best clubs competing from around the world.

Events generally take place both in a swimming pool and at the beach. Indoor events include the 'manikin carry,' in which the lifesaver swims a distance (anywhere from 50m to 200m), dives to retrieve a submerged dummy, then swims it back to the finishing line. And there's the obstacle swim, where the competitor must swim as quickly as possible while dodging a variety of obstacles. The main events occur beachside. These include inflatable rescue boat (IRB) racing, where two competitors drag their IRB across the sand a short distance, launch into the surf and drive out to 'rescue' their teammate, which involves hoicking him or her into the boat, zooming back to shore, cutting the engine, and running to the finishing line. And who could forget flags: a kind of beach version of musical chairs, in which the competitors must lay belly-down in the sand, and then race to grab a baton. But when the sand settles, it's clear there are not enough batons for everyone.
MORE INFO International Lifesaving Federation (www.ilsf.org)

JUNE
WEEK.04

AND ANOTHER THING

- - - - - - - - - - - - - - - -

World Worm-Charming Championships (Willaston, Cheshire, UK)

In what was intended to be a fundraiser and a bit of a laff, a worm-charming event was organised in 1980. But Tom Shufflebotham shocked everybody that day by coaxing 511 worms from the ground. And so began the annual Worm-Charming Championships. Competitors have 30 minutes to charm as many worms from their allocated 3m² plot. And, in case you're wondering, charmed worms are released at the end on the day, after the birds have gone home to bed. (www.wormcharming.com)

KIRKPINAR OIL WRESTLING

WHERE Turkey **WHEN** Late June **GETTING INVOLVED** Check the website for schedules and ticketing info.

Most people would think that wrestling – as most of us know it – is strenuous enough as it is. Not so for the people of Turkey. Instead, try covering yourself with oil and fighting for three days and see what you think then. Oil wrestling, one of the country's favourite sports, has been a part of Turkish culture since the days of the Ottoman Empire and the Kirkpinar Oil Wrestling tournament has been running for an astonishing 642 years.

The origins of the contest can be found during the Ottoman campaign to capture Thrace in the 14th century around Edirne. Some 40 or so soldiers took part in a wrestling bout to pass the time between battles. Two of the men were locked in combat for days, with neither able to defeat the other. Eventually both died from exhaustion and were buried by their comrades under a fig tree. Years later when the army passed that way again they discovered natural springs bubbling up from under the fig tree. The water led them to the meadow, which they called Kirkpinar, which means '40 sources'.

Although oil wrestling takes place all around the country during the year, the diamond event takes place at Kirkpinar. All wrestlers begin the Kirkpinar tournament by praying, reading from the Koran and paying their respects to the great fighters of the past, while musicians and dancers take part in the opening celebrations. With heads of state in attendance, lucrative prize money and adoring fans the atmosphere is electric.
MORE INFO Kirkpinar (www.kirkpinar.com)

CALCIO STORICO

WHERE Florence, Italy **WHEN** Late June **GETTING INVOLVED** Participation is not open to the public (and that's probably for the best). It's a very popular event, so book accommodation early.

Verdi and Azzurri players offer up their skill and blood in Florence's Piazza Santa Croce.

There will be blood. Fifty-four players in pantaloons and six referees wearing ostrich plumes fight it out with fists, feet and smoke bombs in a giant sandpit – all for a pile of steaks amounting to the weight of a white calf. What madness is this you might ask? It may seem an unlikely on-field combination, but such are the colours and contradictions of one of the world's oldest tournaments – the Calcio Storico.

Taking place in the Piazza Santa Croce in Florence, the Calcio Storico is somewhere between rugby, football and all-out street fighting. Games are held each year in late June and early July to coincide with the celebration of St John's Day – the Patron Saint of Florence – and each game lasts for an agonising 50 minutes where the opposing teams try to gain the most number of goals.

With the first recorded match taking place on 17 February, 1530 and some historians tracing the origins of the game back another 200 years, the game is steeped in tradition. The teams who take part represent the four old neighbourhoods of Florence: the Bianchi (Santo Spirito), the Azzuri (Santa Croce), Rossi (Santa Maria Novella) and the Verdi (San Giovanni).

People from all over come to take part in the spectacle: bloodthirsty locals, curious tourists and everyone in between make up the merry throng. Proceedings begin with a street parade through the ancient streets of Florence ending at Piazza Santa Croce.

MORE INFO Calcio Storico (www.calciostorico.it, in Italian)

Mosaic from the 4th century
Villa of Casale, Sicily, Italy.

DEAD SPORTS
CHARIOT RACING

The funny thing about the circus is it has nothing to do with clowns. The original circuses were buildings specially designed to host mock battles and equestrian events, notably the traditional chariot-racing contests that enthralled the Romans for a millennia.

Circus Maximus was the greatest arena and could hold up to 200,000 screaming spectators – almost a quarter of Rome's population. Built into a valley between the Aventine and Pallatine hills, it stretched 600m long and 200m wide. The race track within formed an oval separated down the middle by a narrow fence, known as the *spinae*, which featured an ornate silver counting device indicating the number of completed laps.

Each *aurigae* (charioteer) rode for one of Rome's four competing stables and was identifiable by his tunic, which corresponded with the stable's colours of red, white, green or blue. Betting among spectators was widespread as was allegiance to particular stables. Think of the fanaticism of Italian soccer fans, who have been known to hold underperforming players hostage, and you'll get the picture.

Chariots were either *bigae* (for two horses) or *quadrigae* (for four horses), with the *quadrigae* races considered the showcase events. At the time of Circus Maximus' original construction around 600 BC, races were started by a fanfare of trumpets. In later years the pandemonium from spectators meant it was more practical for judges to commence proceedings with a visual cue, namely dropping a white handkerchief.

For each race, the *aurigae* would drive around the spine until they had completed seven laps. Once the race started it was permissible for them to manoeuvre in front of each other to force other riders to crash into the *spinae*. With up to 12 chariots in a race, the most dangerous part

of the track was at the two *meta* – large columns adorning each end of the *spinae* – around which the racers had to turn.

Like modern-day jockeys the *aurigae* wore little in the way of protective clothing and only a light leather helmet. The object was simply to win the race, at all costs. With this, and nothing else, in mind it was customary for *aurigae* to wrap the reins around their waists so they could use their body weight to control the horses. This meant that when something went wrong, it did so spectacularly as the racers were unable to release the reins. Consequently, death and carnage were a major part of a day at the races. Average life expectancy for *aurigae* would have been severely shortened, with many records showing successful athletes dying in their early 20s.

The possibility of being yanked out of a speeding chariot and getting dragged along the course before being trampled to death by rival horses was not terribly appealing to Roman citizens, so slaves made up the bulk of the *aurigae*. Even though it was a deadly profession, chariot racing could and did bring fortune and fame almost beyond comprehension. Successful slaves were able to buy back their freedom and statues commemorating the greatest *aurigae* have been found throughout the Empire.

The last recorded chariot race took place in the Circus Maximus in AD 549.

- - - - - - - - - - - - - - - -

↗ A record 19 challengers signed up to vie for the chance to duel with America's Cup holder *Alinghi* in 2009.

↗ The 1999–2000 contest was the first race in the cup's history to not have an American challenger or defender.

AMERICA'S CUP

 WHERE In the waters of the winning country **WHEN** Every four years **GETTING INVOLVED** Put on a pair of boat shoes and head to the dock for some pre- and post-race excitement.

It's the world's most prestigious sailing race, and yachts representing their country have been duelling it out on the high seas since 1851. Yet most landlubbers had never even heard of the America's Cup until 1983 when a certain boat called the *Australia II* won the coveted cup from the New York Yacht Club, ending the longest winning streak in the history of sport.

For 132 years America retained the cup, successfully fending off challenge after challenge after challenge. Twenty-five of those challenges, over 113 years, were from England who initiated the competition in 1851 and lost – not that graciously either. The English accused the Americans of cheating, souring relations, and prompting the Prince of Wales to personally request that Thomas Lipton (of the tea empire) launch a subsequent challenge – to remove the undignified tarnish of the earlier challenge. But, it

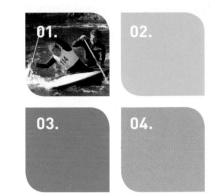

01.
02.
03.
04.

Splendour on the high seas: a flotilla of yachts makes for a stunning sight during the 32nd America's Cup.

'Most landlubbers had never even heard of the America's Cup until 1983 when a boat called the Australia II won the coveted cup'

JULY
WEEK.01

seems, a precedent was set, with much of the America's Cup these days being fought in the courts as much as on the sea.

Following the *Australia's II*'s win, Dennis Connor from the losing American team, challenged the legitimacy of the boat's now famous winged keel. The most controversial race (and court case) occurred in 1988 when the New Zealand team challenged the race with a catamaran. A series of court challenges and appeals named a different winner four times before finally awarding it to America. The 'right to challenge' two-time cup holders, *Alinghi,* won by the Spanish club CNEV was also going through the courts in 2009, testing the Deed of Gift, which governs the rules of the sport and whose stipulations are increasingly being re-interpreted in the courts.

Clearly, times have changed over the course of the competition's history. As have sailing boats due to technological advances. The 1988 dispute over whether a catamaran was a 'legal' vessel, led to the introduction of the International America's Cup Class (IACC) of yacht, which levelled the playing field, ensuring all competitors were racing with boats of the same dimension and design. The IACC boats replaced the 12m class used since 1958, with the main point of difference being an increased sail size.

The America's Cup is one of those races that's more friendly to the spectator who's perched in front of the telly, so able to catch every manoeuvre. Even more so the spectator watching telly in the country of the winning team…

MORE INFO America's Cup (www.americascup.com)

Keven Mealamu leads the All Blacks in a traditional haka before a 2008 Tri Nations series Bledisloe Cup match against the Wallabies.

TRI NATIONS ALL BLACKS HOME GAME

WHERE New Zealand **WHEN** Season runs from July to September **GETTING INVOLVED** Easy; tickets available online.

You've seen the pictures, now see the All Blacks perform their haka and, as is usually the case, outperform their opposition. And, ideally, experience it in the land of the long white cloud, Aoeteroa, among the thousands of rugby-mad Kiwis on their home turf, where rugby is the national sport, at an All Blacks home game.

The All Blacks are famously the world's number one team – ranked as such by the International Rugby Board (IRB), which is responsible for many of the top union competitions, including the Rugby World Cup (held every four years). They have a 75% win average and far outshine their competitors in the Tri Nations Series – the Wallabies (Australia) and the Springboks (South Africa) – the All Blacks with nine wins, and the others with two wins a piece. Tri Nations is the southern hemisphere's answer to the north's Six Nations Series and is played on a home-and-away basis. Games in the Tri Nations between Australia and New Zealand also count towards the coveted Bledisloe Cup.

The All Blacks are also famous for performing a haka (a traditional Maori posture dance) before every international game. Since 1884, the team has performed a haka of some description: some specifically for the opposition, such as Tena Koe Kangaroo (You look out Kangaroo) in 1903, but more regularly since 1914 they have performed the Ka Mate haka (see p109). It comes from the legend of Te Rauparaha and essentially celebrates life over death. Seeing the two teams face off, 10m apart, with the All Blacks chanting and posturing away, is an exciting part of any All Blacks game that's relished by the majority of fans and opposition teams. It's had a few detractors over the years, but, in the end, it's hard to argue with a team, and country, that recognises and celebrates its indigenous people.

MORE INFO The All Blacks (www.allblacks.com)

WIFE-CARRYING CHAMPIONSHIPS

WHERE Sonkajärvi, Finland **WHEN** First Saturday in July **GETTING INVOLVED** The competition is open to all for a nominal entrance fee.

What do the people of Finland, Dennis Rodman and the Guinness Book of World Records have in common? The World Wife-Carrying Championships.

Though the sport is relatively new to Sonkajärvi, it shares close links with the folklore and history of the area. Back during the late 19th century there was a brigand called Rosvo-Ronkainen, who demanded that his fighters prove themselves on a difficult obstacle course. It is on this basis, combined with a love of exercise and laughter that the race has become so cherished. The event celebrated its 18th year in 2009, with 15 of those as World Championship events. The locals are proud and with more than 44 couples registered for most competitions, and chapters popping up in Australia and North America, it's easy to see why.

The course for the wife-carrying championships is not an easy one and, according to the tips provided by the organiser, it is important to gain a mutual rhythm with your wife (be it your wife or someone else's – both are permitted). There are a number of customary positions: 'the piggyback', 'over the shoulder' or 'crosswise', but it is a freestyle event so anything goes.

Competitors must complete the 253m course made up of sand, grass and asphalt, which includes two dry obstacles and one of water about 1m deep. People participate for very different reasons and all are welcomed. It's made for having fun and reconnecting with your partner, so why not sign up and start training.

MORE INFO Sonkajarvi (www.sonkajarvi.fi)

LA MARSEILLAISE A PÉTANQUE

WHERE Marseille, France **WHEN** Early July **GETTING INVOLVED** The competition is open to all players; those without licenses receive special one-week permits.

Pétanque, which literally means 'feet together' in Provencal, has a strange and controversial history. Early forms of the game can be traced back to the Greeks and Romans. The game, not surprisingly, proved unpopular with the all-conquering Barbarians and so fell out of favour for a few hundred years after the decline of the Roman Empire.

By the 14th century, however, the game had become so popular that Charles V, deeming it an idle pursuit, had it banned. It remained that way until the 16th century when Pope Julius II rejuvenated interest in the game and competed against the Spanish and the French. The game was once again banned in the 17th century, this time by defensive tennis enthusiasts, but was rescued by monks who openly flouted the ban. The game even survived a match that took place in a gunpowder room with cannon balls, which left 38 people dead.

The first modern pétanque competition took place in a port outside Marseille in 1908 and now Marseille hosts the largest and the most prestigious pétanque tournament in the world. With a 45-year history and a field of more than 12,000 entrants in the five-day event, the competition is fierce. It is a knockout-style competition and to be champions a team must win 11 consecutive matches – after the first day some 11,000 contestants are eliminated. The finals occur on the fifth day of competition in front of a rabid audience of 5000. Pétanque: a boring game for oldies? Never.

MORE INFO La Marseillaise a Pétanque (www.boulistenaute.com, in French)

a ka mate, ka mate (it is death, it is death)
ka ora, ka ora (it is life, it is life)
ka mate, ka mate, ka ora, ka ora
tenei te tangata puhuruhuru (this is the man above me)
nana i tiki mai whakawhiti te ra (who enabled me to live)
a hupane (as I climb up)
a kaupane (step by step)
a hupane, kaupane (as I climb up)
whiti te ra (towards sunlight)
hi!

The Ka Mate Haka

FOR THE RECORD

- ↗ The overall leading goal scorer in World Cup matches is Ronaldo, for Brazil, with 15 goals in three tournaments.

- ↗ Brazilian Pelé is the only player to be awarded three World Cup medals.

WORLD CUP FOOTBALL FINAL

WHERE Location changes each tournament **WHEN** Every four years **GETTING INVOLVED** A number of finals tickets are made available to the average punter, but you'll have to act the minute they're made available (usually five months in advance).

This is simply world domination. No other sporting event on the planet has as much support, as much cheer, pain and passion as the World Cup. The competition includes more than 200 nations from six continents, there's never an empty seat in the house, and the incredible month of finals are four years in the making.

   To attend even World Cup qualifying matches, which begin three years before the finals, is intense. But it simply doesn't get any better than to follow your team around the host country, along with thousands of other countrymen and women. Add your voice to the thousands of others, and watch your words synch-up and move through

'The competition includes more than 200 nations and the incredible month of finals are four years in the making'

JULY
WEEK.02

Italian football fans get just a tiny bit excited after Italy wins the 2006 FIFA World Cup against France.

the stadium together like an impenetrable swarm of insects. Wear your country's colours with the kind of deliberate flaunting necessary when you're cheering for the other millions at home who couldn't make it. And start preparing for very few hours sleep, and for more worry, magical thinking and pleading with an omnipotent being than you ever thought conceivable.

It's quite possible to feel more at home while travelling around South Africa (2010) or Brazil (2014) with your homies than you do at home. And even if your team is ousted early on, you'll still enjoy the spectacle, maybe even more so now that you can relax a bit.

As well as the thousands of fans who travel to the host nation for their piece of World Cup history, there is an estimated cumulative audience of 26.29 billion people worldwide who watch at least some of the finals from their lounge rooms, making this the most watched and followed event in the world – even more so than the Olympics.

It's a lot of support for an event with a relatively short history. The first World Cup was held in 1930, in Uruguay, which defeated Argentina 4-2. The then FIFA president Jules Rimet initiated it, and the original WC trophy (which would be stolen from Brazil in 1983) was named in his honour. The current trophy is solid gold and spends its years between tournaments in the home of the winning country. It still seems to spend a lot of time in Brazil, which has the most wins, with five. Italy is second with four.

MORE INFO Fédération Internationale de Football Association (www .fifa.com)

01.

02.

03.

04.

NAADAM

WHERE Ulaanbaatar, Mongolia **WHEN** 11 to 13 July **GETTING INVOLVED** All-comers welcome; check the website for details.

Naadam (full name Eriyn Gurvan Nadaam) is a centuries-old tradition that is a celebration of 'manly sports' – although women participate in all but one. What began as a ritual to honour the gods of the mountains, turned into a recruitment exercise for Genghis Khan, and one helluva festival for visitors to attend.

Perhaps the most quintessentially Mongolian event is the horse racing, a tribute to the animals used by nomadic herders on the Steppe. The proceedings begin with around 1000 jockeys (aged between five and 13) shrilling a song to calm their horse. After the heated gallop across the plains, the overall winner is commended with a song. The loser is consoled with a kind of encouragement-award ditty.

Music is also an important part of the archery event, with contestants singing to their arrows to implore a straight trajectory, while the judges sing their commentary. Archers use horn-and-bark bows, and arrows made of willow branches and vulture feathers.

Wrestling is the only game in which women do not compete. The wrestlers' open-fronted jackets were supposedly designed to out female infiltrators after a woman pretending to be a man toppled her opposition. Costumes also include not-so-macho silk briefs and knee-high boots with twirly toes. Aiming to make a part of their opponent's body (other than their feet or hands) touch the ground, the contestants vie for the grand titles of *nanchin* (falcon), *zang* (elephant), *arslan* (lion) and *avarga* (titan). The loser removes his jacket and ducks under the bulging arm of the victor who performs an 'eagle dance'.

As much a part of the festivities as the official sporting events is the unofficial downing of bowls of Mongolia's beloved *airag* (fermented mares' milk). Opening and closing ceremonies include a parade, mock battles, dancing and a guard of honour in traditional uniforms.
MORE INFO Mongolian Tourism Association (www.travelmongolia.org)

JULY
WEEK.02

AND ANOTHER THING

- - - - - - - - - - - - - - - -

World Flying Disc Federation Overall Final (Location changes annually; mid-July)

What started as a little promotion for a toy company swiftly turned into a worldwide organisation. The World Flying Disc Federation is responsible for international championships events in disc sports (also known as frisbee). Events include 'guts' (like dodgeball, but with a disc instead of a ball), 'ultimate' (like rugby) and 'freestyle' (tricks). There are also competitions for distance throwing, accuracy and self-caught flight. (www.wfdf.org)

OPEN INTERNATIONAL BRENNBALL TOURNAMENT

WHERE Wurzburg, Germany **WHEN** Second Saturday in July **GETTING INVOLVED** Tickets are available at the door; check the website for a schedule.

Brennball literally means 'burning ball' in German. It is the closest thing the Swedish have to a national sport and is popular among students in Germany.

At a glance the game resembles softball, with a batter, players on bases and the opposing team in the field. On closer inspection, however, there are marked differences that appear to have more in common with a socialist manifesto than a competitive sport. The rules, or lack thereof, may seem strange to followers of baseball or cricket. There is no pitcher (batters toss the ball in the air before striking), if your ball is caught by the opposing team you're not out and any number of players may congregate at the bases.

There seems to be little point to the game other than to have fun and it is because of this that many a sceptical tourist has been won over on the field. Not much practice or fitness is required, and the egalitarian nature of the game ensures no one gets too upset. It's all part of the appeal – competition Swedish style.

The Open International Brennball Tournament occurs each year in the German town of Wurzburg and is half serious competition, half party. There are accompanying concerts, activities and even beer brennball, which simply involves adding beer consumption to the list of rules.

While you're in town, take a walk up the hill to the foreboding Fortress Marienberg and have lunch overlooking the city.
MORE INFO Brennball (www.brennball.de/english)

Wrestlers perform
the 'eagle dance' as
part of the annual
Naadam Festival in
Ulaanbaatar.

CAMEL CUP

WHERE Alice Springs, Australia **WHEN** Second Saturday in July **GETTING INVOLVED** Buy your ticket at the gate.

Normally a sedate, outback outpost of Australia's central desert region, come July Alice Springs explodes with belly dancing, bands, rickshaw rallies and, most importantly, camel races.

Camel racing may sound a trifle surreal to anyone not acquainted with Australia's 30,000-odd camel population and desert-town antics, but the sport's appeal, nay, challenge, lies in the beasts' unpredictability and irascibility (also in their rather amusing loping gait). Camels snarl, bite and spit – up to 3m. At the start of a race, they might stay right where they are or even reverse. On the other hand, if they get going, jockeys have to do their utmost to stay astride.

Held at Blatherskite Park, part of the Central Australian Show Society grounds, the race meet includes all sorts of trophies and events. The program begins after the Australian anthem is sung, followed by the US anthem (Alice has a large population of Americans working at its US military facility, Pine Gap). In the Honeymoon Handicap, 'grooms' race halfway around the track before lowering the camels to their knees and handing the reins to the 'brides'. There is also a Mr and Miss Camel Cup Fashions on the Field award, and children compete in the Kids Kamel Kapers events.

Outside race day, Alice's Frontier Camel Tours, owned and operated by a local indigenous collective, provide unique transport atop a camel to a few of the area's equally unique features, such as the town's dry river, which flows only every 20 or so years.

MORE INFO Camel Cup (www.camelcup.com.au), Frontier Camel Tours (http://cameltours.ananguwaai.com.au)

FOR THE RECORD

- - - - - - - - - - - - - - -

↗ Lance Armstrong is a legend of the tour, winning seven consecutive races (from 1999 to 2005), after surgery and chemotherapy treatment for cancer in 1996.

↗ In 1990, Greg Le Mond won the overall tour without once wearing the yellow jersey.

↗ The prize money for the winner is around US$750,000.

TOUR DE FRANCE

WHERE France **WHEN** July **GETTING INVOLVED** Entry to compete is by invitation. For spectators, primo roadside positions are hard-won, with people camping out to claim them up to a week before – especially in the mountain stages. It goes without saying that you should book accommodation in any of the host towns early.

Its purpose was simple: to make supermen. The harder the race and the longer the course, the more public interest that it would generate. The more sensational, the better. That, after all, is what sells newspapers. And that was the intention behind *L'Auto* newspaper instituting the world's most famous bicycle race in 1903.

L'Auto editor, Desgrange, burst the boundaries of bicycle racing when he determined the first race's course, around the perimeter of France, which would endure for five weeks. When only 16 riders entered, he halved the distance and waved a cash-carrot as incentive to attract more entrants – increasing the number of competitors to 60.

These days, there's close to 200 cyclists, each competing in teams of nine

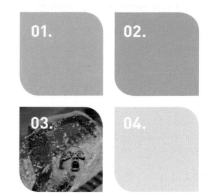

'The course changes every year, but it will always end in Paris after running its spectacularly scenic route through France'

JULY
WEEK.03

Cyclists, cobblestones and the Arc de Triomphe - this must be the Tour de France. Carlos Sastre of Spain in the yellow jersey and Team CSC Saxobank spin through Paris in 2008.

members. All riders in a team record the same time as their leading rider, with the overall winner of the tour determined by an accumulation of per-day times. The rider with the least accumulated hours wins.

The course changes every year but a few things are certain. One: it will traverse flat terrain (graded as easy) through to *hors catégorie* (beyond classification), such as the gruelling Tourmalet pass – the highest road in the Pyrenees. Two: the entire length of the race won't exceed 3500km (with limitations also on the number of kilometres covered in each day's stage) and will include two rest days. And three: it will end in Paris after running its spectacularly scenic course through France.

As well as the yellow jersey *(maillot jaune)*, worn by the rider with the least elapsed time each day, there's a green jersey *(maillot vert)* for the rider with the most sprint points.

A polka-dot jersey *(maillot a pois)* for the king of the mountains (the first to the top), and riders are awarded for their chutzpah with the *Prix de la Combativite* – for breaking from the peloton and leading, rather than sitting in another's slipstream.

The tour takes over towns that are en route, each hosting a veritable carnival and barely able to contain the excitement as the word spreads that the riders are on their way. If you have your bike, each day's stage is open to anyone in the morning. But be quick, or risk being swallowed by the publicity caravan – a 20km-long train of fancy floats advertising commercial products by handing out samples, sweets and souvenirs.

MORE INFO Tour de France (www.letour.fr)

Germany's Andreas Stoldt (R) and David "Double D" Depto of USA partake in a bout of chess boxing during the 2008 world championships in Berlin, Germany.

WORLD CHAMPIONSHIP CHESS BOXING

WHERE Location changes each championship **WHEN** Mid- to late in July **GETTING INVOLVED** Competitors must be under 35 years and proficient in both chess and boxing.

In the chess-boxing arena, life imitates art in a comic-book clash that combines brains and brawn in one larger-than-life contest. It begins with a four-minute session of speed chess, followed by a three-minute bout of boxing, followed by four minutes of speed chess, and so on, until 11 rounds have been played. There's also a one-minute break between disciplines to allow the players to get in and out of their gloves and gowns.

A relative newcomer to the sporting scene, chess boxing was originally a performance piece by Dutch artist Iepe Rubingh to promote a healthy spirit in a healthy body and aggression management, which would later inform the sport's motto: 'Fighting is done in the ring and wars are waged on the board'. Rubingh cites his inspiration as graphic novelist Enki Bilal's *Froid Equateur (Cold Equator)*, the third in the Nikopol trilogy. Rubingh won the first world championship match (as Iepe the Joker) in 2003.

Competition champions are decided either by checkmate (chess), exceeding the time limit (players have a total of 12 minutes for each game of speed chess), retirement of an opponent (chess or boxing), knockout (boxing) or the referee's decision (boxing). Competitors are proficient at both disciplines, having an amateur boxing career and a minimum Elo rating (relative skill rating) in chess of 1800.

The chess-boxing world is seeking new recruits. If your chess skills have never been rated, the WCBO website has an online test, which will help determine your eligibility for the sport. Although matches to date have been for male competitors only, the call is out for women to join the competition. The WCBO is currently scouting in the Ukraine and Russia where there's said to be great potential for competitors to join the growing number of chess boxers.

MORE INFO World Chess Boxing Organisation (www.wcbo.org)

SAN FERMIN RUNNING OF THE BULLS

WHERE Pamplona, Spain **WHEN** 6 to 14 July **GETTING INVOLVED** Runners must be over 18 and not influenced by alcohol.

Just before 8am, the crowd of all-night revellers falls silent. And the last 10 or so hours of drunken wandering focuses sharply on the sea of mostly men dressed uniformly in white, with red kerchiefs who've begun to sing. 'A San Fermin pedimos...' invoking the patron saint, Fermin, to protect them during their imminent dash through the cobbled, bordered-up streets of Pamplona's old town. Then, rolled-up newspapers are thrust into the air to the cries of 'Viva San Fermin, Viva San Fermin'. A rocket goes off, and they run like hell, recognising the signal that the bulls have been released from the corral.

It's a terror-filled four minutes, the time it takes to complete the 800m run. The runners are constantly checking their backs in fear of finding a set of horns at their heels; the bulls, also terrified, have been released from a dark and quiet pen to pandemonium. There are injuries every year. The injured runners are grazed or bruised from jumping out of the path of a bull or, more commonly, from other runners; bulls sustain broken bones from sliding over on the cobbled streets.

Apart from the Running of the Bulls, other events include the Running of the Nudes where people nude-up and run the course to protest against the festival's treatment of animals. On 6 July, thousands of festival-goers, carnival giants and performers parade the streets with an effigy of San Fermin. And on the 14th, the final night, revellers, spent from nine nights of festivities, convene at midnight at the Plaza Consistorial for a final farewell. Until next year.

MORE INFO San Fermin (www.sanfermin.com)

WORLD MARBLES CHAMPIONSHIP

WHERE Prague, Czech Republic **WHEN** Mid-July **GETTING INVOLVED** The competition is open to everyone for a small fee.

Shooting marbles may not be the most lucrative sport in the world but, despite often being relegated to the quirky pages of the local rag, it is a sport that has survived for thousands of years. Whether it be an anarchic team game from ancient Rome or a tidier version played among Victorian-era boarding-school boys, to this day, marbles maintains a continuous presence on the playground.

With references to marble play as far back as the Egyptian Empire, it's hard to imagine a time when children around the world weren't experiencing the dizzying highs and the heartbreaking lows of a high-stakes game of marbles.

No longer relegated to the playground, the modern game is now riddled with rules and regulations as globalisation in every form takes hold. Rules have been put in place to govern everything from the materials used for marbles and playing surfaces, to who gets to smoke while competing or even have their marble colour of choice.

The World Individual Marble Championships celebrated its fifth anniversary in Prague, the capital of the Czech Republic, in 2009. Players from across the globe descended on the home of Dvořák and Kafka to battle it out among the world's best. Despite its lofty title it is an inclusive competition that welcomes competitors of all skill levels.

It's also easy to find something worth seeing after a long day on the marble field. Visit Prague Castle (the world's largest) and see the glorious St Vitus Cathedral.

MORE INFO Czech Marble Federation (www.kulicky.com)

'The Tour de France's status as the world's most physiologically demanding event is largely unquestioned...[comparable to] running a marathon several days a week for nearly three weeks [and] climbing three Everests.'

Daniel Coyle, *New York Times*

FOR THE RECORD

- - - - - - - - - - - - - - - -

 Evgueni Skorjenko holds
the record for men's fin
swimming (50m apnea)
at 14.34 seconds, which
is around 30% faster than
Alexander Popov's world
record for 50m freestyle
(21.64 seconds).

 Flying disc events constitute
the world's only self-
officiating sport. Athletes
arbitrate their own calls and
rate each other's 'spirit' after
the game.

WORLD GAMES

WHERE Location changes each games **WHEN** Every four years
GETTING INVOLVED The procedure for obtaining tickets varies, depending on
the host city.

It's a familiar scenario: the tall, athletic kids are picked for the A team, leaving behind
a bunch of kids whose talents are less mainstream. And so, all the games that aren't
picked for the Olympic Games come here, to the World Games, which provides a
world stage for elite athletes to compete in lesser-known sporting events.

First held in 1981, the World Games are an international multi-sport event
representing the highest level of competition in each discipline. Around 3000 athletes
from different sports and countries compete in the interests of promoting unity across
all boundaries.

The world's best tug-of-war teams, body builders, squash players and waterskiers
prove their mettle and flout their skills quadrennially at the World Games, in the year
following the Olympics. It includes extravagant opening and closing ceremonies, and
around 35 sporting disciplines are represented, such as artistic roller skating, korfball

'Around 35 sporting disciplines are represented, such as artistic roller skating, korfball, canoe polo and swimfinning'

JULY WEEK.04

Competitors flex and fly during a beach handball match at the 2005 World Games in Duisburg, Germany.

(see p20), canoe polo, dragon-boat racing and swimfinning (swimming distances underwater using flippers, without arm strokes). And while the World Games represents the highest level of competition for these sports, most athletes hope that, one day, their sport will be included in the Olympics. This used to be the case, with the 'worlds' either hosting past Olympic events (the tug of war) or providing a springboard into the Olympics for others (triathlon). These days though, the International Olympic Committee (IOC; who grants patronage to the World Games) must keep Olympic participant numbers capped at 10,500 – which leaves little room to move for the likes of powerlifting and orienteering.

The games are run by the International World Games Association (IWGA), which is made up of 32 international sports federations' governing bodies. Unlike its more famous sibling, the IOC, the IWGA doesn't require its host cities to construct purpose-built facilities for the events. So, the climbing may take place at the local junior high, and the precision sport of casting (as in fishing) event at a pre-existing sporting oval.
MORE INFO International World Games Association (www .worldgames-iwga.org)

01. 02.

03. 04.

GOODWOOD

WHERE Goodwood, Chichester, England **WHEN** First weekend and third or fourth weekend in July **GETTING INVOLVED** Tickets and hospitality packages are readily available online.

It's not all roaring engines, lightning fast pitstops, impatient idling and burnt rubber for motor-sport enthusiasts. There's a softer, more genteel side to the sport too, and it's celebrated at Goodwood every year.

The grounds of the elegant Goodwood Estate – home of the Dukes of Richmond for 300 years – are famously and lovingly transformed each July to relive the golden age of the Goodwood Motor Circuit, which operated between 1948 and 1966. Old-school motoring fans have two separate weekends in which to revel in the good old days of racing.

The Goodwood Revival attracts around 120,000 fans of grand prix cars from the '50s and '60s, GT cars, historic saloon cars and Formula Juniors. There are around 360 cars performing in 16 races, which are driven by some well-known names of the era: Stirling Moss, Damon Hill, Giacomo Agostini and Wayne Gardner. All-comers are dressed in period costume.

The Festival of Speed (a few weeks prior to the Revival) gathers together the most significant cars in the history of international motor sport. Entrants are invited by the Duke of March, and the field is chosen thematically – with like vehicles racing one another. The Friday of the festival is a parade of the competing cars, with the subsequent Saturday and Sunday being days for racing. Each competitor's fastest time over the two days determines the final result. Not all cars race; many are simply showpieces on display.

It's a rare tribute to motor racing, and a whopping knees-up. As well as the English country house replete with antique French and English furnishings and fine art, there is an 18-hole golf course, a sculpture park, a self-sustaining organic farm, a forest, a horse-racing track and an airfield – should you fancy a joy ride or a few lessons in between festivals.

MORE INFO Goodwood (www.goodwood.co.uk)

JULY
WEEK.04

AND ANOTHER THING

- - - - - - - - - - - - - - - -

World Lumberjack Championships (Wisconsin, USA)

Dedicated to the traditions and skills of the timber industry, lumberjack events include chopping, sawing, tree climbing and log rolling. Also known as birling, log rolling involves two competitors who step onto a floating log and roll it using quick steps, attempting to unbalance their rival and ultimately see them topple into the drink. The Championships attract competitors from a number of countries, including Australia, New Zealand, the USA and Canada. (www.lumberjackworldchampionships.com)

WORLD TOE-WRESTLING CHAMPIONSHIPS

WHERE Bentley Brook Inn, Ashbourne, England **WHEN** Third weekend in July **GETTING INVOLVED** Open to all for a small fee, and free to watch.

Bentley Brook in Derbyshire is the unlikely home of the Ben & Jerry's World Toe Wrestling Championship. The roots of the event go back 30 years to when the first tournament was held there in 1976. The following year however, much to the chagrin of the locals, a Canadian took the top prize and the competition was duly abandoned.

It wasn't until the landlord of the Bentley Brook Inn, George Burgess, uncovered the rules in 1990 that the tournament rose again and is now one of the biggest events in the Derbyshire calendar.

The rules are quite simple – basically arm wrestling with feet. Why it's not called feet wrestling is anyone's guess, but it seems toe wrestling gags are easier to come by. A constant stream of puns like 'toedium' and 'toedown' appear on programs and posters, and this goes a long way to explaining the town's fascination with the other 10 digits.

The competition is open to anyone with clean feet – referees inspect the trotters of every entrant and disqualify anyone not up to standard. Competitors sit opposite each other with toes locked and, after the count-in, attempt to pin the opponent's feet to the floor for three seconds.

All proceeds go to charity, and the locals ensure a great day out with over-the-top wrestling outfits and personas to match. Alan 'Nasty' Nash is a five-time winner and even managed to take the title in 2000 with a broken foot.

MORE INFO The Bentley Brook Inn (www.bentleybrookinn.co.uk)

BEER-CAN REGATTA

WHERE Darwin, Australia **WHEN** Late July **GETTING INVOLVED** Just turn up, entry by gold coin donation; events begin at 10am.

Darwin has taken a battering in its time. It was the only Australian city bombed during WWII (in 64 separate attacks). Then, on Christmas Eve 1974, Cyclone Tracy levelled 60% of the city in just six hours. Construction workers and builders from across the expanse of Australia came to help rebuild. Now, tradesmen have a reputation for beer drinking anyway, but when they're not accustomed to Darwin's tropical conditions, the consumption goes up. The by-product of which, apart from a lot of headaches, dry mouths and sleep-ins, was mountains of empty cans. A local resident came up with the solution to the litter problem: build boats out of them, and hold a regatta.

And it's been providing Darwin-dwellers an excuse to drink ever since. Today's race attracts up to 30 'boats', each capable of holding four crew members. And if building a boat from beer cans that actually floats, let alone holds four people, isn't worth travelling to Australia's tropical north for, how about boats that reach up to 12m in length *and* have additional novelty value (because being built from beer cans is clearly not novelty enough), resembling Viking ships or crocodiles – the latter of which inhabit the very waters on which these flimsy vessels perch (or not, depending on their seaworthiness).

Other events on race day include a soft-drink can race for children, a thong-throwing event (a 'thong' in these parts being a flip-flop, as opposed to underwear) and the boat-carrying regatta in which contestants run their 'boats' along the searing sands of Mindil Beach.

MORE INFO Beer Can Regatta (www.beercanregatta.org.au)

Competitors row their vessel along Mindil Beach during the annual Beer-Can Regatta in Darwin.

- - - - - - - - - - - - - - - - - -

 The 2006 games were to be held in Montreal; however, the city's organising committee and the games committee couldn't agree on the size of the event and the finances, which led to the games being held in Chicago that year. Montreal continued with its game plans, launching the inaugural Outgames, which are held almost simultaneously.

GAY GAMES

WHERE Location changes each event **WHEN** Every four years
GETTING INVOLVED You can get involved as a participant (for a fee), a volunteer, an artist or a spectator; see the website for details.

What, you may ask, does sexual orientation have to do with the high jump? The answer is nothing, per se, but, if it's the high-jump event at the Gay Games, then it's all to do with reaching new heights in acceptance, self-esteem and community. There are no qualifying standards to enter, and no tests: for athletic or artistic ability, nor for 'gayness'. The Games are open to all comers, and exist so that participants can do the best that they can do and have a good time doing it. The Games are not focused on winning or commercial gain; it's a good games when participants achieve a personal best and organisers break even financially.

   The inaugural Gay Games were in San Francisco – a city where outlandish behaviour comes with the territory. Its population is famously free-thinking, and, as anyone who's clung to the side of a cable car can attest, the city gives one hell of a ride. In the beginning, in 1982, the games were known as the Gay Olympics. One of the original

American Kelly Brennan shows what she's made of before the 2006 Gay Games physique competition.

01. 02. 03. 04.

'The Games are open to all comers, and exist so that participants can do the best that they can do and have a good time doing it'

AUGUST
WEEK.01

organisers, Tom Waddell, was a former Olympiad, representing the USA in the decathlon in 1968. But the IOC sued the organisers for using the word 'Olympics' in the title, and forced the name change.

Thirty-four athletic events are staged, as well as five cultural disciplines. In all, there are more than 12,000 participants, and up to 30,000 spectators attend the opening and closing ceremonies. The cultural events, though fewer in number, are equally important to the games. Its 'rainbow run', like the Olympics' torch relay, carries a rainbow flag through many of the games' participating cities. The cheerleading sees men and women with giant pompoms and short shorts. And the Band Festival includes well-regarded musicians, such as the 178-piece Lesbian and Gay Band Association, who've played such illustrious events as Obama's inauguration.

In the sporting events, participants represent their cities, not their countries. Events include bodybuilding, diving, ice hockey, swimming and dancesport. Stages and performance spaces are part and parcel of the Gay Village, which hosts a range of concerts and parties.

MORE INFO Federation of Gay Games (www.gaygames.com)

The mountains of Tyrol, Austria, make for both spectacular views and treacherous terrain for the Ischgl Ironbike competitors.

CALISTHENICS

WHERE Australia **WHEN** The CVI Victorian State Championships are held in the first week of August while other club, state and national competitions run year-round **GETTING INVOLVED** You can pretty much just turn up to most events, but it would be wise to book for the National Championships.

It may not be set to take over the sporting world, but for the thousands of Australian girls who participate, calisthenics is their chance to shine, to wear false eyelashes and to pretend to be Kylie for a while.

Seeing calisthenics anywhere else in the world pales in significance. Not necessarily because Australians are the best in the world. More so because in the US, for example, it means something different entirely: a routine of simple exercises, such as sit-ups and squats. In Australia, calisthenics is an extravaganza. A unique sport that combines dance, gymnastics, singing and ballet – everything a girl could ever want, except a pony.

Practiced since the 1890s, calisthenics has spread, with plenty of clubs in all Australian states (except Tasmania), mostly found in Australian suburban areas. The various levels of competition range from none (with some clubs just there to promote exercising and staging an end-of-year concert), through state competitions (such as the CVI Victorian Championships) to the National Championships each July. Calisthenics, however is one of those sports that is entertaining to watch no matter what the level of competition.

Events are categorised by age group (from around five years old up to masters classes where it's polite not to ask the competitors' ages) and type. The majority of events are team, with a few solo and duet performances as well. The pinnacle event is the 'spectacular', which incorporates all aspects of calisthenics: gymnastics, flex, singing, dancing, comedy, acting and, often, costume changes.

Derived from the Greek *kallos* (beauty) and *thenos* (strength), calisthenics competitions are a unique window into Australian suburban life.

MORE INFO Australian Calisthenics Federation (ACF; www.calisthenicsaustralia.org)

ISCHGL IRONBIKE

WHERE Tyrol, Austria **WHEN** 1 to 2 August **GETTING INVOLVED** The race is open to all participants; however, there are stringent safety requirements that must be followed. See the website for entry forms and details.

To some, ironbiking may seem like just one-third of an ironman race, but it's a gruelling 154km race over some of the toughest mountain terrain you're likely to encounter. Taking place in the ranges around Tyrol Ischgl – Europe's 'Ibiza of the Alps' – the ironbike is the most prestigious mountain-bike event on the circuit. With a prize purse of €20,000 the competition attracts a field of more than 800 contestants including the world's best professional riders along with the most dedicated amateurs.

The race is divided into three stages: a small route of 27km, a medium stage of 48km and the final course that runs for 79km. The route cuts through the snow-capped mountains and takes in spectacular views of the Alpine peaks. Riders are taken to their limit and even the most accomplished competitors comment on the difficulty of the course.

The town of Ischgl has become a mecca for mountain-bike enthusiasts the world over, and with 1000km of bike trails catering to every level of rider, a mountain-bike school, as well as the 'Ischgl Trailground' (a 15-part practice park) it's easy to see why.

It's when night falls on Ischgl that the town really wakes up. Bikes are cast aside, DJs from across Europe take to the stage and the small community of 1500 joins with tourists and hangers-on to dance the night away – it's enough to get even the most ardent wallflowers out on the dance floor.

MORE INFO Ischgl Ironbike (www.ischgl.com/en-ironbike.htm)

01.

02.

03.

04.

WORLD WATERSKI CHAMPIONSHIP FESTIVAL

WHERE Location changes each championship **WHEN** First week in August **GETTING INVOLVED** Tickets are available online from the host country's website.

In 1922, Ralph Samuelson tied two boards to his feet and, using a clothesline as a tow-rope, became the world's first waterskier. It wasn't long before he was travelling around the US performing tricks, jumps and generally spreading the gospel of waterskiing. Meanwhile, the Swedish had a waterski patent registered all the way back in 1841, and by 1921 the word *vattenskida* (meaning waterski), was already in their dictionary, yet credit for inventing the sport has been paid to Ralph Samuelson, an American expert at the aquaplane and a turkey farmer from Minnesota.

The sport has come a long way, and the world championship is the highlight of an already busy annual calendar. The competition is divided into three events: the slalom, the jump and the short-board. In the slalom, entrants must navigate their way through six floating obstacles; the jump is based on distance; while the short-board is more akin to a diving style of scoring, with entrants performing tricks of varying difficulty.

The World Waterski Championship is held in a different city each year, and the host city is always brought to life with superb free concerts, extreme sports events and a long list of family entertainment.

MORE INFO International Waterski Federation (www.iwsf.com)

'I am thrilled to be involved with the Gay Games. For more than two decades the Gay Games have turned a well-deserved spotlight on athletic and cultural performances by members of the lesbian, gay, bisexual and transgender community and their friends from around the world.'

Sir Elton John, Gay Games Ambassador

FOR THE RECORD

↗ The US has the most World Championship medals with 234. Russia is next with 121.

↗ Two world records still stand from the first championships held in 1983, both by Jarmila Kratochvilova of the Czech Republic: the 400m run (47.99 seconds) and the 800m run (one minute 54.68 seconds).

WORLD ATHLETICS CHAMPIONSHIPS

WHERE Location changes each championship **WHEN** Biennially, from mid- to late August **GETTING INVOLVED** Tickets are readily available from the local organising committee's website.

Track and field athletics has a certain panache that distinguishes it from other sports. It has a lot to do with its age. As a category it constituted the only event in the very first Olympics in 776 BC and remains the backbone of the modern Olympics, in existence since 1896. Kudos comes also from the fact that many events rely solely on an athlete's raw ability. There's something quintessentially human in individuals simply running against each other with few rules, no apparatus and no team members to influence the performance.

Until the early '80s, the Olympics was where world champion athletes made names for themselves and world records. But as the number of sporting disciplines

Xiang Liu of China starts to pull ahead in heat two of the 110m hurdles at the 2007 World Athletics Championships in Osaka, Japan.

01.

03.   04.

'There's something quintessentially human in individuals simply running against each other, relying solely on raw ability'

**AUGUST
WEEK.02**

included in the Olympics increased, all of which advanced to the Olympics from other competitions, pressure mounted for athletics to have its own competition. The first Athletics World Championships were held at the Helsinki Olympic Stadium – site of the 1952 summer Olympics. World Championships, then took place every four years until 1991 when they began to be held every two.

The Worlds are outdoor, with a separate indoor competition in the northern hemisphere's winter. The events at both are more or less the same, with the exclusion of events requiring space, such as the javelin (hate to think: a javelin thrower outdistancing expectations and hitting the running track…) Over the years there has been an increase in the number of events contested at the World Championships. Many of the added events have been women's, such that by 2009 men's

and women's events were equally represented, with the exception of the men's 50km walk. In all there are close to 50 separate disciplines (24 men's and 23 women's), plus qualifiers for almost all, and the associated entertainment, including opening and closing ceremonies.

An average of 50,000 people attend each day – in either the morning or evening session – with the event amassing 450,000 spectators. There are around 2500 athletes and officials hailing from 213 member associations of the International Association of Athletics Foundations, which manages international events. It was founded in 1912 and has its headquarters in Monaco.
MORE INFO International Association of Athletics Foundations (www.iaaf.org)

A freestyler puts in some stylish jumps during the 2007 Corona Extra PWA World Cup on the Hebridean island of Tiree, Scotland.

KING'S CUP SEPAK TAKRAW

WHERE Bangkok, Thailand **WHEN** Mid- to late August/early September **GETTING INVOLVED** Obviously, booking early is best, but you should be able to secure a ticket at the door if you've left your run late.

In the great Thai tradition of honouring its king, there are a number of competitions called the King's Cup. The competitions range across a variety of sporting disciplines, from jet-ski racing to regattas. Despite sharing its name, there's nothing quite like the King's Cup Sepak Takraw tournament. Except maybe a game of volleyball played with the feet in zero gravity. The acrobatic skill of elite takraw players is stunning.

A kind of kick volleyball, the game requires players to keep a woven rattan ball off the ground on their side of the court, and attempt to make it touch the ground of the opponent's court. There are three players per side, and three touches of the ball allowed (all by the same player if it works out that way) before it must fly over the net to the opposition's side of the court.

The game is played almost entirely with the feet, and, to a lesser degree, the head, knees, chest and shoulders. The only time hands touch the ball is during service. One of the team sets up the spike by lobbing the ball above net height. Meanwhile, the server has readied their leg, like a windmill blade, then jumps into the air inverting his or her body and kicks the ball down into the opposition's side. Almost simultaneously, a member of the opposition will have a leg up and at the net ready to block the serve. The whole manoeuvre looks like a choreographed acrobatic routine. The winner is the best of three sets, with 21 points in each set.

Popular throughout Southeast Asia, both at competition and social level, takraw was standardised in 1960 when a set of rules and regulations was established. The King's Cup – the highest level of competition – includes doubles, team and hoop events for both men and women from more than 30 countries.

MORE INFO Takraw Association of Thailand (www.takraw.or.th, in Thai), Sepak Takraw in Bangkok (www.bangkok.com/sport-sepak-takraw)

PROFESSIONAL WINDSURFERS ASSOCIATION WORLD CUP

WHERE Location changes annually **WHEN** Second week in August
GETTING INVOLVED Check the website for scheduling and ticketing details.

There are a number of conflicting theories about when and where the origins of windsurfing lie and, as always, there are many who are willing to take credit. Various trademarks and patents were registered in the late '60s and early '70s and by the '80s the sport was well and truly on the rise.

The sport is now popular all over the world and the Professional Windsurfers World Cup makes up a large part of the pro-windsurfing tour. World Cup tournaments are held throughout the year and each one focuses on a different event with a couple of Super Grand Slam tournaments combining all three. The tour destinations highlight the international appeal the sport holds, with tournaments in Austria, Germany, Scotland, Korea, Portugal and Turkey. There are a number of different events that a champion windsurfer must master, including wave, freestyle and slalom.

In the wave category, sailors cut up waves, like surfers with sails, and are judged on the number and degree of difficulty of their manoeuvres. Freestyle is similar in that sailors have a specified amount of time to impress the judges with as many double forward loops, funnells and flakas as they can muster. Those who can display tricks on both the port and starboard sides of the board garner the highest points. Slaloms are high-speed races, with sailors cutting a fast figure-eight

Anywhere with consistently high winds and safe shallow waters is fair game for the World Cup tournaments, which attract the world's most proficient windsurfers.
MORE INFO PWA World Tour (www.pwaworldtour.com)

ISC WORLD FASTBALL TOURNAMENT

WHERE USA **WHEN** Second week in August **GETTING INVOLVED** Check the website for scheduling and ticketing details.

Whether you call it kitten ball, mush ball, pumpkin ball or indoor-outdoor, one thing's certain, fastball (also known as fast-pitch softball) has plenty of devotees around the world. It is the most popular participation sport in the US with more than 40 million people playing at least one game a year, and there are recognised softball associations in more than 100 countries abroad.

A fellow by the name of George Hancock invented the game at a Yale/Harvard boat club gathering in 1887. A Yale man threw a boxing glove at a Harvard student who then swatted it back with a stick. Hancock jumped up and shouted 'play ball!' and the game Indoor-Outdoor was born.

The sport grew in popularity as baseball players seized upon it as a way of maintaining their form during the off-season and, because it is often played indoors, when the weather turned sour. Over the years the sport evolved through many variations with different names, rules, ball sizes and pitching actions before finally settling on its current format, as a type of traditional softball with a quicker style of pitching.

Around 30 teams compete in the World Fastball Tournament, which returned to the Quad cities of the Mid-Mississippi Valley (which curiously refers to the five cities of Moline, Davenport, Rock Island, Bettendorf and East Moline) in 2009 after a 40-year break – the event was staged there for 10 years in the 1960s.
MORE INFO International Softball Congress (www.iscfastpitch.com)

AND ANOTHER THING

- - - - - - - - - - - - - - - -

World Sauna Championships (Heinola, Finland)

Although it had been going on unofficially for years, the sauna championships became an official event in 1999. Including qualifying rounds, it attracts up to 90 contestants from around 15 countries and 10,000 spectators. The rules are simple: contestants must maintain an upright sitting position in the 110ºC hotbox for as long as possible; last one left wins. (www. saunaheinola.com)

FOR THE RECORD

- ↗ The first *palio* ran in 1701 to honour the Madonna dell Asunta, who protected the Sienese army in the battle of Monteaperti against the Florentines in 1260.

- ↗ Tuscany's *contrade* formed in the 15th century when they numbered around 60.

IL PALIO

WHERE Siena, Tuscany, Italy **WHEN** 2 July and 16 August
GETTING INVOLVED Arrive four hours before the race starts for a position near the rails. You can also watch the warm-ups on previous days.

The Italians' factional tendencies can be seen in all their swaggering glory at Il Palio, a bareback horse race – on the back of which rests an entire district's pride. The crazy gleam in the mares' eyes is reflected in the stands; this event strikes at the very heart of Sienese civic pride. Each horse represents one of the city's *contrade* (districts) – of which there are 17 in total, but only 10 competing. All have their eye on the victorious *pallium* (silk banner), which is created by a different artist each race and awarded to the winner – the first horse across the finish line with its head ornaments intact, but not necessarily its jockey.

The race consists of three laps of a steeply sloped track around the perimeter of the Piazza del Campo. Riders are allowed to use whips, and not just to give their gee-gees a giddy-up, but to upset the competing horses and their riders. The short dash lasts

Siena's remarkable Piazza del Campo hosts one of the world's craziest horse races.

01. 02.
03. 04.

'The crazy gleam in the mares' eyes is reflected in the stands; this event strikes at the very heart of Sienese civic pride'

AUGUST
WEEK.03

all of around a minute and a half, but for the winning district, the celebrations last more than a month. The displays of loyalty from members of each district are often as much of a spectacle as the race itself.

Held twice a year, the first race takes place on 2 July. It's both the Feast of Visitation and the date of the local festival Madonna di Provenzo, which honours a painting said to have miraculous curative power. The second race, on 16 August, the day after the Feast of the Assumption, is also dedicated to the Virgin Mary.

Before the race, horses are blessed in the *contrade's* churches and there are flag-waving processions by pageboy types wearing medieval costumes, and demonstrations of a traditional mounted charge. Medieval parades accompany the competitors when they register at the Palazzo Comunale;

the whole shebang attracting a capacity crowd to the palazzo every race.

Historic adversaries, the Siena-Florence rivalry continues to this day, as every traveller seems to strongly identify with one over the other. It often boils down to aesthetic preference: while Florence saw its greatest flourishing during the Renaissance, Siena's enduring artistic glories are largely Gothic – though there's also the eternal question of who has the best patron saint (Siena, obviously). A World Heritage site, Gothic Siena also makes a great base for touring the medieval Tuscan towns of San Gimignano and Voltera.
MORE INFO Palio de Siena (www.ilpalio.org)

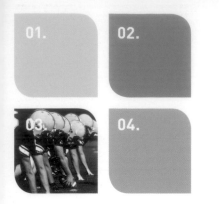

01.

02.

03.

04.

SUPERPESIS PESÄPALLO

WHERE Finland **WHEN** Season starts May; finals held in the second and third weeks of August **GETTING INVOLVED** Tickets are readily available online; book early for finals.

Transplant all the fervour and excitement of a Major League Baseball game to the chic capital of Helsinki, then mess with the rules a little, and you have the essence of *pesäpallo*. Finland's national sport is played at a variety of levels, but the Superpesis series is the highest. The start of the season heralds the start of summer, when the Finns emerge from indoors and reconvene at the country's most popular summer league.

Built on baseball's principles, *pesäpallo* has three out-bases and a home base. But if you're expecting to see baseball, you might think the batters have forgotten in which direction to run, as first base heads off to the left, with second and third zigzagging off to the right, then left. The *pesäpallo* pitch is also a surprise to baseball aficionados: the pitcher stands with the batter and tosses the ball vertically up above the batting plate. The ball must bounce within the field, making precision batting a priority over whacking it out of the field (which is a foul).

A game consists of two periods, of four innings each. An innings is when each team has played offensive (batting) and defensive (fielding), and an innings is decided when the offensive team has three outs or if two runs haven't been scored by the time all 12 batters have had a turn. Although there are nine players per side, in Superpesis, three jokers are allowed. They are batters who can breach the batting order and who specialise in either advancing the field, forcing the play or switching runners between bases.

Pesäpallo was developed by Lauri 'Tahko' Pihkala some time between 1910 and 1920. The idea behind the game's genesis was to develop the skills required to excel at high-profile track-and-field events in the hope that Finland – then under the shadow of the Russian Empire – would be better represented at the Olympic Games.
MORE INFO Pesäpalloliitto (www.superpesis.fi, in Finnish)

AUGUST WEEK.03

'Serious sport has nothing to do with fair play. It is bound up with hatred, jealousy, boastfulness, disregard of all rules and sadistic pleasure in witnessing violence. In other words, it is war minus the shooting.'

– – – – – – – – – – – – – –

George Orwell

EUROPEAN MINIGOLF CHAMPIONSHIPS

WHERE Location changes each championship **WHEN** Biennially, mid-August
GETTING INVOLVED Check the website for scheduling and ticketing updates.

Putt putt, goofy golf, shorties, garden golf, miniputt: they're all names for a game that most people in the West associate with cheap cartoon cut-outs, faux tropical scenes, castles, volcanoes and clown faces. It's not a sport many participants take seriously, and nor should they, but its origins lie in the same moneyed world as the conventional form of the game.

The first minigolf course in the world was founded in 1867 at St Andrew's Golf Club in Scotland – the world's oldest golf club and home to the Masters and its accompanying conservative traditions. A number of women had expressed an interest in playing golf, and rather than let the ladies partake in such a masculine sport, or worse still, outshine the men, a group of members designed and built the 18-hole short course and called it, 'the Himalayas' – since then themes have been synonymous with the game. It wasn't long before many luxury hotels in Europe and America sported themed minigolf courses onsite and soon they could be found on thousands of rooftops across the USA.

The European Championships are one of the highlights of the minigolf calendar and staged every two years by the World Minigolf Sport Federation (WMF). It is one of the most prestigious tournaments in the world and never fails to attract the world's best players.
MORE INFO World Minigolf Sport Federation (www.minigolfsport.com)

HENLEY-ON-TODD REGATTA

WHERE Alice Springs, Australia **WHEN** Last Saturday in August **GETTING INVOLVED** Turn up on the day with your boat or register online.

The desert town of Alice Springs has hosted an annual regatta since 1962, despite the absence of any substantial body of water. Alice's Todd River runs with water every 20 or so years; in the meantime, they make do with bottomless 'boats' crewed by barefoot racers (a la the Flintstones). Crews run along the sandy riverbed with their lightweight vessels hauled up around their waists. The boats come in all 'classes', each with their own dedicated event. There are events for yachts, rowboats and bathtubs – in which four crew carry a lady in a bath to a marker where they bucket in water before heading back to the finishing line.

Other events on the program include sand-skiing, which involves four people strapped to waterskis attempting to 'walk' through the sand; sand-shovelling, the first to fill a 44-gallon drum; and the surf rescue where one team member 'paddles' a trolley along rails (using a shovel) to a waiting 'damsel in distress' who is bundled aboard and 'paddled' back to the finishing line.

One of the most famous fixtures in Australia's Northern Territory, the Henley-on-Todd began, like many Australian traditions, as a piss-take, in this case, an ironic take on the very English Henley-on-Thames tradition. In its 50-odd-year history, the Henley-on-Todd has only ever been cancelled once, in 1993, when there was too much water in the river. The regatta is run on a volunteer basis, with all money raised donated to humanitarian projects.

While the Henley-on-Todd is well worth travelling for, there are plenty more attractions to draw you to Australia's 'red centre', particularly the iconic rock formations of deep significance to the local Anangu – Uluru and Kata Tjuta.

MORE INFO Henley-on-Todd Regatta (www.henleyontodd.com.au)

Land ahoy! 'Boats' battle it out on the dry riverbed during the Henley-on-Todd In Alice Springs

FOR THE RECORD

- - - - - - - - - - - - - - - - -

↗ Michael Phelps (USA) holds the record for winning the most career gold medals, tallying 14 (plus two bronze) in swimming.

↗ Larissa Latynina (former Soviet Union) has the most career medals, totalling 18, including nine gold, five silver and four bronze.

OLYMPIC & PARALYMPIC GAMES

WHERE Location changes; in London, England in 2012 **WHEN** Every four years **GETTING INVOLVED** Popular events such as the opening and closing ceremonies sell out in no time; most events usually sell out, so get in early.

It's among the defining moments of a life: graduated from uni, first overseas trip, married, attended the Olympics… Whether as an athlete, an official, a performer or a spectator, the Olympics are a momentous occasion for millions of people around the world. Some train for years to get there, some volunteer their skills, some just watch it on the telly and others travel to the other side of the globe to see the world's best compete. Of course sports and competition are central to the games, but they're also the stage for stunning artistic performances, a long history of symbols, politics, peace, unity and tradition.

The first international competition recognised as the Modern Olympics was held in 1896 – the same year that the International Olympic Committee (IOC) was established.

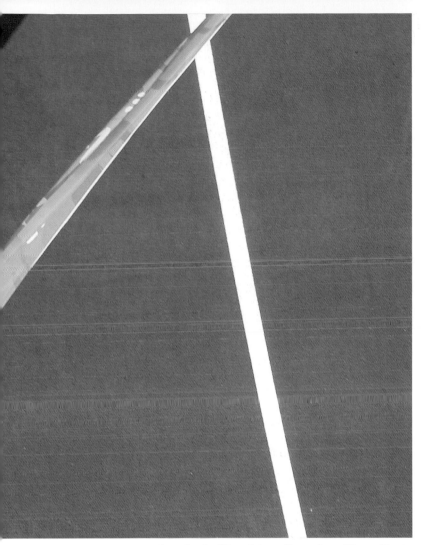

'In those games of the First Olympiad, first-place getters received a silver medal, an olive branch and a diploma'

AUGUST
WEEK.04

Capturing the ribbon of victory: Kenyan Samuel Kamau Wansiru wins gold in the 2008 Olympic Games men's marathon.

In those games of the First Olympiad, 241 amateur sportsmen from 14 countries competed in nine sporting disciplines. First-place getters received a silver medal, an olive branch and a diploma, athletes who placed second received a copper medal, a branch of laurel and a diploma. Nine bands and 150 singers performed at the opening ceremony, which attracted around 80,000 spectators.

In today's Olympics, more than 10,000 men and women, professional and amateur, from 200-plus countries compete in 38 disciplines. Winners receive a gold medal (which was solid gold until 1912), second receives silver and third bronze; all receive a bouquet. The opening and closing ceremonies adhere to an unwritten traditional order of events that includes the parade of nations, hoisting of the Olympic flag and spectacular cultural performances from the host country. As

well, the Olympics includes the Paralympics in which athletes with disabilities compete.

The Paralympics run alongside the Olympics, using the same venues. Many of the same events are contested, but with particular rules, depending on the athletes' physical or intellectual ability: be they amputees, blind or have cerebral palsy. The Paralympics were first held in 1960. Their precursor was the 1948 Stoke Mendeville Games for British war veterans with spinal cord injuries.

Spectators have their own sport – of sorts. Pin-swapping is pursued with passion by many Olympics spectators. And though some pins are more valuable than others (most valuable being the Olympic committee pin of a small country) it's apparently the act of swapping that is most valued, providing an opportunity for Olympic fans to swap life stories at the same time as swapping pins.

MORE INFO International Olympic Commitee (www.olympic.org)

WORLD BOG SNORKELLING

WHERE Llanwrtyd Wells, Wales **WHEN** August Bank Holiday weekend
GETTING INVOLVED Sign up on the day, and pay a teeny registration fee (which is donated to charity).

Other towns have their world-famous monuments, but the tiny town of Llanwrtyd Wells has the World Bog Snorkelling Championships and the Man versus Horse Marathon.

Llanwrtyd Well's moorlands consist of peat bogs, or areas of wet, marshy ground largely consisting of decomposing plant material. The kind of stuff that's as conducive to snorkelling in as, say, chutney. And every year the Waen Rhydd Peat Bog is the site of a mucky challenge that demands that its contestants throw themselves into the sludge and complete two lengths of a 55m trench. Competitors are not allowed to use their arms, just their feet, which are fitted with flippers. Wetsuits are also an obvious advantage in the mucky water, which is home to frogs, tadpoles and newts. The 2007 champion, Joanne Pitchforth, still holds the world record with a time of just one minute and 35.18 seconds.

And if bog snorkelling is too humdrum, how about the triathlon (held in July), which, along with the snorkel, includes a 30km cycle and a 20km run? Also in July, the town hosts the Man versus Horse Marathon. It began in 1989 to test a comment made in a pub about man's endurance. Huw Lobb was the first man to finish the race before a horse, completing the 22-mile course five minutes 19 seconds ahead of the first hooves.

The town's tiny population (around 600) has a famous resident in Robin 'Rob the Rubbish' Kevan, who quietly cleaned up Llanwrtyd Wells and the surrounding countryside, then gained notoriety when he set out to clean up Ben Nevis in Scotland, Snowdon in Wales and Everest's base camp in Nepal.

MORE INFO Green Events (www.green-events.co.uk)

AUGUST WEEK.04

CARNEGIE CHALLENGE CUP

WHERE London, England **WHEN** Last week in August **GETTING INVOLVED** Tickets available online; get in early.

The Carnegie Challenge Cup is the oldest and most prestigious prize in the world of club rugby. Running since 1896, the competition has evolved from a solely northern British tournament to a truly international event. Comprised of teams from the Royal Navy, the British Army, numerous Russian and French clubs, as well as universities and schools around the country, both professional and amateur teams are represented. The number of clubs entering often reaches 100.

Fifty-six teams competed for the trophy in the first Challenge Cup in 1896 and the final was held at Headingley in Leeds in front of an eager crowd of 13,500 people. But since 1929 the final has been traditionally held at Wembley Stadium in London. Though London has never been a rugby-loving city (its citizens are too devoted to football to make room for anything else), the extra media attention the sport receives from the final taking place in the capital has benefited the game enormously.

Thousands of northerners make the pilgrimage down to the big smoke each year for a chance to cheer on their boys on the biggest stage of all. Wigan is the hero of the modern Challenge Cup with a record eight consecutive wins between 1988 and 1995.

There is plenty to see in London after the end of proceedings. Wander down to the Thames to check out Big Ben and the splendour of the House of Lord's, or spend some quiet time in Poet's Corner, Westminster Abbey.

MORE INFO The Rugby Football League (www.therfl.co.uk)

AND ANOTHER THING

La Tomatina (Tomato throwing; Buñol, Spain)

For one morning a year, the small town of Buñol dissolves into the world's greatest tomato fight. Some 140 tonnes of the squishy red beauties are trucked in for the running battle, which is concentrated around Plaza del Pueblo and attracts 30,000 visitors. La Tomatina began in 1945, possibly as an anti-Franco protest or simply as a food fight between friends. (www.latomatina.es)

COWAL HIGHLAND GAMES

WHERE Dunoon, Scotland **WHEN** Last week in August **GETTING INVOLVED** Dunoon's population doubles during the games; book early.

The bagpipes, the caber toss and the kilt are all emblems of Scotland that are both well loved and made fun of the world over. Quintessentially Scottish, the Cowal Highland Gathering (as the games are also called) has been occurring every year since 1894 and has grown to become one of the most popular sporting events on the Scottish calendar. About 2000 people attended the first gathering and more than 100 years later that number has increased more than 10-fold, with 20,000 visitors and more than 3500 competitors (many from abroad) now taking part.

The Cowal Highland Gathering is no ordinary event: it combines sporting activities such as the 'sheaf toss' and the 'weight over the bar' with dance and music competitions including the 'sword dance' and 'solo piping'. There are musical events, such as the massing of the pipe bands, which play crowd favourites like 'Amazing Grace' and 'Scotland the Brave' to thunderous applause. Traditional clans harking from all around Scotland make appearances at the Parade of Clans and visitors can later trace their lineage back hundreds of years and take part in ongoing clan activities.

As well as the competitive events at the Highland Games there is a large number of associated activities to explore. Local artisans showcase their wares, as do Scottish artists and collectors. Memorabilia auctions, armoury displays, dog trials and mock battles are just some of the events on offer. The entire gathering is enveloped in an atmosphere of inclusion and tradition and is well worth the trek to gain insights into Scottish history and traditions.

MORE INFO Cowal Highland Gathering (www.cowalgathering.com)

A helmet, a stick, a ball, and a bucketload of courage – the basic ingredients required to compete in the All-Ireland Hurling Championships.

ALL-IRELAND SENIOR HURLING CHAMPIONSHIP FINAL

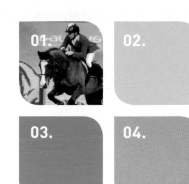

01.

02.

03.

04.

WHERE Dublin, Ireland **WHEN** First or second Sunday in September **GETTING INVOLVED** The season runs from May. Finals tickets are highly prized; check the website for availability.

It's 70 of the fastest moving, stick-locking, wincingly dangerous minutes you're likely to spend. The ancient Irish game of hurling is similar to hockey except that players are permitted to whack the ball (known as a *sliotar*) through the air, as well as along the ground, resulting in many a hurley (stick) passing, at terrific speeds, mere millimetres from players' faces.

There are 15 players per side in a seniors game. The object is to outscore the opponent by hurling the *sliotar* through a H-shaped goal; the underside of the crossbar is netted and fiercely guarded by a goalkeeper (who has a hurley twice the size as the others), getting past him and into the net earns a goal (three points), getting above the crossbar is equal to a point.

Players are allowed to handle the ball: giving it a little toss into the air before whacking it with everything they've got. As a result, balls frequently fly across the field at 150km/h, reaching distances of around 100m. It's little wonder that hurling is generally regarded as the fastest field team sport.

The origins of the game go back some 2000 years, and are intertwined in Irish folklore and legend. In 1884, the Gaelic Athletic Association standardised the game, with a formal written set of rules. Three years later, the first All-Ireland Senior Hurling champion was decided, between five teams representing their counties. It's still the highest level of competition. These days, the top 12 teams play the premier knockout competition, vying for ownership of the Liam McCarthy Cup.

The finals are always played at Croke Park, which, until 2005 when the rules were relaxed a little, was reserved for the exclusive use of Gaelic games – there being four: hurling, football (p152), rounders (a precursor to baseball) and handball (like squash). It's the country's largest stadium, with a capacity of 85,000, and you can expect every seat to be filled with roaring, nationalistic fans during the finals.

Now the second-most popular game in Ireland (after Gaelic football), hurling hasn't always been so popular. Gaelic games were feared to be dying out in the 19th century, and experienced a resurgence in popularity as a result of the Gaelic Revival, along with language, folklore and songs with pre-conquest heritage.

MORE INFO Gaelic Athletic Association (www.gaa.ie)

SEPTEMBER WEEK.01

FOR THE RECORD

↗ Kilkenny is by far the most victorious team, with 31 titles as at 2008.

↗ Cork is the only team to have won the championship on four consecutive occasions.

'Balls frequently fly across the field at 150km/h, reaching distances of around 100m'

Peter Besenyei of Team Red Bull (L) and Mike Goulian of Dragon Racing take part in a fly-over of Budapest ahead of the Hungarian leg of the Red Bull Air Race.

BIRDSVILLE RACES

WHERE Middle of nowhere, Queensland, Australia **WHEN** First Saturday in September
GETTING INVOLVED See the website for ticketing and further information. Accommodation is limited; bring a swag.

Some years there are a few hundred light aeroplanes parked in the dust outside Birdsville's only pub. For the majority of horse-race enthusiasts, flying is the most practical means of getting to Birdsville – a remote town, with a population of 100, perched on the edge of the Simpson Desert.

This is cattle-station country, with some stations equal in area to a small European country and equally populated by beef cattle. European settlers first ventured into Queensland's outback in 1870, looking for a living in minerals and cattle-grazing land. A few set up tents, and by 1882 there was a fully fledged town and the first of the now famous Birdsville Races.

Race day at the dusty Birdsville track, which runs anti-clockwise, is on Saturday with the running of 12 races. There's no mobile-phone coverage and it's at least 400km from anywhere, but you can still bet with one of the dozen or so bookies. All money raised from entry fees goes to the Royal Flying Doctor Service. (Out here, it's got to be pretty serious before you call for the doctor, who comes by plane.) The main race is 1600m long and the total prize money is more than A$100,000. Fashions on the field here still include a range of hats, only they're the wide-brimmed Akubra style. And the only heels will be boot heels – the outback is no place for stilettos.

Don't think for a second that the 6000 revellers who travel for hours to get here come just for the day. There's a week's worth of entertainment and adjunct activities. Nights at Birdsville, especially the Friday before the races, host a range of musicians, comedians and entertainers, not to mention the world's last boxing tent show. Integral to early 20th century outback life, boxing tents are like a travelling circus troupe, only the entertainers are boxers who fight challengers from the towns they visit.

MORE INFO Birdsville Races (www.birdsvilleraces.com)

RED BULL AIR RACE

WHERE Takes place across eight cities worldwide **WHEN** From April through to November **GETTING INVOLVED** Check the website for up-to-date scheduling and ticketing info.

If you love planes, and thrill to heart palpitations, this is the event for you. From Abu Dhabi to Perth, Detroit to Budapest, the Red Bull Air Race visits eight cities around the world and brings with it all the fear and excitement usually reserved for military air shows.

The Red Bull Air Race pilots must have nerves of steel and the concentration of Buddhist monks. The lightweight racing planes navigate their way through a series of inflatable pylons on land or sea, depending on the course. The race is one of the most dangerous in the world with split-second timing required as planes reach speeds of 370km/h while flying only metres off the ground.

Pilots who choose to participate must pass a rigorous screening process before being accepted. They need to have a record of top honours in international flying competitions as well as low-flying air show experience. Around a dozen pilots are generally on the tour, with more waiting in the wings ready to prove their mettle.

Running since 2005, the race was developed over two years by the Red Bull sports team and aimed to combine the best elements of aviation and motor racing. The blend has proved a success as the event has become wildly popular in a relatively short space of time.

Races also take place in San Diego, Rotterdam, London and Porto, and package deals are available for the pay-anything enthusiast all the way down to the nothing better to do tourist.
MORE INFO Red Bull Air Race (www.redbullairrace.com)

FIS GRASS-SKIING WORLD CUP FINAL

WHERE Location changes annually **WHEN** First week in September **GETTING INVOLVED** The World Cup events run from mid-March through September in various locations around the world. Check the website for details.

If you love winter sports but live in a part of the world where snow falls for only a few weeks a year, then this is the activity for you. Buy a pair of grass skis (they're cheaper than regular skis), grab a helmet and find a green slope to hurl yourself down.

The equipment required is fairly similar to conventional ski gear with the exception of the skis themselves (and parkas). Instead of the flat smooth surface, grass skis contain either wheels or tracks on the underside. Wheeled versions are ideal for multi-terrain skiing, while the tracked skis are better suited to smooth downhill slopes.

Grass skiing was invented back in the '60s by a fellow called Richard Martin. He was trying to develop a way for skiers to train and get into shape before the winter ski season began, and soon found it could be enjoyed in its own right. And with the onset of global warming it's perhaps prudent to keep an open mind to such variations of sport – you never know, in 20 years time there may not be much snow left for conventional skiing.

Though it's a long way off qualifying as a mainstream sport, grass skiing is gradually gaining in popularity. Originally, the majority of devotees hailed from Europe, but grass skiing is spreading further afield and has associations in China, Iran, Japan and Taiwan among others – each of which has members competing in the World Cup.
MORE INFO Federation Internationale de Ski (www.fis-ski.com)

'The men of Ireland were hurling when the gods of Greece were young.'

PJ Devlin, author

Sweet mower, man. A competitor moves his modified motor around the course during the 2007 12-hour lawn-mower racing champs.

WORLD CHAMPION LAWN MOWER RACING

01. 02. 03. 04.

WHERE Wisborough Green, West Sussex, England **WHEN** Mid-September to early October **GETTING INVOLVED** To race, you must be a member of the British Lawn Mower Racing Association; info online.

A bit like motor racing in miniature, lawn-mower racing allows English suburban men to cut loose with their mowers. No more Sundays spent thanklessly pushing a mower in symmetrical rows in the backyard. Mower racing is tough, attracts an adoring crowd and is so rebellious that the mowers don't even cut grass.

As much a part of the actual racing, tinkering is paramount to the sport. Each of the four groups of mowers eligible for racing requires weeks of preparation, handyman know-how and time in the shed – usually with a cohort or two and a number of beers. All mowers must have their blades removed – this isn't a blood sport. Group 1 mowers are the upright type that you run behind. These are recommended for beginners, as they require the least amount of prep to race. Group 2 are self-propelled, roller-driven mowers with a towed seat attached. It takes a lot of work to prepare this type of mower for racing, as with the group 3s. These ride-on wheel-driven mowers are generally the fastest group, capable of 50mph. And, finally, there are the group 4s, which differ from the 3s only in that they have a bonnet. All mowers must be approved by the association for racing to ensure they meet the strict specifications of each category.

Lawn mower racing has its origins in a pub (surprise). A few gentlemen were propped at the Cricketers Arms bar, bemoaning the prohibitive costs associated with motor racing, particularly the increase in sponsorship. What to do? The answer was in the bottom of a pint glass. As Jim (founder of the BLMRA) emptied his pint, he saw the lawnsman mowing the pitch outside. And the rest, as they say, is history.

The racing season begins in May and runs through to October. It includes the British Championships, the British Grand Prix, the 12 Hour Race (which, as the name suggests, runs for 12 hours – through the night) and the World Championships. The pinnacle of the racing calendar is a two-day event, and attracts entrants from Zimbabwe, America, New Zealand and Hong Kong. In keeping with the sport's ethos of being utilitarian (and keeping costs low), there is no prize money and no sponsorship allowed. Those magnificent men in their mowing machines do it for the love. And for a small marble trophy.
MORE INFO British Lawn Mower Racing Association (www.blmra.co.uk)

SEPTEMBER WEEK.02

FOR THE RECORD

- ↗ The lawnmower land speed record is 130km/h set by Bob Cleveland on a modified machine that wouldn't qualify for BLMR races.

- ↗ In the US, Xtreme Mower Mayhem Championships takes mower racing a step further, using heavily modified monster-truck type mowers.

'All mowers must have their blades removed – this isn't a blood sport'

01.

02.

03.

04.

O'DUFFY CUP

WHERE Dublin, Ireland **WHEN** Second Saturday in September **GETTING INVOLVED** Tickets are available through Ticketmaster (www.ticketmaster.ie).

The gutsy game of camogie is Irish through and through. The female version of hurling, which dates back 2000 years, camogie is a celebration of Gaelic heritage. Camogie differs little from its older brother. Both have similarities to hockey in that a stick propels a ball into the opposition's H-shaped goal. Getting the ball (*sliotar*, which is slightly lighter in weight for camogie than in hurling) past the goalie (who, in camogie, wears the same jersey as the outfielders; in hurling, the goalie wears a distinctive jersey) into the netted area beneath the crossbar is equal to a goal (three points). Getting the *sliotar* above the crossbar scores one point.

Camogie, like hurling, allows for players to flick-up, kick-up (but not pick-up) the ball into their hands, so they can toss it into the air before grasping the stick with both hands and whacking the ball with all their might. It makes for some fast-moving, nail-biting action as sticks swing dangerously close to players' faces.

Camogie is played at all levels, from schools, through colleges and counties. The premier competition, the All-Ireland Seniors, is played from June, with the top seven teams making it through to the knockout finals. They play for the O'Duffy Cup, named for Sean O'Duffy who was a trade union leader and freedom fighter imprisoned for his involvement in the North King St uprising. He was also an active advocate for popularising camogie, which was first played in 1904 as part of the Gaelic League Fair. The first All Ireland Seniors Championship was played in 1932, with the finals played at Croke Park since 1934.

September is a fine month for Gaelic games at Croke Park, with the hurling championship held the week before the Camogie final, and the Gaelic football final held the week after.
MORE INFO Camogie Association of Ireland (www.camogie.ie)

SEPTEMBER WEEK.02

AND ANOTHER THING

- - - - - - - - - - - - - - -

World Gurning Championship (Egremont, England)

Every year, the Egremont Crab Fair celebrates the harvest in staunchly traditional ways. The fair does 'not involve the mechanised swings and roundabouts that became part of so many fairs from the late 19th century.' It opens with the Parade of the Apple Cart, where crab apples are thrown to the crowds, then proceeds with the games, including the World Gurning Championship, in which contestants have to pull their ugliest face with their head stuck through a horse's collar. (www.egremontcrabfair. org.uk)

BOSSABALL

WHERE Location changes **WHEN** Check the website **GETTING INVOLVED** Contact one of the Bossaball clubs; details are online.

Bossaball has more energy, colour and exaggerated antics than a children's television program. A cross between 'volleyball, soccer, trampolining, samba and inflatables', bossaball is a look-at-me sport.

The volleyball similes come from bossaball's main objective, which is to ground the ball in the opponent's side of the court. A court that is notably entirely inflatable and fitted with trampolines. One of the team's three to five players is stationed on the tramp and it's his or her job to perform dramatic spikes, several metres above the ground. Unlike in volleyball, which allows three touches per side before the ball must be sent over the net, bossaball allows for eight touches, meaning more opportunities to wow the audience. In bossaball, players are permitted to propel the ball with their hands, head and feet. Given the generally bouncy nature of the court, there is little chance of players injuring themselves, which results in some spectacular manoeuvres, with players free to throw themselves around in pursuit of the ball. Grounding the ball on the opponent's side of the court scores a point. If the ball lands on the opponent's trampoline, that scores three points.

Bossaball was dreamt up as a franchise by Brazilian music entrepreneur Filip Eyckman. It's mostly played at festivals and corporate events as an exhibition sport, so rarely requires a referee. But look out if there is one; known as Samba Referees, judges 'have a whistle, a microphone, various percussion instruments and a DJ set'.
MORE INFO Bossaball (www.bossaball.com)

YANGPHEL OPEN ARCHERY TOURNAMENT

An archer takes aim
at the Yangphel Open
in Paro, Bhutan.

WHERE Bhutan **WHEN** From mid-July, with the finals in mid-September **GETTING INVOLVED** To visit Bhutan costs a minimum of US$200 per day, and all travel must be undertaken through an authorised agent.

In a deeply Buddhist country that survives as the last great Himalayan Kingdom, it's not surprising that Bhutan's national sport is archery. It's integral to the country's identity, with links to Lord Buddha, self-preservation and spirituality. In Bhutan, Gross Domestic Happiness is more valued than Gross Domestic Product and giant protective penises are painted on most doors. But far from being a nation of saintly, other-worldly hermits, Bhutan straddles the ancient and the modern world. Archery tournaments here are razzed up by Dha-Lo (Bhutanese cheerleaders) and enjoy half-time entertainment of the Royal Dance Troupe ilk. But they still adhere to traditional elements.

Tournaments are played between teams of 13 archers. Each archer has two arrows per turn, with the order in which they shoot determined by the team captain (and, apparently, the star sign of each archer). The targets angle slightly skyward, the lower portions of which are painted with Bhutanese designs (such as flowers and clouds) in colours that match those of the painted bullseye. A bullseye *(karey)* equals three points, hitting the target equals two points and landing within an arrow's length of the target equals one point. The first team to reach 25 wins the game; to win the tournament, the team must win two of three games.

All archers wear traditional dress (a *dha*, or tunic), and the rules of play stipulate that no one will bring cigarettes or alcohol onto the course, nor speak ill of their opponents. The open tournament attracts up to 7000 spectators, including Bhutan's king.

MORE INFO Yangphel Archery (www.bhutanarchery.com)

FOR THE RECORD

- - - - - - - - - - - - - - - -

↗ In 1999, Bertrand Piccard and Brian Jones were the first to fly a balloon around the world, making records for the longest flight duration (477 hours and 47 minutes) and the greatest distance (40,814km).

↗ The 1961 record for the highest flight still stands at 34,668m.

FAI WORLD HOT-AIR BALLOON CHAMPIONSHIP

 WHERE Location changes each championship **WHEN** Biennially, mid-September **GETTING INVOLVED** Spectators, look skyward for the mass start each day (at 7am and 5pm).

A blue sky polka-dotted with 100-plus enormous multicoloured balloons makes spectacular viewing. There's a certain romance attached to hot-air ballooning. It's not just that it was in a hot-air balloon that humans first attained the wondrous faculty of flight. It's the non-mechanised nature of the balloon, and the pilot's understanding of the elements – working with air currents and temperatures – that's equally amazing.

Strictly speaking, it's not possible to steer a balloon; there's no mechanical device that can manoeuvre a balloon laterally. It is possible to tap into different wind speeds

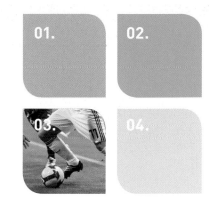

01.

02.

03.

04.

'Ballooning is an early-bird's sport, with weather conditions most friendly just after dawn'

SEPTEMBER
WEEK.03

Flying over Albuquerque, New Mexico – is there anything more spectacular than an indigo sky freckled with a festival of hot-air balloons?

and directions that vary according to altitude. A pilot can drop down into a layer of the atmosphere that has a strong, directional wind, travel the required distance, then raise the balloon up out of that wind into another layer. But there are no guarantees: pilots must rely on their knowledge of weather patterns and go hunting for the right conditions.

The main means of control available to a pilot is the ability to go up and down, which is achieved by opening and closing the envelope (as the balloon is called) and adding hot air. The hot air makes the balloon buoyant, as it has a lower density to the cooler air that surrounds it.

Competition ballooning involves a number of tasks that test a pilot's skill in manoeuvring their balloons over a set course, with goals, targets or scoring areas, and time or distance limits. A common task requires a pilot to fly over a target and drop a marker (a small sand bag attached to coloured streamers) as close to the target as possible. Other tasks involve flying a minimum or maximum distance within a specified time or achieving the greatest change in direction. The winner of the competition has the highest number of points across all set tasks. The World Championships attract more than 150 balloons from around 35 countries, and thousands of spectators. Ballooning is an early-bird's sport, though, with weather conditions most friendly just after dawn.

Most championship events allow for spectators to go for a ride. Seeing familiar surroundings turn into patchworks of colour and become like architectural models from hundreds of metres on high is a holiday in itself.

MORE INFO Federation Aeronautique Internationale (FAI; www.fai .org/ballooning)

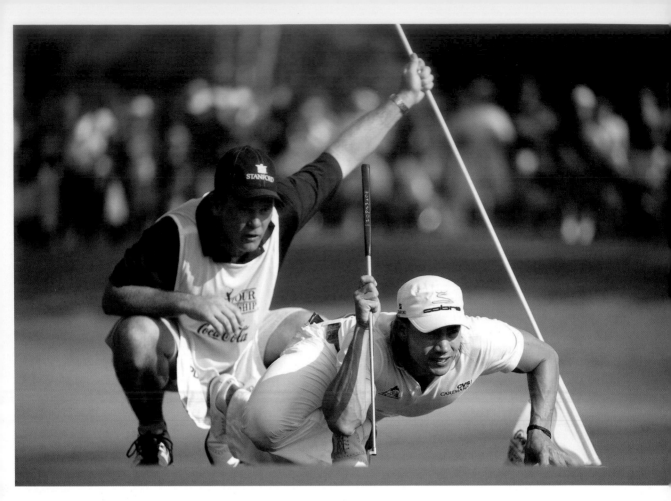

Camilo Villegas lines up a putt as caddie Gary Matthews looks on during the Tour Championship at the East Lake Golf Club in Atlanta, Georgia.

INTERNATIONAL WHEELCHAIR RUGBY FEDERATION WORLD CHAMPIONSHIPS

WHERE Location hanges each championships **WHEN** Every four years, mid-September **GETTING INVOLVED** Tickets are available through the host city's federation.

Originally named murderball, wheelchair rugby is a full-contact sport, where wheelchairs – given a *Mad Max* makeover – constantly clash as an integral part of the game. Composed of elements of basketball, rugby and ice hockey, wheelchair rugby is an indoor sport involving two teams. Each team has four players on the court at a time, all vying for possession of the ball so they can carry the ball across the goal-line, thereby scoring a point for their team. In order to score, two wheels must cross the line while the player is in possession.

It's a fast and furious game, with the prized 'possession' changing teams at lightning speed. Players must bounce or pass the ball within 10 seconds. Courts measure the same as basketball courts: 28m long by 15m wide. Teams have just 12 seconds to advance the ball from their back court to their front court, and a total of 40 seconds to either score or concede possession. Games consist of four eight-minute quarters.

All players are quadriplegic, with limited function in both the arms and legs. Players are classified according to their mobility: 0.5 points being the lowest and 3.5 the highest. The total points allowed per team is eight. Players' wheelchairs are specially modified: fitted with hubs to protect the spokes, wings over the wheels to limit opponents obstructing their progress, an anti-tip device and a front bumper to strike and hold opponents.

Wheelchair rugby developed in Canada in 1977. Previously, only wheelchair basketball existed, which requires the use of the upper limbs. At least 25 countries now participate in international competitions, with the first world championships thrashed out in 1995.

MORE INFO International Wheelchair Rugby Federation (www.iwrf.com), Canadian Wheelchair Sports Association (www.cwsa.ca).

PGA TOUR CHAMPIONSHIP

WHERE Atlanta, Georgia, USA **WHEN** Third week of September
GETTING INVOLVED Check the website for scheduling and ticketing details.

Woods, Singh, Mickelson and Villegas. Big names and big money on the big stage – this is what the Tour Championship is all about.

After sharing the glory for a number of years with the Champions Golf Club of Houston, the East Lake Golf Club of Atlanta is now the permanent home of the Tour Championship – a confusing combination of the PGA tour tournament and final event for the year-long FedEx Cup competition (championship trophy for the PGA tour).

Running since 1991 (earlier known as the Nabisco Championship), the Tour Championship has changed its stripes a number of times over the years. Already one of the most prestigious and richest tournaments on the tour with a winner's cheque of more than a million US dollars, the tournament was rescheduled in 2007 to also become the last event in the FedEx Cup, which has its own separate and very lucrative winner's prize of US$10 million. Unlike previous years, where the top 30 money earners were invited to play the championship, it is now only open to those with the highest number of points. This season-long points-based competition is the richest golf tournament in the world today and dishes out a staggering US$35 million in prize money.

People travel from all over to watch the best battle it out, so if you want to see your heroes in the flesh it's prudent to book a bed nice and early. After a day on the green, visit the High Museum of Art, one of Atlanta's finest galleries, which specialises in works by artists from the Southern United States.
MORE INFO The Tour Championship (www.pgatour.com)

WORLD TRAMPOLINING CHAMPIONSHIPS

WHERE Location changes each championship **WHEN** Dates change, but generally sometime between September and November **GETTING INVOLVED** Tickets are readily available; check the website.

Despite a healthy following, trampolining attracts none of the flag-waving, handmade signs, chants and cheers of other sports. It's a hushed crowd, as though holding its collective breath until the high-bouncing acrobat is back safely on solid ground. Trampolining is a form of gymnastics where athletes perform impressive feats 8m up in the air – somersaults, twists and pikes both forwards and backwards.

Invented in 1935 by US gymnast George Nissen after he watched acrobats bounce off safety nets, trampolining became instantly popular in the US, with the first national championship held in 1948. The first world championship was held in 1964 in London. Competitions generally have individual and synchronised events for men and women. An individual performs three routines, each with 10 elements. Synchronised routines involve two facing gymnasts performing the same routine. (As anyone who has been sent flying by sharing a trampoline will appreciate, gymnasts perform on adjacent but separate trampolines.) Judges look for control, form, execution and height – particularly that a gymnast is maintaining height throughout the routine. In all positions of a routine, the gymnast must have their legs together, their toes pointed, and must start and finish on their feet. A routine is also marked for its degree of difficulty, with each element in the routine attracting a differing degree, calculated by factoring in each twist or quarter somersault.
MORE INFO Federation Internationale de Gymnastique (www.fig-gymnastics.com)

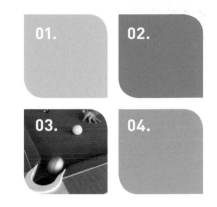

'The balloon seems to stand still in the air while the earth flies past underneath.'

Alberto Santos-Dumont, aviator

Premiership Cup in hand, Luke Hodge celebrates Hawthorn's win over the Geelong Cats in the 2008 AFL Grand Final.

AFL GRAND FINAL

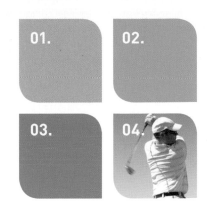

WHERE Melbourne, Australia **WHEN** Last Saturday in September
GETTING INVOLVED Finals tickets don't come easily – the reserve of MCG members and family. Watch the telecast with hundreds of others at the city's public plaza – Federation Square.

Come September, most Australians believe the world to be oval-shaped, so complete is their focus on football; specifically, Australian Rules football and the colossal final about to determine the year's premier team. Like a fever, it infects even the unwary arty type with no apparent interest in footy who can't help but watch in wonder as the population amasses in colour-coordinated groups to watch the game, kick footballs to one another in deserted streets on match day, and partake in the numerous public events that accompany the Grand Final every year.

Around 300,000 people crowd the city's streets for the parade on the Friday before the game. The two teams' players ride in open-top cars so fans can catch a glimpse of their heroes. The Monday night before the game is the red-carpet Brownlow Medal, when the year's best and fairest player is revealed – along with many players' wives' cleavages adorned with diamonds that flare with hundreds of camera flashes.

Football at the top level (the Victorian Football League) was a local Melbourne-based affair until the 1980s when the original 12 teams became 16, with the addition of four teams representing other states. Despite nine of the 16 teams still being based in Victoria, football has national appeal, being the country's most popular winter sport. It's simply a beautiful game to watch: fast moving, high marking, long kicking and with gutsy tackling and crafty athleticism. There is no off-side rule in Australian Rules, so players run awfully long distances in pursuit of the oddly shaped ball that can bounce up in any direction with the unpredictability of a lotto ball. Australian Rules is one of the only sports that awards players for missing, with players scoring a point if the ball is kicked either side of the goal posts (but within the small posts). Kicking the ball between the main posts scores a goal, equal to six points.

The recently refurbished Melbourne Cricket Ground (MCG) fills with a 100,000 crowd on Grand Final day – the highest attendance of any club championship in the world. Even regular games attract around 40,000 people who sing their club's song, wear their team's colours (even if it means a less-than-fashionable ensemble in brown and yellow), scream, clap, yell and stomp along with the play.
MORE INFO Australian Football League (www.afl.com.au)

SEPTEMBER WEEK.04

'It's a beautiful game to watch: fast moving, high marking, long kicking and with gutsy tackling and crafty athleticism'

FOR THE RECORD

- ↗ The Grand Final between Geelong and Hawthorn in 1989 is regarded as one of the toughest, with players knocked out, playing with punctured lungs, and hospitalised after the game.

- ↗ Best on ground in 1995, Greg Williams, had 32 possessions on grand final day, which was also his 32nd birthday.

Italy's Alfredo Rota (L) duels with France's Ulrich Robeiri during the men's team épée final at the 2007 Fencing World Championship in St Petersburg, Russia.

ALL-IRELAND GAELIC FOOTBALL FINAL

WHERE Dublin, Ireland **WHEN** Third Saturday in September **GETTING INVOLVED** Join the hundreds of thousands of others without a finals seat and watch the game from a local pub.

With 80,000 tightly packed bodies emitting fiery screams, anxious energy and anticipation, things get pretty hot inside Croke Park during a football final. The inter-county All-Ireland Gaelic Football final is the pinnacle of Ireland's most popular game. (So don't expect to come by a ticket easily.) Apart from winning adoration from hundreds of thousands of fans, the premiers take home the Sam Maguire Cup – named after a man who was a footballer himself and a prominent member of the Gaelic Athletic Association (GAA), which is credited with organising the game.

Although football existed in some form or other as early as 1308 (when it was reported that a spectator was arrested for accidentally stabbing another man), there was no formal organised play or competition. Collectively known as *caid*, the GAA organised the playing code in 1887 – when the first All-Ireland Football final was played. Gaelic Football has similarities to Australian Rules (both do not have an off-side rule), and it is often posited that Australian Rules is derived from Gaelic football, brought to Australia by the many Irishmen transported there in the mid-19th century.

The 15 players in a Gaelic football team robustly struggle for possession of the round ball in order to kick or hand-pass (strike with hand or fist) it through the H-shaped goal. Landing the ball beneath the crossbar (and past the goalie) scores three points; above the crossbar equals one point. Players must progress the ball towards their goal, and dispose of it within four steps. A game lasts for 70 minutes, but the post-game buzz lingers for a long time afterwards.

MORE INFO Gaelic Athletic Association (www.gaa.ie)

FENCING WORLD CHAMPIONSHIP

WHERE Location changes each championship **WHEN** End of September
GETTING INVOLVED Check online for up-to-date scheduling and ticketing info.

Though it's a sport that's rarely in the headlines, there are still a lot of Errol Flynn wannabes out there and the best place to find them is at the World Fencing Championships. The event is an annual competition organised by the Fédération Internationale d'Escrime (FIE) and, except for the Olympic Games, it is the most important event on the world fencing calendar.

Sadly, fencing matches no longer involve leaping from rooftop to rooftop with sword in hand; instead it is now a highly regulated and tactical sport. Records of fencing schools date back as early as the 12th century, and from the 14th century interest in the sport grew rapidly. Members of the aristocracy felt it gentlemanly and 'knightly' to attain skill with the sword and pursued these ambitions with relish while treatises on the subject became commonplace.

The first international meet was held in 1921 by the FIE and at that point it was a European competition. The politics of the time played a role in the development of the tournament; Mussolini offered national recognition and privileges to world and Olympic champions and soon the Italian fencing team successfully requested the European competition be transformed into the world title in 1937.

In the conventions of the modern sport, competitors don white suits and mesh masks, which have inbuilt electronic scoring devices. They compete for points won by touching the other player with the three different weapons available: the sabre, épée and foil.
MORE INFO Fédération Internationale d'Escrime (FIE; www.fie.ch)

KRYSTAL SQUARE OFF HAMBURGER EATING CHAMPIONSHIP

WHERE Chattanooga, Tennessee, USA **WHEN** Late September or early October
GETTING INVOLVED Register online for this all-you-can-eat frenzy.

Perhaps slightly familiar to those from big families – where meals require speedy eating before siblings snatch the better morsels – competitive eating is a big deal. In fact, some competitions are so fervently contested that the queasy are advised to stay away. Competitive eating is particularly popular in the US, which boasts a number of governing bodies, including the International Federation of Competitive Eating (IFOCE).

Most eating competitions are dedicated to a single foodstuff, such as hotdogs, hamburgers or chicken wings. Competitions require competitors to stuff as many of said foodstuffs down their gullets in the allotted time frame. Vomiting, known in the trade as 'a reversal' is permitted, as long as it doesn't leave the competitor's mouth.

Eating competitions come from the small-time local comps held at county fairs, which usually involved that area's main food product, such as watermelons or cherries. It's not surprising then that many of the 'major league' eating comps are sponsored by food outlets. The Krystal Square Off is one such event, organised by the Krystal hamburger restaurant chain. The current world record holder is Joey Chestnut who consumed 103 small square hamburgers in eight minutes, in 2007. It's a harrowing eight minutes for spectators, as a line of competitors stuffs tray upon tray of burgers into gaping mouths. There's no time for chewing, just the occasional swill of liquid. The Krystal Square Off purse is a healthy US$50,000 – which'll surely buy more than enough antacid.
MORE INFO Krystal Square Off (www.krystalsquareoff.com)

AND ANOTHER THING

Mountain Cheese Olympics (Galtür, Austria)

The antithesis of competition eating, the Cheese Olympics focus on handmade products from small local producers. Around 90 dairies from all over the Alps enter their cheeses in the Olympics, which are judged according to category (soft, hard etc). And, as cheese-tasting is hardly a spectator sport, all producers make their products available for tastings and to buy. (www.galtuer.com)

DEAD SPORTS
LAVA SLEDDING

Even before they saw off Captain Cook in 1779, the word on the seven seas was that the Hawaiians were hard-core. After all, these were the warriors who, after a battle, would remove their enemy's entrails and break every bone in their body so they could carry them off to be sacrificed. Traditionally, Hawaiian sport was the preserve of the men, and reflected the fearless abandon by which warriors lived and died. Given this background, it's no shock to learn that the mountain-sized dudes who gifted the world big-wave surfing over razor sharp reefs have another, albeit more obscure, extreme sport tucked under their *malos*. Introducing *he'eholua* or lava sledding.

Imagine luge gone crazy. Or, more precisely, luge on a 3.5m-long wooden sled hurtling down a totally unforgiving mountain runway formed by ancient lava flows. You'd almost need to be crazy to contemplate doing it.

Lying, kneeling and even standing on their *papa holua* (the traditional name for the sleds), aristocratic islanders would take it in turns to race down specially prepared tracks at speeds in excess of 60 km/h. The primary objective was to get to the end unscathed and still attached to your *papa holua*. Whoever was deemed to have travelled the furthest would be judged champion. If several riders managed to go the distance then the winner would be decided based on style, grace and recklessness.

Tracks varied in length and composition. Most were around 200m long although one slide at Kahikinui on the island of Maui runs for 1.5km. Novice tracks run down grassy slopes but it's the dangerous, razor-sharp lava runways that were used for competitions. More than 50 ancient tracks have been discovered across the Hawaiian archipelago.

The name *he'eholua* means 'to slide

into the pit' and in a sense, competitors were physically and spiritually entering the realm of Pele, the Hawaiian goddess of the volcano. Legend says that Pele herself once competed against the warriors. Unfortunately for them she hated losing and would destroy with lava anyone who managed to beat her.

Controlling the *papa holua* was not easy. Unlike modern sleds these cruisers measured a meagre 15cm wide and 10cm deep. Riding prone, that doesn't leave much room between your face and the black rock lava whistling by below. The two long runners, similar in design to modern skis, were greased with coconut oil to help them glide quicker. Making the *papa holua* was an art form involving numerous rituals to select the right wood and then find the form of the sled within the wood.

For almost 2000 years, the Hawaiian *Ali'i* (nobility) practised *he'eholua* as a test of strength, skill and courage. The last major competition was held in 1825 after which kill-joy Christian missionaries were successful in their efforts to persuade the chiefs to ban this insane and wondrous sport.

In the 1990s, Hawaiian Tom Stone, professor of Hawaiian culture at the University of Hawaii, single-handedly launched a revival of *he'eholua* by hand-making his own *papa holua* based on the traditional sleds that survived the missionary zeal. If it catches on, perhaps *he'eholua* is set to become the world's first truly insane sport...

FOR THE RECORD

↗ Abudusataer Wujiabudula from China is the current World Highwire Champion, walking the 1km line in 11 minutes and 22.49 seconds.

↗ All 16 World Highwire Championship contestants who finished the course became joint Guinness World Record holders for the longest skywalk.

WORLD HIGHWIRE CHAMPIONSHIPS

WHERE Seoul, South Korea **WHEN** Seoul Citizens Day, October **GETTING INVOLVED** Even if your trip to South Korea isn't in time for the championships, look out for a *jultagi* performance.

Highwire-walking straddles the line between being a sport (generally of a competitive nature) and an art. But seeing as it has many of sport's ingredients (a large following, always entertaining, and 'world championship' in the title) it's worthy of review.

The first World Highwire Championships saw 18 competitors race the clock across a 30mm wire stretched 1km over Seoul's Han River. Two competitors failed to finish: one, tiring halfway across and jumping into the river to a waiting rescue boat, the other put one foot wrong and fell 10m into the river. Both were unharmed. The event was held as part of the annual Seoul Citizens Day, which commemorates the city's 600-year history as capital of South Korea. And although it's uncertain whether the

01.   02.

03.   04.

'Many highwire 'stunts' have been performed without safety nets and without permission'

One of those situations where it's best not to look down... Pedro Carril of the USA takes a walk on the high side as a participant in the first World Highwire Championships.

championships will continue to feature in the celebrations, tightrope walking or *jultagi* performances are frequently held on national days and festivals.

No 55 on South Korea's Important Intangible Cultural Properties list of cultural practices officially designated for preservation, *jultagi* is similar to tightrope walking but has the added dimension of story telling, with a narrative play unfolding from atop the wire. The ensemble cast includes a musician, a clown and the rope-walker. Acrobatics are also integral to the performance, with the rope-walker leaping into a kneeling, lying or sitting position.

The main difference between tightrope walking and highwire walking is the height at which the very thin line is anchored. Although there is no official height at which a tightrope becomes a highwire, it's generally over 6m. The

height factor adds to the danger factor and the necessity for a safety net. Or not. Many highwire 'stunts' have been performed without safety nets and without permission. In 1974 Philippe Petit famously committed the 'artistic crime of the century' when, after six years of planning, he fixed a cable between New York's Twin Towers and walked, danced and jeered at waiting police officers from it for 45 minutes.

You can spot a highwire walker by their very flexible, leather slippers, plus they'll often be carrying a very large pole sideways. The pole distributes a walker's balance laterally, moving it out from the very narrow point directly above the feet. Highwire walking is a great test of agility, balance, concentration and chutzpah.

MORE INFO Official Seoul City Tourism (www.visitseoul.net)

Known first as a snowboarder, Shaun White shows his skill with a different kind of board during the 2008 Maloof Money Cup in Costa Mesa, California.

WORLD MASTERS WEIGHTLIFTING CHAMPIONSHIPS

WHERE Location changes each championships **WHEN** Early to mid-October **GETTING INVOLVED** Check the website for fixtures and ticketing details.

The strong-folk of the sporting world, weightlifters have moved from the circus tent into the arena, where they adhere to strict technical requirements to perform the sport's two events: the snatch and the clean-and-jerk.

The snatch is one smooth continuous movement of the barbell, taking it from a squatting position to above the head. The clean-and-jerk (also known as the 'king of the lifts', as it is with this technique that more weight can be lifted) involves the 'clean' lift to shoulder height, followed by the jumping 'jerk' to above the head. With both men and women competing in differing weight classes (of which there are eight for men and seven for women), each competitor is allowed three attempts at each lift. The lifter who chooses the lightest weight goes first. Each lift is judged and given a white light if correct or a red light if deemed invalid. There are three judges: two or more red lights equates to a 'no lift'. Competitors are marked for individual events as well as an aggregate of both.

Weightlifting as a sport spans three centuries, being one of the original events in the first modern Olympics. The world championships, though, predate even the Olympics by five years, with the first competition (between seven athletes) taking place in 1891. To date, there have been more than 70 world championships (with the masters being for competitors over 35 years) and weightlifting has featured in 21 Olympics (the 2000 Olympics being the first to include women's events).

There's been a return to the strongman antics in recent years, with events like the World's Strongest Man in which contestants pull trains and 18-wheel trucks. Strength-testing activities, like tyre flipping and object loading, have also become part of everyday cross-fit programs, making strongmen and women out of everyday folk.
MORE INFO International Weightlifting Federation (www.iwf.net)

MALOOF MONEY CUP

WHERE Orange County, USA **WHEN** First week in October **GETTING INVOLVED** The website has full details of entry for competitors. Tickets for spectators are available online.

Whether you agree with their methods or not, there's no denying that Joe and Gavin Maloof, owners of the Sacramento Kings (NBA) and Palms Casino in Vegas, know how to put on a show. They're fully aware that the best way to make your tournament stand out from the others is to cough up the most prize money. Athletes go where the money flows and skateboarders (whether they like to admit it or not) are no exception.

The Maloof Money Cup celebrated its inaugural year in 2008 and, though it reeks of the kind of commercialisation long present in sports like basketball and football, it features a stellar field of competitors including such superstars as Ryan Sheckler, Andrew Reynolds and Shaun White. All this combined with a specially designed 'street' course means there are few voices of dissent.

Offering the largest prize pool in skateboarding history – the men's winner pockets US$100,000 while the women's champion takes home US$25,000 – the Maloof brothers have taken a gamble on the saleability of the sport and for now it appears to be paying off. Skaters from around the world have praised both the course design (the brothers worked closely with world-renowned skaters in the design and building stages) and the organisation of the event.

Staged over three days as part of the Orange County Fair, the Money Cup includes three professional US Championship competitions, the men's and women's Pro Street and two amateur events.

MORE INFO Maloof Money Cup (www.maloofmoneycup.com)

COMBAT DES REINES

WHERE Valias, Switzerland **WHEN** First week in October **GETTING INVOLVED** Tickets are available at the gate; check the website for the schedule.

It's cow against cow at Switzerland's cow-fighting events, which take place every spring and autumn. Short-legged, stocky Erdinger cows, famous for being feisty, fight each other to decide who will be queen of the herd. The combatants snort and stamp their hooves before charging, locking horns and trying to force each other backwards. It can be anticlimactic however, with animals sometimes losing interest and drifting out of the ring in search of greener pastures.

A good fight can last for up to 45 minutes. Any cow that backs down is eliminated and the last left standing is the 'queen'. The cows' horns are filed down and no blood is spilled – the main reason that animal rights activists don't object to the showdowns between these naturally aggressive ladies.

While the cow-fighting ritual has taken place here for centuries, Valaisian farmers have been organising regular battles since the 1920s. The 'queen of the queens' will sell for a very high price, such that the cow-fighting circuit has become more lucrative for many farmers – who can earn more from the sport than from their herds' milk and meat. Hence, genetic selection, embryo freezing, oats concentrate (believed to act as a stimulant) and even wine are used to prepare the cows for battle.

The major competitions, such as the rodeo-style event held during Martigny's Foire du Valais exposition, are big events in southern Switzerland, attracting television cameras and tens of thousands of spectators.

MORE INFO Foire du Valais (www.foireduvalais.ch, in French)

'When I see three oranges, I juggle. When I see two towers, I walk.'

Philippe Petit, on why he highwire walked between New York's World Trade Center twin towers in 1974

FOR THE RECORD

- Australia holds Commonwealth Games records for five of the six possible team relay swimming events.

- A stunning 82 new records were set at the 2006 Commonwealth Games.

COMMONWEALTH GAMES

WHERE Location changes each games **WHEN** Every four years **GETTING INVOLVED** Tickets available through the host country's games website.

Sport has been put to use as a diplomat and arbiter of human relations for centuries. Sometimes, it's on such a grand scale, attracting the attention of the multitude, that the arts follows sport into the arena, joining forces to create one whopping event. The Commonwealth Games brings together more than 4000 athletes, hundreds of artistic acts and innumerable spectators from more than 50 countries, all under the rather exalted banner: 'Humanity. Equality. Destiny.'

Athletes swim, cycle, box, bowl and shoot in the name of their country – one of the 53 members of the Commonwealth of Nations. It's a voluntary association of independent sovereign states, the majority being former British colonies or

01.

02.

03.

04.

'The Games brings together thousands of athletes under the rather exalted banner: 'Humanity. Equality. Destiny'

OCTOBER
WEEK.02

Hurtling over the bar, Tatiana Grigorieva competes in the women's pole vault qualifying event at the 2006 Commonwealth Games.

dependencies thereof. Unlike other quadrennial world sporting events, namely the Olympics, the Commonwealth Games allows for constituent countries (such as Scotland) and smaller nations dependent on the Crown (such as Guernsey) to send their own teams. As a result, more than 70 teams compete in the games, established in 1930 to promote the 'good will' of the British Empire, for the ideals of democracy, world peace, free trade and human rights.

The first Games were held in 1930, then called the British Empire Games. Four hundred athletes from 11 countries competed in six sports. From 1954 to 1966, the games were known as the British Empire and Commonwealth Games, which would again change its name in 1970 to the British Commonwealth Games before reaching its current incarnation in 1978 as the Commonwealth Games. Today's games must include a minimum of 10 sports, and usually run up to 17, with a maximum number of four team sports. They also have a fully integrated program of events for Elite Athletes with Disabilities (EAD) and run a separate Youth Games.

Of course it has its traditions – the Queen's baton relay probably being the most conspicuous. With similarities to the Olympics' torch relay, the Queen's baton leaves Buckingham Palace with a written message from Her Majesty. It travels through most, if not all, participating countries, before reaching the host city where it is given back to Her Majesty (or her rep) who reads the welcome message heralding the start of the games.

Host cities generally make the most of their time in the spotlight, staging equally world-class cultural performances representing each of the participating countries.

MORE INFO Commonwealth Games Federation (www.cgf.com)

WORLD CONKER CHAMPIONSHIPS

WHERE Ashton, England **WHEN** Second Sunday in October **GETTING INVOLVED** Entry for spectators is for a small fee. Register online, up to three months in advance, to enter the championships.

What do fishermen do when the weather's too bad to fish? They try to hit each other's nuts. At least that's what a few chaps drinking at Ashton's Chequered Skipper did when they inadvertently invented the inaugural World Conkers Championship.

Conkers is a schoolyard game in which two players each string a horse-chestnut from a shoelace, dangle it, and take it in turns to try to hit and destroy the other's 'conker'. Rules differ between schoolyards, but if a player drops a conker they must yell 'no stamps' before their opponent has a chance to yell 'stamps'. If they're not quick enough, they must watch as their opponent stomps on their nut. Schoolyard rules also generally make provision for the 'strings' rule, which awards the first player who yells 'strings' after the lines become entangled with another shot.

World championship rules, however, do not allow for either the 'stomp' or the 'string'. In fact tangling of strings is seen as bad sportsmanship, which can lead to disqualification. In Ashton's world championships, a coin toss decides who goes first. The 'striker' instructs their opposition at which height to dangle the conker, then (using the non-conker holding hand) draws back the conker to aim for the strike. If the targer is missed, another two attempts are allowed before the striker becomes the strikee. And so on, until one of the conkers is smashed, breaking completely off the string. All conkers are supplied by the event organisers to prevent illegal hardening of competition conkers.

The event attracts thousands of spectators, and raises tens of thousands of pounds for charity. There are stalls, bands and Morris dancers each year. And the original pub in which the championships were devised still provides refreshments.
MORE INFO World Conker Championships (www.worldconkerchampionships.com)

OCTOBER
WEEK.02

AND ANOTHER THING

- - - - - - - - - - - - - - - - -

Polar Circle Marathon (Kangerlussuaq, Greenland)

In a country where -5°C temperatures are described as 'beautiful, not too cold', running over 40km in the snowy wilderness must be a walk in the park. Of course running through Greenland's soundless Arctic desert affords the opportunity to run into musk oxen and reindeer, too. All competitors who complete the course within seven hours receive a medal. Those wishing to drop out should take themselves to the nearest drinks station (every 5km) where they can wait in a sleeping bag for a ride back to town. (www.polar-circle -marathon.com)

BATHURST 1000

WHERE Bathurst, New South Wales, Australia **WHEN** Second Sunday in October **GETTING INVOLVED** Tickets available through Ticketek (www.ticketek.com.au)

Australia's general bulk and the resulting requirements of long-distance travel has led to a very healthy car culture. And you'd be hard pressed to find a race that has exerted more influence on that car culture than the Bathurst 1000, which has affected car manufacturing and given regular citizens the opportunity to drive racing cars.

The Bathurst has run since the '60s, originally as an 800km race held strictly for production cars identical to those everyday Australians would drive out of the showroom. The plaudits and attention heaped on the winning car model led to a rivalry between the country's two car manufacturers that continues today. Ford and Holden battled it out at the Mt Panorama circuit to win kudos for durability, reliability and performance, which of course translated to sales. The marketing slogan went something like: 'Win on Sunday, Sell on Monday'. Both companies would eventually build cars, available on the commercial market, known as Bathurst specials, such as the Holden Monaro and Ford Falcon GT.

By the '70s, Australia had adopted the metric system and Bathurst had added another 200km to its course, making a total of 1000km. Popularly known as the 'great race', the fastest time to complete the course is six hours, 19 minutes and 14.8 seconds in 1991. The race has evolved to only include a specific class of car, the V8 Supercar, and around 187,000 fans make the road trip to Bathurst every year to see and hear them in action.
MORE INFO V8 Supercar Championship Series (www.v8supercars.com.au)

IRONMAN WORLD CHAMPIONSHIP

WHERE Kona, Hawaii **WHEN** Second week of October **GETTING INVOLVED** Check the website and your local clubs for qualifying events and lottery details.

Separating the (iron) men from the boys. World championship competitors create waves in Hawaii.

If 3.8km of ocean swimming and 180km of cycling, followed up with an excruciating 42km run sounds like a good idea, you either have a death wish, or you're a super-fit ironman.

Each year 1800 of the 'luckiest' ironmen from every continent are given the chance to prove themselves on the 'Wimbledon' of triathlons. Despite the gruelling course, tens of thousands of triathletes vie for a place on the starting line in Kona, Hawaii. Entry is gained through qualifying events throughout the year while a small number gain entry via the sanctioned lottery.

The tournament dates back 30 years and began after a discussion between local athletes arguing over who was the fittest – swimmers or runners. Someone suggested the idea of a combined event incorporating the three existing sporting events on the island – the Waikiki Roughwater Swim, the Around-Oahu Bike Race and the Honolulu Marathon. John Collins, a US Navy commander, stood up at the party and declared that the winner of this new endurance race would be called 'the Ironman'.

Over the years there have been many copycat events, some sanctioned by the governing body and others simply called triathlons. But the spirit of the ironman series resides in the giant swell of the Hawaiian waves, the blinding heat of the lava desert and the gusting winds that sweep across the cycle route.

Many tourist operators offer package deals to cater for the influx of athletes, officials and spectators, but be early to avoid missing out.

MORE INFO Ironman World Championship (www.ironman.com/worldchampionship)

FOR THE RECORD

↗ US athlete Barbara Bedford has held the Pan Am record for the women's 200m freestyle event since 1975 with her time of one minute 58.43 seconds.

↗ As of the 2007 Games, the British Virgin Islands, Curaçao, Saint Kitts and Nevis, and Saint Marten were all ranked equal 41st (last), not having won a medal.

PAN AM GAMES

WHERE Location changes each games **WHEN** Every four years
GETTING INVOLVED Tickets available through the host city's games website.

As much as we all love stories about unknowns who come out of nowhere to suddenly become stars, it rarely happens that way. (Except if you happen to be very good at being locked up in a house with a group of strangers and have every movement broadcast to the general public, without being voted out.) And so it is with sports. Athletes don't just go from the backyard pool to the Olympic pool. There are a number of precursors to the Olympic Games; athletes work their way up an established ladder of competitions, rung by rung. Regional games, like the Pan Ams, are one of those rungs.

Supported by the International Olympic Committee (IOC), regional games allow for countries to compete at an international level with a view to competing in the Olympics. At the regional level, the IOC provides scholarships and administrative support to countries that might otherwise not have the means to dedicate to

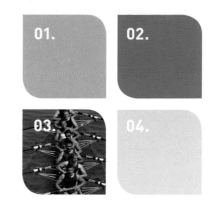

'Athletes don't just go from the backyard pool to the Olympic pool. There are a number of precursors to the Olympic Games'

Spurred on by an enthusiastic crowd, American Sarah Haskins (L) and teammate Julie Ertel pace out the final stretch of the women's triathlon at the 2007 Pan Am Games in Brazil.

developing sport, and provides the international-competition platform of the Pan Am Games. Countries competing in the Pan Ams include those from the continents of North and South America, its islands and the land bridge of Central America.

Forty-two countries compete in the Pan Am Games. And although they share a landmass, they speak one or more of around a dozen languages: primarily Spanish and English, but also Portuguese, French, Quechua and Aymara. They unite under the banner, 'America, Espirito, Sport, Fraternite', which throws together words from four languages to loosely translate as, 'American spirit of friendship through sport'.

The Pan Am Games were first held in 1951, in Argentina. These days around 5000 athletes compete in the same sports as sanctioned by the IOC, as well as some that are not. In between events in swimming, cycling, wrestling and roller sports, you could also expect to see some hat dancing at the 2011 games held in Guadalajara.

This southern Mexican city has contributed many cultural icons to the Mexican lifestyle. These include tequila, mariachi music, the broad-rimmed sombrero and *charreadas* (rodeos), and these days it is also known for its outstanding food. Watching athletes exert themselves is hungry work for the average spectator; refuel at a street-side taco and *torta ahogada* stand, a neighbourhood cafe or a fine dining room in a restored colonial mansion.

MORE INFO Pan American Sports Association (www.odepapaso.org)

The rugged landscape surrounding Afghanistan's Kabul provides a dramatic backdrop to boys practising the age-old art of kite flying.

BRIDGE DAY FESTIVAL

WHERE West Virginia, USA **WHEN** Third Sunday in October **GETTING INVOLVED** To jump, you must have experience skydiving and register online. To watch, just turn up.

The New River Gorge Bridge is one of those exhilarating, much anticipated moments on long country drives, where slow, winding roads walled in by foliage open out to a bridge crossing with a stomach-turning drop. While the drive only lasts a minute, it's an awesome minute – passing 260m above rapids. And that's the end of it for most of us. But for skydivers, without an aeroplane, it's a delicious opportunity to jump. And jump they do. Every year, the bridge is closed to vehicular traffic and opened to jumping and rappelling traffic, as well as those who like to watch.

The 'base' in base jump is derived from all the very big things from which you could possibly throw yourself: a building, an antenna, a span (bridge) and earth – as in a cliff. The competitive element of base jumping is in the wrestle with the rational mind required to overcome that internal voice that warns 'DON'T YOU DARE'. More than 400 people jump from the bridge on Bridge Day, with prize money awarded for landing accuracy. But the majority of jumpers do it for the rush: all eight seconds of it, which is how quickly you come down to earth after such a jump. Organisers anticipate 100,000 spectators, which includes those who simply want the opportunity to walk the 900m-long bridge surrounded by the gorge's stunning scenery. Just expect to see people throwing themselves off the bridge at regular intervals. Vendors set up stalls at either end of the bridge should you be taken by a sudden urge to buy souvenirs in the middle of the countryside.

The festival has been operating since 1980, primarily as a promotion for the area, which boasts white-water rafting, fly-fishing, hiking and various other festivities including the Appalachian String Band Festival.
MORE INFO Bridge Day (www.officialbridgeday.com)

KITE-FIGHTING

 WHERE Afghanistan **WHEN** Most Fridays **GETTING INVOLVED** Just look to the skies.

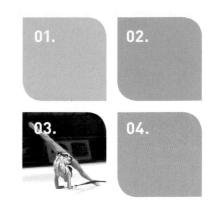

Kite-fighting takes the gentle recreational activity of releasing a kite and watching it bob about on the air, and transforms it into a do-or-die competition that sees one contestant going home kiteless. Two kites dual midair until one's line is severed, sending the kite off into unchartered currents and into the hands of whoever finds it when it lands. Kite-running, as it's known, is almost a sport unto itself. Mostly boys give chase, running through streets, over rooftops and fences, and across roads. All the while with their eyes on the prize, rather than where they're going, which can prove dangerous.

Fighting-kites are made with an abrasive line, made with a mixture of very finely crushed glass and rice adhesive. Kite-fighters manoeuvre their kites to cut their opponent's line. It takes two to fight a single kite: one to fly (the leader) who releases the line until the kite's nose points in the desired direction; the other to hold the *charkha* (or reel).

Banned in Afghanistan under the Taliban, kite-fighting (*Gudiparan bazi*) is making a comeback, and each *kocha* (block) has its kite-flying champion. Kite-fighting is a mostly impromptu affair, but if you look skyward on a Friday in autumn you're almost certain to see a fight or two, with boys running over rooftops in pursuit of the losing kite. All kites are handmade, using bamboo for the skeleton and a very thin paper for the skin. They range in size, colour and design, with the all-important line also made by hand.

MORE INFO Afghanistan Directory (www.afghana.com)

RUBBER DUCKY REGATTA

 WHERE Santa Clarita, California, USA **WHEN** Third Sunday in October **GETTING INVOLVED** Adopt a duck online, or buy a ticket at the gate.

It's as though all the rubber ducks in all the bathrooms across America have escaped. After years of collusion they've managed to break out of the bath, and made it to the wild open waters. Thousands of rubber ducks are released on race days. Although it's a race, there's nothing particularly pacey about a rubber duck's gentle bobbing motion. But don't think those inanimate painted smiles are oblivious to the thousands of cheers coming from the spectators who line the race course.

Thousands of rubber-duck races are organised around the world to raise money for charities. Organisers release the ducks into the water whose course is strictly controlled in order to limit the number of escapees finding their way into the oceans. At some of the larger events up to 100,000 ducks turn the water a cheerful yellow. Each duck has a number painted on its underside, which correlates to the number on a ticket being clenched by a spectator nearby. The first ducky past the finishing line wins the person holding the corresponding ticket number a holiday, a food basket, a juicer…whatever the organisation has raised for the event.

Santa Clarita's ducky regatta raises money for the area's health centres. Participants can adopt a duck online before the event, and enjoy a range of family activities throughout the day. Events run across America and Europe, and have even been reported in Australia's Northern Territory – where the ducks have to contend with local crocodiles.

MORE INFO www.derbyduckrace.com

Every winter, districts in Kabul held a kite-fighting tournament. And if you were a boy living in Kabul, the day of the tournament was undeniably the highlight of the cold season. I felt like a soldier trying to sleep in the trenches the night before a major battle. And that wasn't so far off. In Kabul, fighting kites was a little like going to war.

Khaled Hosseini, *The Kite Runner*

↗ In 2008, Australian Christian Sprenger won an outstanding nine World Cup titles, and came fifth overall.

↗ Cameron van de Burgh of South Africa was the overall male winner in 2008 and Marieke Guehrer of Australia overall women's winner.

FINA SWIMMING WORLD CUP

 WHERE Location changes with each meet **WHEN** From mid-October to mid-November **GETTING INVOLVED** Check the website for scheduling and ticketing news.

Until recently, 'real' swimmers only swam in 50m pools. Whatever the distance of the event, be it 50m or 800m, it would only be recognised internationally if swum in a 50m-long pool. Understandably, an 800m swim with 16 turns is a different beast to an 800m swim with 32 turns. It's necessary to ensure all swimmers compete using identical parameters. But in 1991, the international federation for swimming, FINA, decided to acknowledge short-course (25m) records and created the World Cup short-course competition series in 1993, thereby increasing the overall opportunities for swimmers to compete internationally.

Olympians and world record holders from around the globe compete in the World Cup competition, which runs for a month. The entire circuit is composed of seven

'The circuit is made up of seven meets, each held in a different country to spread the love of short-course swimming'

OCTOBER
WEEK.04

With almost perfect symmetry swimmers hit the pool at the start of the FINA Swimming World Cup men's 50m freestyle in 2008.

meets, each of which is held in a different country – to spread the love of short-course swimming. Freestyle, backstroke, breaststroke, butterfly and medley events comprise the World Cup calendar – same as at long-course events – only they're swum in a 25m pool. All events are raced in heats and finals, except for the 800m and 1500m freestyle, which are timed finals. Generally, all host countries adhere to the same format of competition: the suspension builds throughout the day, with the heats raced in the mornings, and all the tension of the event finals is realised in the afternoon.

Scoring is a tad complicated, and specific to the event. Swimmers are ranked according to their top performances. The top 10 women and men of each meet are awarded World Cup points, with the overall points winner receiving first prize (US$100,000); the next highest points scorer is second (US$50,000) and third place is also acknowledged

(US$30,000). World Cup points double at the final meet, and bonus points (and money) are awarded to those who break a world record (20 points, plus $10,000) or equal a world record (10 points, $5000).

There's a good chance you won't have to travel too far to attend at least one of the World Cup rounds. The most recent World Cups have followed the same order of proceedings, beginning in South America, then moving to Africa, Oceania, Asia and Europe for the final. But then, if you're looking for an excuse to skip continents, you could follow the whole circuit and see the world using 25m pools as pegs.

MORE INFO Fédération Internationale de Natation (www.fina.org)

WORLD ROCK-PAPER-SCISSORS CHAMPIONSHIP

With an almighty 'Arr' a determined pirate throws down a scissor stroke to cut a landlubber's paper during the 2006 World Rock-Paper-Scissors Championships.

WHERE Toronto, Canada **WHEN** Third or fourth Saturday in October **GETTING INVOLVED** Tickets available online through the society.

The means for deciding a multitude of scenarios, from who goes first to who has to take out the rubbish bins, rock-paper-scissors is now a world-class competition unto itself.

In 2002, the World Rock Paper Scissors Society, based in Canada, standardised the rules of play for international competitions. The game is played all over the world, so variations on rules are to be expected. The Rock Paper Scissors Society believes that human nature is predictable. The shrewd observer can quickly read an opponent either by their body language, their gender, their game history or a combination of these and more factors. Even in our attempts to be random we are, apparently, predictable. Experts also believe you can influence an opponent's play by brushing up on basic precepts of human psychology. Competitors at the World Championships routinely dress garishly and in costume, to try to throw their opponents and give nothing of their true selves away, attempting to hide anything that that the opposition may exploit.

In international competition there are only three elements – no bombs, no water, just rock, paper and scissors. A rock is indicated with a clenched fist, thumb showing (it's considered bad sportsmanship to hide the thumb). Paper is represented by a flat hand, palm down, and scissors by extending the middle and index fingers like scissors. The competitors' 'prime', or count before the throw, must be in sync, which is one of the roles of the adjudicator.

So, do you plan your next holiday around the World Rock-Paper-Scissors Championship or, as your companion wishes, Toronto's International Film Festival? Only one way to find out...

MORE INFO World RPS Society (www.worldrps.com)

RUSSIAN COLLEGE LAPTA CHAMPIONSHIP

 WHERE St Petersburg, Russia **WHEN** End of October **GETTING INVOLVED** Check the website, or ask around while in town.

Lapta is sport's version of the national anthem in that it's terribly important culturally and everyone knows about it, but very few know the lyrics. Chances are that everyone you ask in Russia will know about Lapta, but they won't be able to tell you how to play. It's no reflection on the general populace's lack of attention to one of the country's national games, more a reflection on the lack of standardised rules of play. But, with a history that can be traced back to the 14th century, it's not surprising that there are regional differences.

Leather balls and bats were uncovered during excavations of Veliky Novgorod, which loosely translates as the 'Great New City', which is actually quite ancient. Archaeologists have dated materials back to the 10th century, and put the bats and balls somewhere in the 14th century. Claimed by the Lapta Federation to be the precursor to baseball, Lapta has elements of many modern games, including cricket.

Batters must run to a 10m line and back. If successful, they score two points for their team. Five fielders from the opposition try to hit the runner with the retrieved tennis ball, and there can be multiple people (up to six) running after each hit. We're not 100% sure on the rules either...but it's the idea of the game that counts. And St Petersburg has long been a city of ideas. It's not only Rastrelli's architecture and Tchaikovsky's operas that entice visitors, but also beatnik bands, contemporary art galleries, underground clubs and delectable dining.

MORE INFO Russian Lapta Federation (www.lapta.ru, in Russian)

WORLDWIDE FESTIVAL OF RACES

 WHERE Wherever in the world you are **WHEN** Changes, but usually late October **GETTING INVOLVED** Register online.

The Festival of Races is a running event that brings participants together virtually, from around the world. Unfortunately, you can't virtually run, and are required to actually physically exert yourself. Entrants can run 5km or 10km and do so in the knowledge that they have thousands of other virtual companions all running at the same time. Or nearly the same time, allowing for time differences. And everyone's a winner, as every person who runs, partners up with a buddy, and uses the online training schedule is fitter than they were before they started.

It's loosely organised – participants can run at an event that's officially sanctioned in their home town or just make up a course that suits them. Making up your own course means it's just you and your mate running and probably along the same training course you've been running for months. It may lack the cheering multitudes you imagined, as you break the finishing ribbon, sweating and exhausted but victorious; however, it's likely to be more conveniently located to home.

It costs nothing to enter the Festival of Races, which is open to all and is non-commercial. To validate your run, organisers ask that you simply register, run, then report your time. The more competitive participants can then check back into the website after the event and see how they placed. Of course, partnering up, as is recommended by organisers, also gives you someone 'real' to compete against each time you train together and provides the external motivation sometimes necessary to get off the couch.

MORE INFO World Wide Festival of Races (www.worldwidefestivalofraces.com)

AND ANOTHER THING

Karaoke World Championships (location changes each championship)

The Karaoke World Championships is a serious singing competition – as opposed to those impromptu ones down at the local. To participate, contestants need to have first sung their way through trials held in their home country. Often, depending on the host country, karaoke restaurants allow the public to belt out songs during breaks in the competition. (www.kwc.fi)

FOR THE RECORD

 The 'Austrian Oak', as he was called in his bodybuilding days, Arnold Schwarzenegger has played a leading role in popularising bodybuilding. He was seven-times champion of the Mr Olympia competition, and is commemorated in the naming of the Arnold Sports Festival (early March).

WORLD BODYBUILDING CHAMPIONSHIPS

WHERE Location changes each championship **WHEN** First week of November **GETTING INVOLVED** Check the website for scheduling and ticketing information.

Essentially a beauty contest for the bulked-up, bodybuilding and its fraternity constantly fight for its recognition as a 'sport'. If it were, then it might finally be included in the Olympics. And who wouldn't prefer to win an Olympic medal, rather than a sash and crown, for all their hard work?

Apart from hours of lifting weights, to build up even tiny muscles that most of us never knew we had, bodybuilders eat up to seven meals a day that are high in protein and low in fat. Weeks before a competition, they'll avoid ingesting salts and fluids (other than protein drinks) to remove the fluid that sits just under the skin. Less fluid under the skin means more visible muscle definition, separation and density, and more visible

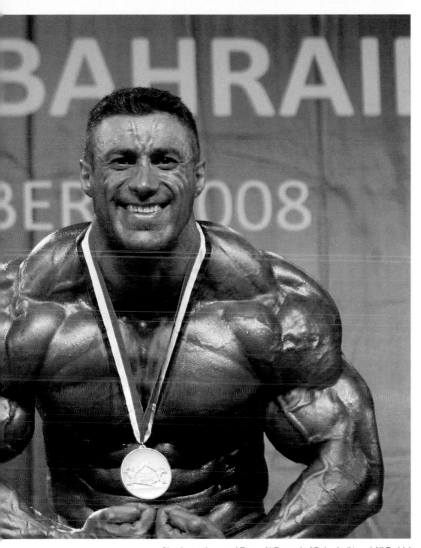

'There are breakaway events that exploit the body's 'classic' figure – where bigger is not necessarily better'

NOVEMBER
WEEK.01

Check out the pecs! Tareq Al Farsani of Bahrain (L) and Ali Trabizi Nouri of Iran strike a pose after receiving their medals in the 90kg category at the World Men's Bodybuilding Championships in 2008.

veins. Then there are the layers of artificial tan and coconut oil, which give competing bodybuilders an unnatural orange glow and help to create shadows – again defining muscles. That fetching shade of ochre could be what separates one tower of bulging muscle from the next in the eyes of the judges.

Judges award higher points to the body with the biggest muscles. But there must be an all-over bulk, with a body proportionally and aesthetically correct. That means a broad shoulder area, narrow waist and adequately long legs and shorter upper body. Contestants perform 10 compulsory exercises, which show off their bods, and do so in various weight categories. Contestants are barefoot and wear only a loincloth-like pant, or bikini for women. The idea behind all the sweat, coconut oil and protein shakes? To resemble the chiselled statues of the ancient Greeks and Romans, considered to represent the perfect physique.

As a bulging upper body atop two solid trunks isn't a particularly feminine ideal, separate women's events have developed, which focus on athletic appearance rather than bulk. Even in the men's competition, there are breakaway events that exploit the body's 'classic' figure – where bigger is not necessarily better – and there's a separate 'natural' fraternity of bodybuilders who eschew any kind of synthetic substances in their craft.

The World Bodybuilding Championships are organised by the International Federation of Bodybuilding and Fitness; they're for male competitors only, with the female equivalent held in October. A number of national federations also organise coveted events, like Mr Olympia (end of September).

MORE INFO International Federation of Bodybuilding and Fitness (www.ifbb.com)

MOTORCYCLE GRAND PRIX

WHERE Season consists of 18 grands prix, and visits more than a dozen countries **WHEN** From April to November; check the website for the latest schedule **GETTING INVOLVED** Each host country has its own ticketing procedure; go directly to their respective websites for ticketing details.

Spanish rider Jorge Lorenzo of the Fiat Yamaha team takes a concentrated corner during a practice session before the Malaysian MotoGP.

You won't see these beasts every day. Specially built for racing, grand prix motorbikes use the latest technology to enable as near a perfect performance as possible. And these world championship performances are the nearest to perfection you'll see. The grand prix season constitutes the pinnacle of motorcycle racing. It ought to, given that it's the oldest motor sport world championship, and that it's had since 1949 to cultivate a word-class event.

Run over a distance of between 95km and 130km, each race lasts for around 45 minutes. Unlike car racing, pit stops are the exception, rather than the norm. This makes tyre selection integral to a bike's success on the track, with the rider attempting to strike a balance between a softer tyre (providing better grip, but that wears relatively quickly) and a harder-wearing tyre.

During its venerable history, the race format has seen a number of changes. None of them would be more revolutionary than 2002's ushering in of a new era in the sport by allowing four-stroke engines. It's the four-stroke category that is considered the ultimate of the three individual race categories and riders in this event must be over 18 years. The 250 category is for twin-cylinder machines and riders over 16, and the 125 single-cylinder race allows youngsters between 15 and 28 the opportunity to compete at world level.

But it's not just bikes; paddock girls are an integral part of motor racing. Invariably gorgeous, it's their job to hold umbrellas over the riders while they wait for the other riders to take their places on the grid. The shade provided by the ladies ostensibly shields riders from the heat, but actually provides eye candy for the mostly male audience. Demonstration rides are as much a part of the program as the official races, and might include stunt riders and parades.

MORE INFO The Official MotoGP Website (www.motogp.com)

BADMINTON GRAND PRIX

WHERE Around 10 grands prix held every year, each hosted by a different country **WHEN** Year-round **GETTING INVOLVED** Contact the World Federation for updated schedules and ticketing info.

It seems paradoxical, but badminton – the genteel sport once played by Britain's well-to-do – is lightning fast, physically demanding and high energy. It's hard to imagine the pampered upper classes of yesteryear exerting themselves beyond a playful, limp-wristed thwock of the shuttlecock, but indeed they did.

Definitively launched by the Brits in 1873, badminton is derived from a popular children's game from the 17th century called 'battledore and shuttlecock'. It involved simply hitting a shuttlecock back and forth as many times as possible without it hitting the ground. The origin of the shuttlecock is a mystery, but one plausible theory posits that perhaps writing quills stored in corks proved too much of a temptation to the children of the house. It became known as badminton after Badminton House in Britain, where a netted version of the game became popular in the 1850s.

Today's game involves players rallying the shuttle back and forth with often dramatic and swift play. The fastest recorded badminton slam is 332km/h (compared to tennis' 246km/h). And, although faster, the feathers exert a significant drag on the shuttle, slowing the overall trajectory. Forcing the shuttle to ground on the opponent's side of the court earns a point; earn 21 and you win the game. The best of three games wins the tournament. Each year's grands prix are open to all players who are members of a national association affiliated with the world governing body – the Badminton World Federation, established in 1934.

MORE INFO World Badminton Federation (www.internationalbadminton.org)

CANOE & KUNDU CANOE RACE

WHERE Alotau, Papua New Guinea **WHEN** First week in November **GETTING INVOLVED** A number of organised tours visit the festival, or you can get along independently.

Nestled in a hillside on the shore of Milne Bay, Alotau is a sleepy little town…most of the time. Not so during the first week in November however, when the bay fills with boats made to traditional specifications that are pitted in races against one another.

While the festivities last for seven days, preparations for the festival take months of work. Communities from all corners of the province take part, each community known for a specific type of vessel. The single-person wooden dugout canoes, sometimes fitted with tarpaulin sails, are popular along the Huhu Coast, Bwanabwana and Eastern Sua areas for example, while the elaborately designed *sailaus* are popular among the D'Entrecasteaux and Trobriand Islands as trading vessels. All of the boats are made by hand, with elders disseminating how-to knowledge to the youth – keeping tradition alive, while providing a spectacle for tourists and a cultural event that brings together an entire province.

Races are by class of vessel and include the spectacular short-distance war canoe races. These enormous dugouts require a captain to coordinate his 40-strong crew – all dressed in traditional garb – via the steady thrum of a traditional drum. Kewokewo outrigger canoes, designed for speed and swift manoeuvrability, race from nearby Samurai Island to Alotau.

A range of nighttime and off-water events are a part of the festivities. Take in a variety show PNG-style or witness the official exchange of gifts, food and pigs on Kundu Day.

MORE INFO Papua New Guinea Tourism Promotion Authority (www.niuginitourism.com)

'When they get a 50in waist and a gorilla butt, it's ugly looking – and I think bodybuilding has become ugly looking.'

- - - - - - - - - - - - - - - -

Joe Gold, owner and operator of California's famous Gold's Gyms and World Gyms

Asashoryu of Mongolia knows how to throw – unbalancing the Bulgarian Kotooshu and going on to win his 19th Emperor's Cup.

GRAND SUMO TOURNAMENT

WHERE Fukuoka, Japan **WHEN** For 15 days from the first Sunday in November **GETTING INVOLVED** The earlier rounds of lower-ranking wrestlers are easier to attend. Check the website for up-to-date ticketing info.

A sumo bout carries a lot more weight than the *rikishi* (wrestlers) themselves when you consider the rigours of training they endure. Although each bout usually lasts only a minute or so, that burst of push-and-shove is loaded with personal sacrifice; each minute could mean the difference between living like a slave or like a king.

To enter the sumo profession is to enter a life segregated from family and the rest of society. *Rikishi* live in training stables *(heya)* within a strict system of social standing, such that wrestlers of higher rank are waited on by wrestlers ranked below them. High-ranking wrestlers *(sekitori)* live in separate apartments within the compound and have no duties to attend to other than to eat, drink beer and answer fan mail. Lower ranked wrestlers do all the chores around the stable, including cleaning, cooking and holding a towel for the *sekitori* after his bath.

Eating is an important part of training for sumo wrestlers. Generally, they skip breakfast and eat a huge lunch that's washed down with beer. After lunch they'll have a sleep. It's a routine that helps to stack on weight, and, controversially, increase the incidence of liver disease, diabetes and heart failure. *Rikishi* reportedly have a life expectancy that's 10 years below the average for a Japanese male.

Tournaments are dictated by a long history of tradition that relates to the Shinto religion. Immediately before a bout, *rikishi* face the audience, clap, then stomp to drive out evil spirits. After a cleansing ritual in which *rikishi* rinse their mouths with a ladleful of 'power water' and dab their lips dry with 'power tissue', they squat, clap and spread their legs – traditionally to show they weren't carrying any weapons. *Rikishi* then return to their corners to throw salt into the ring to purify the space. And this is all before they eye each other off in an attempt to stare down their opponent before charging one another and locking shoulders.

There are six Grand Sumo tournaments every year, roughly every two months. The final day of the 15-day competition comes down to the top six wrestlers, which have been determined over the course of the preceding days – the *rikishi* with the most wins essentially wins overall. He's the one at whom the referee is pointing a war-fan for successfully pushing his opponent out of the circle or into a forced touch of the ground with a part of his body other then the soles of his feet. **MORE INFO** Nihon Sumo Kyokai Official Grand Sumo Home Page (www.sumo .or.jp/eng)

NOVEMBER WEEK.02

FOR THE RECORD

- - - - - - - - - - - - - - - -

↗ There are no weight categories in sumo wrestling, so a wrestler can come up against an opponent twice his size.

↗ If the highest-ranking wrestler is unseated by a lower-ranking opponent, the audience spontaneously throws the cushions from their seats into the ring.

'To enter the sumo profession is to enter a life segregated from family and the rest of society'

Imagine the thunder of hooves during the 2008 Melbourne Cup. Trained by Bart Cummings, Viewed, with jockey Blake Shinn, eventually brings it home by a nose.

MELBOURNE CUP

WHERE Melbourne, Australia **WHEN** First Tuesday in November **GETTING INVOLVED** Join the 100,000-plus others at the race (ticketing info online) or find a big telly (say, Federation Square's screen) at around 3.20pm.

Melburnians love it. And not just because it's a public holiday. The Melbourne Cup is the epitome of the 'fair go' ethos that permeates the Australian identity. It's the only race with international credibility that is a handicap contest – adjusting the weight each thoroughbred carries to give each horse a more equal chance of winning. You don't need to be rich and famous to own a Cup winner (although you will be after it wins); past winners have been owned by school teachers, fishermen and fruit sellers. And everyone can go to the Cup.

More than 100,000 people flock to Flemington Racecourse on cup day, arriving by car, train, tram, boat and helicopter. About half make it to the course, while the other half picnic in the car park. Fashion is a serious undertaking. Each year at least 40,000 ladies' hats and 30,000 pairs of shoes are sold to complete Cup outfits. While racewear imitates Ascot each year, there are perennial outfits worn to the Melbourne Cup seldom seen at other world-class events. Tuxedo jackets are often teamed with shorts and a pair of RM Williams boots, and there are popes, gorillas and various other themed get-ups.

The Melbourne Cup, watched by 700 million people in more than 170 countries, is the feature event of the Spring Racing Carnival, which runs through October and culminates with the Cup. The 3.2km Cup was first staged in 1861. It brings the entire country to a standstill for the three-or-so minutes during which the race is run. The city's once-a-year gamblers come out and form syndicates with other punters, and every television or radio is tuned to the race. And if you're looking for a tip: check the trainer. If it's Bart Cummings, who has trained a record 12 cup winners, you're in with a fighting chance.

MORE INFO Racing Victoria (www.racing.victoria.net.au)

LUCHA LIBRE

WHERE Mexico **WHEN** Year-round **GETTING INVOLVED** Check the websites for event details and ticketing info.

They're like real-life comic-book heroes, in the ring at least, where *luchadores* undertake high-flying antics, perform good-guy–bad-guy routines with loose plot lines, and conceal their true identities behind colourful masks.

The mask is the most immediately identifiable characteristic of Mexican wrestling. The elaborate *mascaras* represent each wrestler's identity and removing an opponent's mask is tantamount to disqualification. While most wrestlers wear masks, those that don't have no face, as such, to lose, so are required to put their hair on the line – committing to shave their head if beaten by their masked opponent as a symbol of humiliation.

Apart from the masks, the high-flying leaps of *luchadores* also distinguish Mexican wrestling. The stunning aerial displays are performed by catapulting from the ropes around the ring. While there are loads of weight categories into which wrestlers fall, they also fall into good-guy *(tecnico)* or bad-guy *(rudo)* categories. *Rudos* tend to be brawlers and bend the rules, though never enough to break the code of conduct, which is considered worse than losing your mask. The winning *luchadore* is the one who holds down his opponent for the three-count or forces his opponent into submission.

Tournaments take a number of formats, but generally are either a three-man tag team elimination match or individual elimination. The main event organisers and promoters are the Consejo Mundial de Lucha Libre (CMLL) and the Asistencia Asosoria y Administración (AAA). Mexico has the largest number of wrestlers in the world, so it shouldn't be hard to find some masked folk hero action when you're next there.

MORE INFO Consejo Mundial de Lucha Libre (www.cmll.com, in Spanish) and Asistencia Asosoria y Administracion (www.luchalibreaaa.com, in Spanish)

WORLD NETBALL CHAMPIONSHIPS

WHERE Location changes each championship **WHEN** Every four years **GETTING INVOLVED** Check the website for event details and ticketing info.

It's the top competition in the most prominent women's sport. Held every four years since 1963, the World Netball Championships bring together the world's best teams. In that time, the Australian national team, known as the Diamonds, has dominated the competition – winning nine of the 12 tournaments.

With its many similarities, netball was originally called women's basketball. It was instituted in the USA in 1895 by Clara Baer, a PE teacher with an interest in basketball – which had been invented a few years earlier by James Naismith, for male students. When Clara received the rules from Naismith, which included a sketch of the court, Clara misinterpreted the lines Naismith had drawn. The sketched lines indicated the areas where various players would be strongest, but Clara interpreted the lines to mean that players were not allowed outside of these areas, inadvertently inventing zones.

The other main differences between netball and basketball are the no-dribble and no-running rule. These moves were purportedly too difficult for women (who at the time wore long bustled skirts), and so were removed from the women's version of the game.

Netball was first played in England in 1895 at a women's college, and quickly spread to Commonwealth countries, including Australia, Jamaica and Antigua. In 1960 representatives from England, Australia, New Zealand, South Africa and the West Indies met to formalise the rules and establish the International Federation of Women's Basketball. It was here that the decision was made to hold a quadrennial competition for associated members, known as the World Netball Championships.

MORE INFO International Federation of Netball Associations (IFNA; www.netball.org)

NOVEMBER
WEEK.02

AND ANOTHER THING

Woz Challenge Cup (location changes annually)

It's an international polo tournament minus the chardonnay and handsome steeds. In the Woz Challenge, named after Apple's co-founder Stever Wozniak, all players are on Segways – two-wheeled upright personal transporters. Played by four teams consisting of five players each, Segway polo simply involves teams trying to score goals by hitting the ball from atop their Segways. (www.segwayhtpolo.com)

High speed stoush: red-clad Princess Slay-Ya of the Kansas City Roller Warriors trips Angela Death of the Denver Roller Dolls in Denver in 2007.

WFTDA CHAMPIONSHIP TOURNAMENT, NORTHWEST KNOCKDOWN

 WHERE Portland, Oregon, USA **WHEN** Second week of November
GETTING INVOLVED Check the website for the latest schedule and
ticketing info

Combining elements of high-camp kitsch, rockabilly, feminism, burlesque
and even wrestling, roller derby has something for everyone. It's high-energy
entertainment that involves two teams of costumed ladies attempting to out-
skate one another, and dirty play is encouraged, within reason. Roller derbies are
enjoying a major revival in the US, with a long history that includes endurance
skating, racing and dance-a-thons.

During the Depression, the dance-a-thon format attracted huge numbers of
participants – all hoping to shuffle their way through days of 'dancing' to win cash.
Take that format and add in the potential danger of high-speed roller skating and
you have a successful entertainment-sport formula.

The revival was swift, with 80-odd all-female leagues springing up in around
three years. Although they are all self-organised, the majority of leagues adhere
to the rules according to the Women's Flat Track Derby Association, which
organises inter-league competitions like the regional Northwest Knockdown. The
rules go a little something like this: a team is made up of five with three blockers
(defence), one pivot (the last line of defence, distinguished by a stripe on her
helmet) and a jammer (or scorer, with two stars on her helmet). To begin, all but
the jammers of both teams form a pack and must stay in the pack at all times.
Once the pack has done a lap of the oval-shaped circuit, the ref blows a whistle
to signal that it's time for the jam. The jam is a two-minute countdown during
which the jammer tries to overtake the pack, while being bumped and obstructed
by the opposition's defence. Each time a jammer passes the pack she earns their
team a point. Are you still with us? It's confusing to watch too, but generally the
more bumps and dramatics there are, the happier is the audience.

Throughout its history, roller derby has struggled to maintain its legitimacy.
Although it thrives on theatrics and a certain churlish charm, it has staunchly
resisted the temptation to fall into fake drama. Instead, the theatricality is
expressed in the characters. Rollergirls often adopt a character and an alias that
oozes sardonic wit, a la Anna Mosity and Skid'n'Nancy.

MORE INFO Women's Flat Track Derby Association (www.wftda.com), Northwest
Knockdown (www.northwestknockdown.com)

*'Although it thrives on theatrics and a certain
churlish charm, roller derby has staunchly
resisted fake drama'*

NOVEMBER
WEEK.03

FOR THE RECORD
- - - - - - - - - - - - - - -

↗ Wearing of helmets became
compulsory in the 1960s to
maintain the sport's integrity.

↗ The Roller Derby revival is
spreading, with leagues
forming in both England and
Australia.

The outfits are a bit much, but the breakfast more than makes up for it – elephants at the Surin Round-Up enjoy a feast of some 60,000kg of fruit.

ASIAN GYMNASTICS CHAMPIONSHIPS

WHERE Location changes each championship **WHEN** Late November **GETTING INVOLVED** Check the website for scheduling and ticketing details.

Seeing gymnasts leap, somersault, twist and bend the way only gymnasts can has a mesmerising thrall for the spectator, like watching another species entirely. And gymnasts are a particular breed, particularly women: small-framed, petit, pixie-like. It figures, scientifically, that it's easier to throw yourself around if you're of a lighter frame.

Officially known as artistic gymnastics, this is the most prominent form of the sport. Involving various purpose-designed apparatus, men and women display almost super-human flexibility, agility, precision and plain guts – it takes a brave person to run full-speed at a solid object, and, the millisecond before impact, to spring onto it and contort the body into various shapes before landing solidly on the other side on two feet. That's the vault, which is more recently called the tongue or table after the wider-shaped apparatus used since 2001. Other events include the floor, in which both men and women compete, performing choreographed routines (women to instrumental music); the pommel horse, in which men with arms made of steel fling their legs about with humbling agility; and the uneven bars performed by women who swing their bodies between two horizontal bars set at different heights. There is also the rings (men), balance beam (women) and horizontal bar (men).

Around 250 gymnasts from 20-odd countries compete in the Asian Championships, in team and individual events. There are qualifying rounds and finals, and each performance is judged according to the 'new life rule' in which every performance is stand-alone – not dependent on previous performances. Two panels of judges assess different aspects of each performance. One gauges the degree of difficulty and looks for technical elements, the other assesses execution, composition and artistry; both scores combine to give the final score. Apart from regional competitions, gymnastics is also well represented in world events such as the Olympics. **MORE INFO** Federation Internationale de Gymnastique (www.fig-gymnastics.com)

SURIN ELEPHANT ROUND-UP

WHERE Surin, Thailand **WHEN** Third weekend in November **GETTING INVOLVED** As the festivities run for a week, people arrive in dribs and drabs; getting there is no problem. Book transport back to Bangkok early.

As far as sports goes, this event has elements of competitive eating, football and ironman. More of a display sport, the 300 or so elephants that participate in the Surin Elephant Round-Up are earning their keep. With shrinking natural habitat and less work available, many of Thailand's elephants are forced to perform to make a living.

It's no dancing-bear routine though; these animals are generally revered. The elephant breakfast, usually on the Friday morning, is a huge smorgasbord. Fruits and vegetables line the street for these gentle giants to feast on, and any leftovers are taken home by the locals for themselves.

Thousands of Thais and travellers stampede into provincial Surin for the show, which demonstrates these working elephants' skills and strength, as well as honours their role in Thai history. You'll see elephant football, obstacle courses in which elephants sprint and pick up objects, and tugs of war that pit an elephant against 70 soldiers. There are demonstrations of log pulling, a job for which elephants were once commonly employed, and re-enactments of old hunting and war scenes featuring vintage costumes. The trunk-waving finishes with an eight-act play about elephants: their role in royal traditions, war and work. It typically features hundreds of elephants and thousands of human performers.

Located some 450km northeast of Bangkok, near the Cambodian border, Surin is famous for its festival, and for its locals who are skilled *mahouts* (elephant handlers). After the festival, slip over the border to Cambodia and visit world-famous Angkor Wat and Prasat Preah Vihear.

MORE INFO Tourism Authority of Thailand (www.tourismthailand.org)

WORLD SENIOR KARATE CHAMPIONSHIPS

WHERE Location changes each championship **WHEN** Biennially, mid- to late November **GETTING INVOLVED** Check the website for scheduling and ticketing information.

If only you could see inside the karateka's mind. It's there that the other half of the competition is waged. Karate practice is as much about mental adeptness as physical agility and precision. Of the myriad martial arts, karate is primarily characterised by linear punching and kicking movements, while the rest of the body remains in a stable fixed stance. But a decisive and almost intuitive demeanor also characterises karate.

Gichin Funakoshi, the father of karate, said that 'the ultimate aim of karate lies not in victory or defeat, but in the perfection of the character of its participants'. He encouraged practitioners to have a clear conscience, to be courteous, humble and determined. So, as well as seeing some impressive karate moves at the world championships, you can rest assured that they're all nice fellows, too.

Sport karate differs from the martial-art practice of karate, foremost in that sport karate deliberately looks for a fight. The everyday practice of karate is essentially opposed to conflict. At a world championship level, protective gear is compulsory, including mitts, shin pads and mouthguard. The two areas of competition are in the kata events, which involve a sequence of movements that are assessed by a panel of judges, and the kumite events, which are sparring competitions with points awarded to karatekas by a referee. Sparring partners are matched according to weight and age. The refs are karate masters, able to recognise the thinking behind particular moves.

MORE INFO World Karate Federation (www.karateworld.org)

01.

02.

04.

'To win one hundred victories in one hundred battles is not the highest skill. To subdue the enemy without fighting is the highest skill.'

- - - - - - - - - - - - - - - - -

Master Gichin Funakoshi, father of karate

↗ Muhammad Ali is the only man to have won the linear heavyweight championship three times.

↗ Amateur boxing features in the Olympic Games, in which boxers must wear protective head-gear, matches run to four rounds and are scored according to skill rather than damage inflicted.

HEAVYWEIGHT BOXING

 WHERE Primarily the USA, but also England **WHEN** Intermittent; check the website **GETTING INVOLVED** Check one of the major boxing organisation's websites for up-to-date scheduling and ticketing info.

The raw bare-chested bouts of professional boxing matches are about as elemental as a sport can get. In the same way that humans crowd around an accident scene or pub brawl, organised fights attract thousands of frenetically engrossed onlookers, particularly when the combatants are in the heavyweight category (more than 90kg), wear no protective head-gear and intend to inflict physical harm on one another, ideally, by knocking their opponent unconscious.

Partly because of its finality, but also due to its drama, the knockout is the preferred way to end a fight. Fights generally consist of up to 12 rounds of three-minute bouts. If both boxers go the distance, without being knocked out or sustaining injuries that the

'Partly because of its finality, but also due to its drama, the knockout is the preferred way to end a fight'

NOVEMBER
WEEK.04

Sweat, saliva and dreams of victory fly as heavyweight boxers Jameel McCline (L) and Michael Anthony Mollo Jr, both of the USA, take to one another in a 2008 WBC elimination round.

referee deems to put the boxer in danger if he were to continue fighting (a technical knockout), then the winner is nominated by the referee and/or judges. There are generally three judges who score the number of punches that connect, defence movements and knockdowns. From inside the ring, the referee stays close to the action and ensures that all fighting is legal, according to the Marquess of Queensberry Rules.

Instituted in 1867, the 12 rules basically ensure a fair fight. They also revolutionised the sport by introducing the compulsory wearing of gloves, which placed more emphasis on defensive fighting and altered the fighter's stance. Bare-knuckle fighters had a backwards lean with arms straight out, which was replaced by a forwards lean with the hands closer to the face.

The in-fighting between professional boxing's sanctioning bodies is almost as fierce as the fist fighting that goes on in the ring. With four organisations claiming to be *the* major sanctioning body for the sport, the famous cry of 'heavyweight champion of the world' is never heard these days. The modern-day western boxing (as the sport is also known) champion is now known as the 'undisputed champion'.

The most respected and indisputable way to win the title of world champion is to win the linear championship. By this method, the fighter beats the current world champion title holder, who beat the current world champion title holder and so on, which can be traced back to an almost unbroken 100-year history.

MORE INFO International Boxing Federation (IBF; www.ibf-usba-boxing.com), World Boxing Association (WBA; www.wbaonline.com), World Boxing Council (WBC; www.wbcboxing.com), World Boxing Organization (WBO; www.wbo-int.com)

FLANDERS SYNCHRO OPEN

WHERE Kortrijk, Belgium **WHEN** Last weekend in November **GETTING INVOLVED** Check the website for ticketing details.

Like a human kaleidoscope, brightly coloured beings slip through the water in such deliberate lines to form perfect patterns. In synchronised swimming group events, individuals become one very attractive amorphous and constantly moving mass. To the spectator it may seem like those swimmers jutting out of the water in a perfectly straight line are not moving, which is part of their skill – we never see the 'egg beater' treading-water motion below the water.

Synchronised swimming owes much to Hollywood star of the 1950s, Esther Williams. The graceful moves and glinting smile of this doyenne of the pool helped to define the era as wholesome, artful and elegant. She famously broke her neck (but survived) during a dive while filming MGM's *Million Dollar Mermaid*, she had numerous burst eardrums and an enviable set of lungs that could keep her underwater for minutes. But she always came up smiling, coiffed and composed – the signature of a synchro swimmer.

Part swimming, part gymnastics, synchronised swimming competitions are judged according to the artistry of the routine, as well as the technical proficiency with which it is performed. Swimmers generally perform two routines: one predetermined and one freestyle. There are obviously team events, but also duets and solos – in which the swimmers are synchronised with the music, rather than with each other.

The Flanders Open competition is unique in that the maximum age for competitors is 13 years. An international competition, recognised by the European governing body (LEN), it's here that you're likely to see future Olympians. The program includes a St Nicolas (better known as Santa) celebration in which delegates do a little dance routine to earn their presents.

MORE INFO Flanders Synchro Open (www.flanders-synchro-open.be), Ligue Européenne de Natation (LEN; www.lenweb.org)

NOVEMBER WEEK.04

UNDERWATER HOCKEY

WHERE Location changes **WHEN** Check the websites for competition details **GETTING INVOLVED** Underwater hockey is a better participatory sport; look for a local aquatic club or check out the rules online and form your own.

Some sports are simply more spectator-friendly than others. Underwater hockey would have to be one of the least friendly to watch, seeing as all the action takes place at the bottom of a pool. But if you're a diver looking for something to do in the off-season, which is how underwater hockey came about, then this could be just the sort of action you're looking for.

Also called octopush (in England: 'octo' for the eight players that originally comprised a side and 'push' for the pushing motion of the stick), the rules are fairly straightforward whereby two teams of six players attempt to push a lead puck through its opposition's goal. All players wear diving masks, snorkels and gloves (to guard against scraping the bottom of the pool) and carry a 35cm stick. There are usually two referees in the pool with the players, plus one or two poolside who keep score and track of the time and substitute players.

A recent schism resulted in two international bodies governing the sport. As if promoting a sport that no one can see wasn't hard enough, competitions organised by the two bodies seem to conflict time-wise, which reduces the number of supporters and participants at each – split into two comps as they now are. International events are run every two years, but there are numerous local organisations and comps with which to get involved. A surprisingly high number of cities around the world play, so there's likely to be one nearby.

MORE INFO World Aquachallenge Association (www.thewaa.org), Confederation Mondiale des Activities Subaquatics (www.cmas.org)

AND ANOTHER THING

- - - - - - - - - - - - - - - -

Cannabis Cup (Amsterdam, Netherlands)

The Cannabis Cup pre-empted the whole public-vote thing by decades when it created a festival in which the public voted for the best weed or hash. Started by the editor of NY-based magazine *High Times* (supposedly modelled on *Playboy*, but for recreational drug users), the festival has been going strong since 1987. It costs 250 euro at the door, and visitors (aka judges) are expected to vote on the weed, which is supplied by the local legal coffee shops. (www.hightimes.com/public/cancup)

ASIAN GAMES

WHERE Location changes each games **WHEN** Every four years **GETTING INVOLVED** Check the website for scheduling and ticketing details.

This gigantic event provides a platform for around 50 Asian countries to compete in a range of sports. Many disciplines familiar to other regions are represented, such as swimming, cycling, gymnastics and weightlifting. But it's the uniquely Asian events that are generally of most interest. Competitive dragon boat races (p88) involve long, thin decorated boats packed with a crew. Twenty rowers sit tightly in pairs, while a drummer at the front of the boat sets the pace and a steerer at the rear keeps them on course. You could also catch all the action of a kabaddi (p18) match, sepak takraw competition (p128) or wushu competition. Wushu is the Chinese martial art made famous by Jet Li; it takes two forms at competition level: the non-contact gymnastics-like routine *(taolu)* or full-contact fighting method *(sando)*. Chess is often an official event, along with dancesport (p27) and roller skating.

The games were first held in 1952, but were born out of a much smaller event, the Far Eastern Championship Games, which were held since 1913 and organised to promote harmony between the Asian nations. They, naturally, became defunct in 1938 when Japan invaded China, sparking the expansion of WWII in the Pacific. The Asian Games has had its political hiccups in the past too, mainly with some member countries opposing the inclusion of Israel (now excluded), but the games continue to promote goodwill. Run under the auspices of the Olympic Council of Asia, other regional games include Winter, Indoor, Beach, Youth and Martial Arts Games. **MORE INFO** Olympic Council of Asia (www.ocasia.org/Game)

Indonesian striker Husni Uba (L) goes head over heels in the sepak takraw men's double at the 2006 Asian Games in Doha, Qatar.

FOR THE RECORD

↗ All HWC players are first-timers (so may not have competed in previous tournaments). It's just as well then that a large percentage of ex-players don't qualify as homeless by the time the next tournament comes around. Organisers estimate that 73% of players change their lives for the better, moving into jobs, education, homes, training, reuniting with families, and coming off drugs.

HOMELESS WORLD CUP

WHERE Location changes each cup **WHEN** Dates from year to year are radically different, any time from July to December **GETTING INVOLVED** Matches are not ticketed and are free; however donations are welcomed year-round. To play, contact your local team – details online.

From the shadows of government-housing towers in Australia to a patch of dirt in the backblocks of Zambia, street football players turn up to training. An estimated 25,000 people around the world, from more than 56 countries, call that designated training patch home every week – turning up from whatever makeshift or temporary housing that shelters them, to physically work out, hone their skills and work as a team. Ultimately, they're working to represent their country, whose team will travel together to take part in the Homeless World Cup.

Unlike other world cups, this one is played annually and the standard of play varies wildly. But the same passion is present. All players are either homeless, in drug

01. 02. 03. 04.

'All players have come from experiencing significant hardship to representing their country in a world event'

DECEMBER
WEEK.01

Melbourne's architecturally diverse Federation Square holds a sea of supporters cheering on Russia and Afghanistan in the men's final of the 2008 Homeless World Cup.

rehabilitation (and have experienced homelessness in the preceding years) or are asylum seekers. They've come from experiencing significant day-to-day hardship to representing their country in a world event. The tournament lifts them out of obscurity and onto a world stage where they are cheered rather than jeered and rewarded for the great personal effort they've put in over the preceding year of training.

Makeshift stadiums pop up in the streets of the host city during the week of the tournament. Often, there are three separate stadiums – which is what it takes to stage 400 matches in such a short space of time. Three rounds play out: the preliminary and secondary rounds determine the six categories in which the teams will play, while the final round sees teams playing for their respective cups. Each category has its own mini competition, with the top eight teams playing for

the Homeless World Cup and teams ranked 33 to 40 playing for the Community Cup; the intervening four categories have their own cup.

There are four players per team, which can be all-male, all-female or mixed, who play on a pitch that's just 22m by 16m. Games are 15 minutes long, so the action is fast and never far away. Given the short bursts of play, you could sit for an hour and catch four games – all guaranteed to be wildly different – or flit from pitch to pitch. As with most world events, there are usually arts and cultural events staged in association with the cup, which may include anything from film nights and public lectures to parkour demonstrations.
MORE INFO Homeless World Cup (www.homelessworldcup.org)

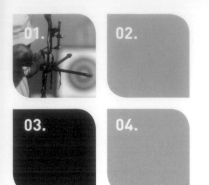

01.

02.

03.

04.

KING'S CUP

WHERE Bangkok, Thailand **WHEN** 4 and 5 December **GETTING INVOLVED** All-inclusive packages are generally offered, which guarantee not only a seat, but good seats.

It has all the intensity and violence of a world heavyweight boxing title fight and more – the equivalent of each boxer fighting with eight fists. Known as the 'art of eight limbs', muay thai (Thai boxing or kick-boxing) moves incredibly fast: fighters *(nak muay)* strike and block using their gloved fists, elbows, knees and shins. Within seconds, the two bare-chested bodies have exchanged straight punches, elbow slashes, jump kicks, knee slaps and reverse foot thrusts. Each round lasts for three minutes, and fighters go five rounds with their opponent. The fight ends when one of the *nak muay* is knocked out, technically knocked out (deemed to be in bad shape by the ref) or at the end of the five rounds. If both fighters are still standing, then the winner is the fighter who landed the most blows, who was the more aggressive fighter and who used the most counter-defence moves (ie ones that don't just block an attacking strike, but that simultaneously cause damage to the opponent). Like in western boxing, fighters are matched according to weight category.

Before every fight, *nak muay* show their respect for their teachers and positive influences by performing a series of movements to traditional music in the ring. They then return to their corners where their teachers utter an incantation, blow on their foreheads three times and ceremonially remove the headband given to them when they graduated as *nak muay*.

The international King's Cup commemorates the Thai king's birthday, so attracts an enormous crowd. Before the fight is the candle-lighting ceremony. Considering the hundreds of thousands of people that turn up with candles aloft, it's fortunate His Majesty doesn't have to blow them out.

There are regular top-level bouts, including 17 March, which is National Muay Thai Day. **MORE INFO** World Muay Thai Council (www.wmcmuaythai.org)

DECEMBER
WEEK.01

WOMEN'S WORLD SQUASH CHAMPIONSHIPS

WHERE Location changes each championship **WHEN** Biennial, from late November to early December **GETTING INVOLVED** Tickets are easy to come by online.

Its heritage is humbling in its longevity, which has bounced through 14th-century monasteries, prison life and English public schools. Squash is a hybrid of a number of racquet sports. At its most basic level, it evolved from hitting a ball up against a wall. The monks of the 16th century weren't alone in pursuit of that solitary activity (who hasn't whiled away a few hours as a youngster with a ball and a wall?) Only the monks used webbed mitts, which developed into racquets at the notorious 18th-century Fleet Prison (where bankrupts were incarcerated). More recently, squash became a popular school sport, with various rule variations, which weren't standardised until the early 20th century.

Squash players are renowned for their superior athleticism – running around inside a human-sized terrarium will earn you a reputation for fitness. At this level, too, strategic deceptive shots are frequently played, which have the opposition running all over the court. Long rallies, lasting up to 30 shots, draw out the tension to breaking point. The ball, whose squishy nature informs the name of the game, comes in various degrees of bounce – to account for temperature and skill level. At competition level, a super-slow yellow double-dot ball is used, which characteristically dies in the corners rather than sitting up to allow for easy slam shots.

The World Squash Federation officiates over a number of international competitions, including the Women's World Championships, which attracts players from around 20 countries, including the highest ranking in the world.
MORE INFO World Squash Federation (www.worldsquash.org.uk)

'You are never really playing an opponent. You are playing yourself, your own highest standards, and when you reach your limits, that is real joy.'

– – – – – – – – – – – – – – –

Arthur Ashe, tennis player

HOCKEY CHAMPIONS TROPHY

WHERE Location changes each year **WHEN** Changes annually, but often November or December
GETTING INVOLVED Tickets are readily available; check online for details.

Bedecked in royal orange, a Dutch player lunges forward during a 2008 match against Germany.

If it weren't for the Champions Trophy, hockey fans would only see the world's best teams clash every four years. Apart from the Olympics and the World Cup, the Champions Trophy is hockey's most prestigious competition, and it happens annually. Without it, we'd have to fill the ensuing years with hockey in its various other guises: on ice (p90), roller skates or underwater (p186). But, here, we have pure field hockey, where the top six men's teams in the world compete in a round-robin format on a field outdoors. Twenty-two top-ranking athletes clash sticks each game, each trying to thwack, push or putt the ball through the opposition's goal, which is fiercely guarded by a man wearing the equivalent of modern-day armour.

Basically known as 'the ball and stick game', references to hockey date back around 4000 years, with evidence to suggest it was played in ancient Rome, Scotland, Egypt and South America. It seems picking up a stick and hitting a ball around against an opponent comes as naturally to humans as putting one foot in front of the other. In 17th- and 18th-century England, the entire male population of neighbouring villages would clash, with hundreds of players hitting a ball around for weeks on end. It goes without saying that there was no 'sticks' rule back then either. The modern game developed primarily in English schools in the early 20th century. The sport underwent a dramatic change with the introduction of artificial turf in the 1970s – which changed the speed at which the ball travelled, leading to new tactics, techniques and rules.

MORE INFO International Hockey Federation (www.fihockey.org)

Helmets reflecting the luge ahead, American bobsleigh team Shauna Rohbock and Valerie Fleming launch their craft.

BOBSLEIGH SKELETON WORLD CHAMPIONSHIPS

WHERE Location changes each championship **WHEN** Annually, except in a Winter Olympic year; dates are variable each year depending on the host, and can be anywhere from October through to March
GETTING INVOLVED Tickets are available online.

Of all the events at multi-sport showstoppers, like the Winter Olympics, it's the sliding sports that are among the most popular. Maybe it's due to the fact that most people can relate, having skidded down a grassy knoll, sand dune or snow-covered slope on an Esky lid at some stage in their childhood. So, seeing the skill and speed of elite sliders is awesome.

Skeleton is an individual event for men and women who compete in separate categories. The simple aim is to reach the finishing line in the quickest time. But there are sharp twists and turns in the track, which becomes rougher and harder to handle as the day progresses. There's also nothing with which to steer; sliders shift their legs and shoulders to adjust their weight on the sled and alter its direction. Wearing aerodynamic helmets, spiked shoes and skin-tight speedsuits that look like they've been painted on, sliders take a running start, pushing their sleds for about 15m before leaping on them: head first and face down. These first 50m are crucial for sliders; finishing times are differentiated by hundredths of a second, so they need to be up to speed right from the start.

Bobsleigh (or bobsled), in comparison, is a team event: two-man, four-man or two-woman. Each team has a standing start, whereby they push the sled, and consists of a braker and a pilot who steers the sleigh via a mechanism rigged up to the two front steel runners. Bobsleighs are more pod-like: semi-enclosed and with the competitors in a supine position. Bobsleighs use the same runs as the skeletons.

It's exhilarating to watch, with 130km/h speeds on the straights the norm. In world competitions, such as the World Championships and World Cup, four heats are run over two days. Being positioned earlier in the day, before the track deteriorates, is advantageous for athletes. The running order is decided according to world rank – the higher ranked athletes are the first to go.

It's hard to believe watching the precision of each millisecond at world competition level that it all started with a couple of English wags on holiday pushing their friends around on the delivery boys' sleds. It was in St Moritz that, to protect his guests from errant sledders, the resort owner constructed the first run in 1903, which is still in use today and one of the last remaining natural tracks.
MORE INFO Federation Internationale de Bobsleigh et de Tobogganing (FIBT; www.fibt.com)

'Wearing aerodynamic helmets and spiked shoes, sliders take a running start before leaping on their sleds: head first and face down'

DECEMBER
WEEK.02

FOR THE RECORD

- - - - - - - - - - - - - - - - -

↗ Along with its stunning beaches and breathtaking coral reefs, the Caribbean island of Jamaica also has a bobsled team, which was the crowd favourite at the 1988 Winter Olympics.

↗ The fastest bobsleigh speed was clocked at just more than 200km/h.

GRAND PIGEON RACE

WHERE Thailand **WHEN** 11 December **GETTING INVOLVED** Check online for entry and pricing details.

Take one large cage, add two mixed martial arts fighters, and stir – there may be a couple of rules in this particular fight club, but being nice is not one of them.

In many Western cities, they're a pest, with councils spending thousands to remove them, but to fanciers all over the world, pigeons are remarkable birds. Nobody is sure how homing pigeons can navigate their way back home from a strange place far away that they've never been to before. And most people never knew the important role in communications pigeons played: that's how Reuters press agency got its start, with a fleet of 45 pigeons. And then there are the racing pigeons; the thoroughbreds of the avian world who are specially trained and bred to fly home fast.

Once the domain of old folks who kept a few birds as a hobby, the sport of pigeon racing was recently reinvigorated with the introduction of one loft races. Favoured for their ability to test the breed of a bird, rather than its training, these races allow breeders from around the world to compete. Thailand's Grand Pigeon Race started in 2008, and is a gruelling 560km flight from Chiang Mai, in the hills, to Bangkok. The humid conditions favour small- to medium-sized birds (in case you were thinking of entering), and first prize is a hefty €24,000 – although all birds become the property of the organisers.

Before being transported to the starting coup and released en masse, which is quite a sight (and an alarming one if you've been forever scarred by Hitchcock's *The Birds*), the pigeons are fitted with microchips. The scanner that's fitted at the entrance to the home coup automatically reads each pigeon's identifying chip the millisecond it lands home. The fastest bird wins.

Researchers differ in their theories on how exactly pigeons' physiology enables them to find home. Most agree that they orient by the sun, but theories tend to differ at the suggestion that they all use magnetic fields. Some researchers believe pigeons use sight to navigate, following roads and manmade structures in the same way as humans do.

MORE INFO Thailand Grand Pigeon Race (www.thailandoneloftrace.com)

ULTIMATE FIGHTER FINALE

 WHERE USA **WHEN** Regular matches throughout the year **GETTING INVOLVED** Tickets are available online.

Cage fighting is not really a sport you'd want to take your mother to. Well-built fighters wearing only gloves, shorts and tattoos combine moves from any number of martial arts, including judo, ju-jitsu, karate, kickboxing and wrestling – the ultimate fight. Made even more so apparently by the fact that it takes place on an octagonal mat behind a cyclone-wire 'cage'.

Fighters fight in various weight categories for five rounds of five minutes each. As with western and Thai boxing, the fight ends with a knockout or technical knockout or at the end of the five rounds with the winner being the fighter with the highest score. Bouts are judged, with points awarded for each strike (be it delivered with the hands, the feet, elbows or knees) and for grappling (choke holds, throws, takedowns – that sort of thing).

Made for television, ultimate fighting began in 1993 in the USA when the Ultimate Fighting Championship organisation hosted a cable-TV show that televised the bouts They were promoted as no holds-barred fights, with very few rules. Since then, more limitations to the amount of damage a man can do to another (especially on TV) have been instituted in an effort to bring some integrity to the sport and to protect the fighters. No eye-gouging, biting, small joint manipulation or fish-hooking is tolerated. Each fight features the obligatory MC-type dude who constantly yells in an effort to whip up the crowd. That's also the job of the Octagon Girls who stand around in bikinis looking pretty. **MORE INFO** Ultimate Fighting Championship (www.ufc.com)

WORLD ARM-WRESTLING CHAMPIONSHIPS

 WHERE Location changes each championship **WHEN** Changes annually, but often November or December **GETTING INVOLVED** Build up your fighting arm's bicep, forearm, wrist and hand. Check the website for an up-to-date schedule.

It takes technique to be an arm-wrestling champ. Sure, forearms like Popeye's are desirable, but it's what you do with them that counts. There are two offensive techniques in arm-wrestling: the top roll and the hook. The top roll is an attempt to move the opponent's arm into a weaker position, about a fist-width between the bicep and forearm. This is achieved by rolling the wrist over the top of the opponent's while exerting downward pressure. From here it's just a case of walking the fingers further up the opponent's hand, exerting pressure again, and slamming it home. The hook is like a karate chop to the opponent's wrist – where the wrestler curls their wrist suddenly, attempting to take out the strength in the opponent's hand. The bicep is strictly a defensive muscle, anchoring the arm to the table and resisting the opponent's force.

One tactic to which arm-wrestlers with any kind of nous adhere is to maintain a directed gaze, with the eyes always looking at the hands. To look away could spell disaster. Ask anyone who has heard the sound of an arm break during a wrestle. Looking away forces the shoulder to follow the neck – away from behind the arm where it's needed. Keep it in mind next time you're challenged to an arm-wrestle at the pub or even after a disagreement at Christmas dinner.

There are official tournaments at every level, from regionals to world competitions, with opponents paired according to weight category. **MORE INFO** World of Armwrestling (www.worldofarmwrestling.com)

DECEMBER WEEK.02

AND ANOTHER THING

Action Asia Challenge (Hong Kong)

With a 3am start 'to ensure at least three hours of competition in the dark', the Action Challenge is a multi-discipline event that covers 70km requiring contestants to run, rock-scramble, mountain bike, kayak, abseil and read maps. Then there are the 'special tests of courage, skill, local culture and teamwork'. Still interested? Applications are available online. (www. actionasiaevents.com)

FOR THE RECORD

- - - - - - - - - - - - - - -

↗ Legendary surfer Sunny Garcia won a record five Triple Crown titles.

↗ In 2008, two Australians took out the title: Joel Parkinson and Stephanie Gilmore.

TRIPLE CROWN OF SURFING

 WHERE Hawaii **WHEN** Comprises three separate comps back to back, from mid-November through to mid-December **GETTING INVOLVED** Tickets are available on the day of competition.

It would have to be the only sport with such a wildly variable playing field – the ocean is an unpredictable entity. Although on Oahu's North Shore every winter it tends to throw up predictably huge waves, up to five stories high, which is why you'll find the world's top surfers here every year. The Triple Crown is a series of three separate competitions. There are individual winners of each, plus the Triple Crown for the best surfer across all three.

The series was first organised in 1983, bringing together three pre-existing local events. The Hawaiian Pro kicks things off, followed by the World Cup then, the grand finale, the Pipeline Masters – running since 1971. Not only is the Masters a World

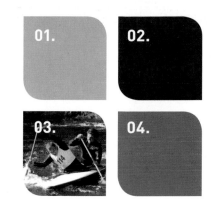

01.   02.

03.   04.

'Watching a surfer disappear into the mouth of one of these monsters, only to re-emerge moments later, is awesome'

DECEMBER
WEEK.03

There must be an easier way to arrive at Hawaii's Sunset Beach, but Greg Emslie does it in style while competing in the 2008 World Cup of Surfing.

Championship title (the other two are qualifiers), it's arguably the most spectacular to watch. The Banzai Pipeline beach break consistently produces 8ft to 10ft waves that arch up into massive tubes over a barely submerged reef. Watching a surfer disappear into the mouth of one of these monsters, only to re-emerge moments later, victorious, is simply awesome. The preceding World Cup is held at Sunset Beach, notorious for a wall of water that crunches surfers and holds them down for excruciatingly long periods. The main break is in deep water several hundred metres out (bring binoculars). By contrast, Haleiwa (the Hawaiian Pro venue) peaks just 90m out. Its main break sections off across a reef to a shallow inside section of reef known as the Toilet Bowl.

Generally, surfers are allowed three or four waves. Their rides are judged and scored (out of 10) according to the size of the wave, the distance ridden and the quality of manoeuvres performed during each ride. Success at the Triple Crown augurs well for success at the Association of Surfing Professionals (ASP) World Championship title – the highest level of competition.

The variety of conditions is considered the proving ground for pro surfers, both men and women (who were included in the competition in 1997). What the Triple Crown doesn't have in world ranking points and prize money, it more than makes up for in kudos – the winner considered to be the most proficient big-wave rider in the world. There's also the inherent cachet of the competition being held in the birthplace of surfing – Hawaii.

MORE INFO Triple Crown of Surfing (www.triplecrownofsurfing. com), Association of Professional Surfing (www.aspworldtour.com)

MONSTER TRUCKS

WHERE USA **WHEN** Year-round **GETTING INVOLVED** Tickets are available online.

Monster truck racing is the spectacle of pick-up trucks fitted with humongous wheels drag racing on a course littered with really big things to run over – aeroplanes, cars, that sort of thing. As a sport, monster truck racing didn't really come into its own until the late '80s. For more than a decade before that, it served as a kind-of half-time entertainment for the more established sports of tractor pulling (in which tractors huff and strain to pull a heavy object less than 100m – popular in rural areas) and mud bogging (where 4WD vehicles sputter through a pit of mud).

Bigfoot is largely credited with being the first-ever monster truck. Built in '75 and a rolling billboard for its owner's 4X4 supply shop, it still tours – in name at least. Currently in its 19th incarnation (there is no number 13, as it's perceived to be bad luck), Big Foot 14 set the world monster truck long-jump record in 1999 when it cleared a 727 jetliner – more than 60m.

It was in the heady days of the late '80s that a separate circuit developed for monster truck racing. As well as racing events, these days such extravaganzas also include freestyle events, in which trucks attempt to perform doughnuts, wheelies and jumps. While competing is a highly specialised field, with trucks owned by promoters themselves or sponsored by corporations, spectators flock to events. Monster truck touring shows are considered family-style entertainment, second only in popularity to Disney on Ice shows. Events are also regularly televised.

MORE INFO Monster Truck Racing Association (www.mtra.us)

DECEMBER
WEEK.03

SOUTHEAST ASIA GAMES

WHERE Location changes each games **WHEN** Biennially, third week of December **GETTING INVOLVED** Tickets available online from the host country's games site.

You only have to look at the history of regional games to see how the world has changed. Since the first edition of the Southeast Asian Games in 1959, for example, half of the founding member countries no longer exist as such. Burma is now known as Myanmar, Malaya is Malaysia and South Vietnam is Vietnam. The political shifts and dynamism of the region is the games' raison d'être: to promote good relations and understanding among neighbours whose administrative structures and borders may shift from one games to the next. And if the 2009 edition of the games is anything to go by, it seems to be working.

Laos, the host country of the 2009 games has been significantly compromised by years of war and isolation. To devote its resources to hosting such an event is a grand gesture, and one that resulted in a number of participating countries to donate funds and people-power to help out. And although fewer sports overall are included, 25 down from 45 in the previous games, there are still events that are particular to the region.

Among them are pétanque (p109), muay Thai (p190) and pencak silat. A collective term for Indonesia's martial arts, pencat silat would have to be the most artful fighting technique – performed like a dance act. Graceful and fluid choreographed manoeuvres make combat almost appealing – if you had to be beaten up, this is the way you'd want to go.

Other participating countries include some of the world's youngest countries, like Timor Leste, which gained independence from Indonesia in 1999, and Brunei on the island of Borneo, which regained its independence from the UK in 1984. Also on the bill: Indonesia, Singapore, Cambodia, Philippines, Thailand and Vietnam.

MORE INFO Olympic Council of Asia (www.ocasia.org)

'Live your life like a warrior, as if every day is your last.'
- - - - - - - - - - - - - - - - -
Wayne 'Rabbit' Bartholomew, surfing legend

NATIONAL FINALS RODEO

Is it a bird? Is It a plane? No... It's Snake Bite, wowing audiences and crushing cars.

WHERE USA **WHEN** First week of December **GETTING INVOLVED** The toughest thing about the finals is getting a ticket, which often sell out a year in advance. The box office sells returned same-day tickets each morning from 10am. Cheaper 'mad dash' find-a-seat tickets let you scramble around to find no-show seats in the balcony area.

Imagine if people paid to watch you work. For most of us that would translate to watching us tap away at a computer, albeit with exaggerated furrows of concentration on the brow. For cowboys, it means roping steers, skilled riding (either on horseback or on a bull) and the potential for thousands of dollars in prize money – all in a day's work.

As a sport, rodeo involves skilled horsemen and women, competing in both timed and roping events. Timed events include barrel racing, in which cowgirls ride around a course of barrels, and steer-wrestling, in which cowboys have about six minutes to bring down a steer by diving from their moving horse onto said steer. Roping events include a single rider lassoing and tying down a calf, or two riders lassoing and roping a steer: one at the head and one at the tail. Such techniques are still used on cattle stations to bring down an animal in order to brand it or administer medical attention. Bull riding and bronco riding, collectively known as 'rough stock', is less common in the real world, with few occasions for riding an 850kg bull or catching wild horses presenting themselves. It's with the bull riding that you'll see the clowns who have good reason for those painted frowns. It's their job to distract the bull after a cowboy has been tossed off and to buy time for the cowboy to leave the ring safely. That means putting themselves forward as bait.

The Professional Rodeo Cowboys Association is the largest of the many governing bodies, overseeing 700 rodeos each year – the finals being the culmination and featuring the best cowboys and girls.
MORE INFO Professional Rodeo Cowboys Association (www.prorodeo.com)

FOR THE RECORD

BA' GAME

WHERE Kirkwall, Scotland **WHEN** 25 December and 1 January
GETTING INVOLVED Better to just get out of the way, but there's nothing to
stop you joining the fray.

Kirkwall might make a nice change from your usual Christmas ritual. Unlike in most
towns on Christmas Day, where families cluster quietly indoors, feast and politely
exchange gifts, the good folk of Kirkwall host a frenzied mass street-football match.
Ball-up is at 1pm, so, theoretically, there's time to squeeze in a quick lunch and
pressie exchange before the big game. But with the boys' ball-up at 10.30am, and
usually still going by the time the men's game starts, Christmas lunch may exclude all
young males.

  Played on Christmas Day and New Year's Day, ba' is a fine example of the kind
of flock-football that has been played for centuries in various parts of the UK. With
around 200 people per side, most players won't even see the ball, let alone touch it.
The writhing surge of humanity moves unpredictably through Kirkwall's atmospheric

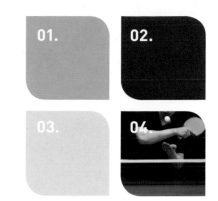

'With around 200 people per side, most players won't even see the ball, let alone touch it'

DECEMBER
WEEK.04

It's either an attempt at the Guinness World Record for massed man hug or it's a pack of Uppies in Kirkwall looking for a small leather ball on Christmas Day. Who can be sure?

paved streets and twisting *wynds* (lanes), as the ball changes possession between the Up-the-Gates and Down-the-Gates (Uppies and Doonies) – determined by on which side of the gate a player was born. Ferryloupers (incomers) determine their side by the route they first took into Kirkwall, or by the influence of family and friends.

The rules are simple: there are none, other than the first team to score a goal wins. The teams' fixed goals are equidistant from the centre of town and from where the ball goes up: the magnificent St Magnus Cathedral. The Doonies must land the ball in the sea, while the Uppies must hit the wall at Sandison's Corner. Tactics range from players breaking away from the scrum making a lot of noise and pretending to have the ball (distracting the opposition and clearing the way for teammates to continue on their way towards the goal)

to players simply punching clear a path. It's also pertinent to have team members loitering in the surrounding streets away from the scrum to cover the possibility of the ba' being tossed to the player out on their own with a clear run to the sea or corner.

The winning team nominates the game's most influential player who is awarded the honour of hanging the ba' (handmade leather-cased ball with a cork core) in the lounge-room window. With that honour comes 399-odd thirsty fellows, as the man of the match hosts the after-game drinks.

MORE INFO Orkney's Official Tourism Website (www.visitorkney .com)

SYDNEY TO HOBART YACHT RACE

WHERE Sydney and Hobart, Australia **WHEN** Departs Sydney 26 December **GETTING INVOLVED** Say 'Hello sailor,' on Hobart's Constitution Dock, especially on New Year's Eve.

You've got to love a race that is open to all-comers. Boats of varying age, size, shape, construction and rig all set sail as part of the legendary Sydney to Hobart Yacht Race. Around 100 boats leave Rushcutters Bay in Sydney and make a Rhumb Line (the shortest route) to Hobart – all 630 nautical miles (1170km). The champagne corks start popping on board the maxi-yachts (more than 21m) little more than a day and a half later, when they sail first into Hobart and win line honours. But there is also a handicap winner, the best in its division, which is among the top honours in sailing.

Running since 1945 and organised by the Cruising Yacht Club of Australia in association with the Royal Yacht Club of Tasmania, the Sydney to Hobart race route hugs the east coast of Australia before negotiating the notoriously rough and windy Bass Strait. Many boats have disappeared without trace in the open sea between the mainland and the island of Tasmania. It took just over six days to complete the race in its inaugural year. And it wasn't until 1999 that the race was completed in under two days.

The Sydney to Hobart race is a testing ground for innovations in yacht design. Entrants now strive to complete the race in under 40 hours – an unthinkably impossible task less than a decade ago. The current race record belongs to *Wild Oats XI* with a time of one day, 18 hours, 40 minutes and 10 seconds, set in 2005.

Sailors already safely docked in Hobart begin celebrating immediately, while the other two-thirds of the entrants are still battling it out on the open sea. Traditionally all the entrants and the public come together at Hobart's Constitution Dock on New Year's Eve.

MORE INFO Sydney Hobart Yacht Race (www.rolexsydneyhobart.com)

BOXING DAY TEST

WHERE Melbourne, Australia **WHEN** From 26 December **GETTING INVOLVED** Tickets sell out fast for Boxing Day, but can generally be bought for the remaining days via Ticketmaster (www.ticketmaster.com.au).

Summer in Australia means long, hot days, holidays at the beach, zinc cream and cricket. And for Melburnians, watching the Boxing Day Test is welcome summer respite. After a busy run-up to Christmas, then Christmas itself, the city heads to its beloved 'G' (Melbourne Cricket Ground) for a sit-down on a grand scale – five days of Test cricket.

Play here at the MCG on Boxing Day began in 1950, but was sporadic until 1980 when the schedule became more concrete. Australia plays the touring opposition over five long, gloriously slow days in traditional whites and with the traditional red ball. They can keep their Twenty20 comps and one-dayers, this time of year calls for as much down time as possible. That's not to say that nothing happens. Boxing Day Tests have seen plenty of headline-making action. It was here in 1995 that umpire Darrell Hair called Sri Lankan spinner Muttiah Muralitharan for throwing, and that Shane Warne took his 700th Test wicket in 2006 against England

Tens of thousands of fans turn out with groups of mates, and Christmas lunch leftovers in an Esky. Recent developments to the hallowed ground have increased the MCG's capacity to 100,000. The spiritual home of Australian cricket, the MCG has been hosting matches since the 1850s. It's linked to the CBD via a footbridge, which leads to the city's public hub – Federation Square. Deck chairs are usually set up in front of Fed Square's giant screen, which beams all the cricket action.

MORE INFO The Melbourne Cricket Ground (www.mcg.org.au)

FESTIVAL OF THE SAHARA

WHERE Douz, Tunisia **WHEN** 23 to 27 December **GETTING INVOLVED** Book accommodation early, and be prepared for open-air entertainment – under the Saharan sun.

While the Christian world focuses on wintry scenes with sleigh bells and snow dashing, Saharan nomads flock to Douz, Tunisia's gateway to the mighty desert, for a celebration of their culture. Festivities include a number of unique sporting events, including camel fights and rabbit hunting using greyhound-like saluki dogs. Fantasias are also a feature, in which riders on Arabian horses skillfully canter, turn, stop and shoot their rifles. Up to 50,000 turban-wrapped visitors from across North Africa pitch their Bedouin tents on the outskirts of town. In the evenings, there are artistic performances, such as the hair dance, where young women rhythmically toss their tresses, and belly dancing. There is, of course, the odd camel tagine on offer, as well as Berber pizza made by the local women – not to mention Tunisia's finest dates, which are harvested in Douz at this time of year.

Having begun as a Berber marriage market, the festival features public weddings, which are invariably the events that incite the most rousing cheers. The festival took its current form in 1967 as a way of preserving and promoting nomadic traditions. The Berbers arrived from the Sahara – which begins 50km south of town – with the decline of the Roman Empire in the late 4th century, bringing with them the first camels seen in Tunisia.

Douz is home to the country's largest palm grove, a museum with a section on camel husbandry and a Thursday market brimming with Berber rugs and Tuareg jewellery.

MORE INFO Tunisian National Tourism Office (www.tourismtunisia.com)

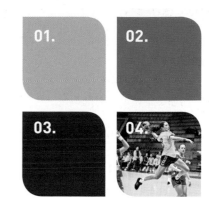

01. 02. 03. 04.

DECEMBER
WEEK.04

AND ANOTHER THING

WCA National Championships (USA)

You may wonder how organised barracking for a football or basketball team could become a sport in itself. As distinct from the chanting, Mexican waving and ad hoc stomping that generally takes place in the stands, cheerleading is a choreographed display of athleticism that combines the skills of dancing and gymnastics. Around 4500 budding cheerleaders compete in the National Championships – held annually. (www.cheerwca.com)

Ballcourt marker from the Maya site of Chinkultic, Chiapas, Mexico, from AD 591.

DEAD SPORTS
MESOAMERICAN BALL GAME

In football, the English Premier league is widely regarded as the fastest-paced version of the game. But compared to the ball-game obsession that gripped pre-Columbian Mesoamerica, watching a Premiership match would be like watching snails playing subbuteo (table football).

Evidence from archaeological sites across Mesoamerica (Greek for 'middle America') reveals the Mesoamerican ball game as one seriously pacy spectator sport.

The ball in question was made of woven bands of rubber. Estimated to be the size of a volleyball it was 15 times heavier, weighing in at around 4kg. The game was played on specially constructed courts made of solid stone, so the balls were able to ricochet like giant rubber bullets. Sixteenth-century Spanish friar, Diego Durán, witnessed the game being played in Mexico and was impressed by the extent of injuries caused by the balls. He

even recorded the deaths of players killed after being struck by a ball in the face or stomach.

It is most likely the game originated with the ancient culture of the Olmecs, who dominated the lowlands of modern day Mexico from about 1400 BC, and quickly spread along trade routes throughout the region as far south as Nicaragua. For more than 3000 years the game was enjoyed in different variations by Olmecs, Maya, Aztecs and the mysterious inhabitants of the Teotihuacan city state.

The exact rules are unknown and appear to have changed over time and place. The general gist of it was that two teams would face each other in a square or rectangular court and try to 'score' by getting the ball into their opponent's end. Ball courts have been unearthed among most major Mesoamerican ruins. The Mayan stronghold at Chichen Itza boasts the most formidable one, which measures

166m by 68m. A cross section of a court would look like somewhere between a U and a V, depending on the degree by which the walls sloped, which presumably added another level of danger for the players. Later courts featured carved stone rings that might have served as goals, although getting the ball through is believed to have been especially challenging.

For the players, games were often a matter of life and death. Representations of male and female players on religious panels, vases and drinking vessels show they wore helmets and kneepads, as well as protective yokes around their waists. Striking the ball with the yoke is believed to have been the primary method for moving the ball, a technique that would have required great timing and skill if injury was to be avoided.

Ball games were major religious and secular events. Spectators would have crowded viewing platforms on nearby temples and even along the walls of the ball courts to get a glimpse of the action. Gambling on the outcome was par for the course, which has led to speculation among some historians that the game was sometimes used to offset costly wars between rival kings.

But the biggest cost of the games was reserved for the players. From about the year AD 700 onwards, several art murals of ball games appear to show the captains and sometimes all of the players of a losing team being ritually sacrificed, usually by decapitation.

INDEX

PHOTO CREDITS

In order

JANUARY WEEK 1
Cameron Spencer, Getty Images
Christopher Lee, Getty Images

JANUARY WEEK 2
DB Volkswagen Motorsports, Corbis
David R. Frazier Photolibrary, Inc.,
Photolibrary

JANUARY WEEK 3
Peter Parks, Getty Images
Peter Jordan, Photolibrary

JANUARY WEEK 4
Xinhua /Landov, Reuters
Eric Miller, Reuters

FEBRUARY WEEK 1
Rob Tringali/Sportschrome, Getty Images
Jens-Ulrich Koch, Getty Images

FEBRUARY WEEK 2
Lisa Maree Williams, Getty Images
Gallo Images, Getty Images

FEBRUARY WEEK 3
Bryn Lennon, Getty Images
Sally Dillon, Lonely Planet Images

FEBRUARY WEEK 4
Yuri Kadobnov, Getty Images
Jonathan Wood, Getty Images

MARCH WEEK 1
Adrian Dennis, Getty Images
Stringer, Getty Images

MARCH WEEK 2
László Balogh, Reuters
Christopher Lee, Getty Images

MARCH WEEK 3
Jamie McDonald, Getty Images
David Cannon, Getty Images

MARCH WEEK 4
Pierre Verdy, Getty Images
Steve Robertson, Getty Images

DEAD SPORTS - BULL LEAPING
Steve Outram, Photolibrary

APRIL WEEK 1
Alex Livesey, Getty Images
David Peart, Reuters

APRIL WEEK 2
Andy Lyons, Getty Images
Heinz Kluetmeier, Getty Images

APRIL WEEK 3
E. Sarkisov, Photolibrary
Wolfgang Kaehler, Corbis

APRIL WEEK 4
Clive Mason, Getty Images
Elsa, Getty Images

MAY WEEK 1
Erik de Castro, Corbis
Bryn Lennon, Getty Images

MAY WEEK 2
Miguel Riopa, Getty Images
Filippo Monteforte, Getty Images

MAY WEEK 3
Mark Thompson, Getty Images
Lee Foster, Photolibrary

MAY WEEK 4
Andrew Yates, Getty Images
Adrian Dennis, Getty Images

JUNE WEEK 1
Mike Clarke, Getty Images
Lou Capozzola, Getty Images

JUNE WEEK 2
Andrew D. Bernstein, Getty Images
Ker Robertson, Getty Images

JUNE WEEK 3
Scott Barbour, Getty Images
Ray Stubblebine, Reuters

JUNE WEEK 4
Carl de Souza, Getty Images
Michael Steele, Getty Images

DEAD SPORTS - CHARIOT RACING
DEA/G DAGLI ORTI, Photolibrary

JULY WEEK 1
Sven Nackstrand, Getty Images
Bradley Kanaris, Getty Images

JULY WEEK 2
Sean Gallup, Getty Images
Stephen Shaver, Getty Images

JULY WEEK 3
Bryn Lennon, Getty Images
Wolfgang Kumm, Corbis

JULY WEEK 4
Sampics, Corbis
Terry Trewin, Getty Images

AUGUST WEEK 1
John Gress, Reuters
Norbert Eisele-Hein, Photolibrary

AUGUST WEEK 2
Ian Walton, Getty Images
Jeff J Mitchell, Corbis

AUGUST WEEK 3
Paolo Sacchi, Getty Images
Robin Smith, Photolibrary

AUGUST WEEK 4
Phil Walter, Getty Images
Peter Turnley, Corbis

SEPTEMBER WEEK 1
Stephen Molumphy, Inpho
Handout, Getty Images

SEPTEMBER WEEK 2
Phil Cole, Getty Images
TG Stock, Getty Images

SEPTEMBER WEEK 3
Holger Leue, Lonely Planet Images
Fred Vuich, Getty Images

SEPTEMBER WEEK 4
Tim Terry, The Slattery Media Group
Anatoly Maltsev, Corbis

DEAD SPORTS - LAVA SLEDDING
Jim Wark, Lonely Planet Images

OCTOBER WEEK 1
Chung Sung-Jun, Getty Images
Michael Bezjian, Getty Images

OCTOBER WEEK 2
Mark Dadswell, Getty Images
Bruce Omori, Corbis

OCTOBER WEEK 3
Donald Miralle, Getty Images
Antoine Gyori, Corbis

OCTOBER WEEK 4
Charles Pertwee, Corbis
Mark Blinch, Reuters

NOVEMBER WEEK 1
Haman I Mohammed, Reuters
Saeed Khan, Getty Images

NOVEMBER WEEK 2
STR, Getty Images
Martin Philbey, Corbis

NOVEMBER WEEK 3
Rick Wilking, Reuters
Epa/Prodprant Rangsawad, Corbis

NOVEMBER WEEK 4
Streeter Lecka, Getty Images
Mark Nolan, Corbis

DECEMBER WEEK 1
Mark Dadswell, Getty Images
Fred Ernst, Getty Images

DECEMBER WEEK 2
Daniel Dal Zennaro, Corbis
Aurora Photos, Alamy

DECEMBER WEEK 3
Sylvain Cazenave, Corbis
Duomo, Corbis

DECEMBER WEEK 4
orkneypics, Photolibrary
Cordaiy Photo Library Ltd., Corbis

DEAD SPORTS - MESOAMERICAN BALL GAME
Tolo Balaguer, Photolibrary

A YEAR OF SPORT TRAVEL
August 2009

PUBLISHED BY
LONELY PLANET PUBLICATIONS PTY LTD
ABN 36 005 607 983
90 Maribyrnong St, Footscray,
Victoria, 3011, Australia
WWW.LONELYPLANET.COM

Printed by Hang Tai Printing Company
Printed in China

Cover image Mitch Diamond/Photolibrary
Lonely Planet's preferred image source is Lonely Planet Images (LPI). www
.lonelyplanetimages.com

ISBN 978 1 74179 883 8

LONELY PLANET OFFICES
AUSTRALIA Locked Bag 1, Footscray, Victoria, 3011
Phone 03 8379 8000 Fax 03 8379 8111
Email talk2us@lonelyplanet.com.au

USA 150 Linden St, Oakland, CA 94607
Phone 510 893 8556 Toll free 800 275 8555 Fax 510 893 8572
Email info@lonelyplanet.com

UK 2nd Floor, 186 City Rd, London, ECV1 2NT
Phone 020 7106 2100 Fax 020 7106 2101
Email go@lonelyplanet.co.uk

A YEAR OF ↗
SPORT TRAVEL

PUBLISHER Chris Rennie
ASSOCIATE PUBLISHER Ben Handicott
COMMISSIONING EDITOR Janine Eberle
PROJECT MANAGER Jane Atkin
IMAGE RESEARCHER Rebecca Dandens
ART DIRECTOR Nic Lehman
COVER DESIGNER Mick Ruff
DESIGNER Yukiyoshi Kamimura
EDITORS Justin Flynn, Saralinda Turner
LAYOUT Wibowo Rusli
PRE-PRESS PRODUCTION Ryan Evans
PRINT PRODUCTION Graham Imeson
Special thanks to Sophie Cunnigham

THE AUTHOR
SIMONE EGGER
Simone is a Melbourne-based writer. She writes regularly for Lonely Planet
(its destination guidebooks, website and armchair-travel books), as well as
for local and international newspapers and magazines. She has travelled to
around 40 countries, and can say 'hello', 'thanks', 'please', 'bye' and 'how
about those [insert team name here]?!' in a dozen or so languages.

THANKS FROM THE AUTHOR
Thanks to: Andrew Cole, Aris Gounaris, Dave Kutcher, Martin Hughes,
Elissa Bates, Warren Egger and Sue Visic for ideas. Also to Sam and Karl for
their words. And especially to Simon, Walter, Warren and Mum for all the
intangibles.

CONTRIBUTING AUTHORS
SAM PANG
Sam is a writer, broadcaster and producer. He has been a co-host of 'The
Breakfasters' on Melbourne's independent radio station Triple R 102.7FM
since 2004. A failed Aussie Rules footballer, he has written for the Age
newspaper and commercial television, as well as producing radio and
theatre. He lives in Melbourne and doesn't have a dog.

KARL SMITH
Karl is an Australian writer and musician – born in New Zealand, raised
in Bangladesh and schooled in South India. He has written for numerous
publications including Limelight, Lonely Planet and Cheap Eats. Despite
being an excitable tennis and soccer fan, Karl has consistently proved he
is better suited to describing the sports he loves, rather than participating
in them.

CRAIG SCUTT
In ancient times Craig would have been a warrior poet but these days he
is willing to settle for being a sporty writer. He has a bi-monthly habit of
announcing he will be training for a marathon, Iron Man, Coast-to-Coast;
only for his admirable intent to languish on the reef of indolence.